finding God
in the graffiti

Other books in the series

Practicing Discernment with Youth:
A Transformative Youth Ministry Approach
by David F. White

Branded:
Adolescents Converting from Consumer Faith
by Katherine Turpin

Lives to Offer:
Accompanying Youth on Their Vocational Quests
by Dori Grinenko Baker and Joyce Ann Mercer

Book, Bath, Table, and Time:
Christian Worship as Source and Resource
for Youth Ministry
by Fred P. Edie

YOUTH MINISTRY ALTERNATIVES

finding God in the graffiti

empowering teenagers through stories

frank rogers jr.

THE
PILGRIM
PRESS
Cleveland

For Hassan Hammoud
(1990–2001)

The wheelchair-bound creator of
Battery Charger Man,
whose deepest wish was
to find the power to keep going and going and going,
and whose deepest fear was
that his power would evaporate completely.
Cancer devoured your body, Hassan, but your power lives on.
It replenishes hope in every soul that follows your lead.
In the fight to tell our story in the face of Lord Death,
your power, in us, keeps going and going and going . . .

SUSTAINABLE Certified Fiber
FORESTRY Sourcing
INITIATIVE
Label applies to the text stock   www.sfiprogram.org

© 2011 by Frank Rogers Jr.

The Pilgrim Press
700 Prospect Avenue
Cleveland, Ohio 44115
thepilgrimpress.com

Library of Congress Cataloging-in-Publication Data
Rogers, Frank, 1958–
     Finding God in the graffiti : empowering teenagers through stories /
Frank Rogers Jr.
          p.   cm.
     Includes bibliographical references (p.   ).
     ISBN 978-0-8298-1802-4 (alk. paper)
     1. Storytelling–Religious aspects–Christianity.   2. Church work with
teenagers.   I. Title.
BT83.78.R63 2011
259'.23–dc23   2011030639

Foreword   vi

Acknowledgments   x

Introduction   1

1. How do stories transmit a faith tradition?
   Narrative pedagogy and religious literacy   21

2. How do stories shape one's sense of self?
   Narrative pedagogy and personal identity   51

3. How do stories mediate a profound experience of the sacred?
   Narrative pedagogy and contemplative encounter   74

4. How do stories nurture a critical consciousness?
   Narrative pedagogy and critical reflection   98

5. How can stories embolden the artist within?
   Narrative pedagogy and creative vitality   124

6. How can stories inspire social transformation?
   Narrative pedagogy and societal empowerment   156

   Conclusion   183

   Notes   189

   Bibliography   204

Foreword

For three decades the task of conceptualizing youth ministry has largely been left to independent commercial enterprises that have failed to recognize the importance of denomination, theology, ethnicity, class, and other cultural particularities for shaping Christian discipleship. In addition, youth ministry as it has evolved over these decades lacks significant critique of the shift in the social roles of young people in the second half of the twentieth century and into the twenty-first century, in which youth are increasingly ghettoized as passive consumers rather than treated as agents of faith influencing the common good.

Decades of domestication, marginalization, and trivialization of youth ministry by theology schools, denominations, and publishing houses have distorted our imagination of what counts as youth ministry. The image of youth ministry as trivial or pragmatic has left many hungry for youth ministry approaches that include social critique and engagement, theological sophistication, faith formation, and a genuine knowledge of and respect for the unique youth of today. The Youth Ministry ALTERNATIVES series has been jointly conceived by The Pilgrim Press, David F. White, and Faith Kirkham Hawkins to address that hunger.

The Youth Ministry ALTERNATIVES series aims to clearly articulate approaches to youth ministry that embody social awareness and theological reflection and foster the distinctive gifts of youth for the church and the world. The series will highlight approaches to youth ministry that embody the following commitments:

1. **Dialogue with Living Communities.** This series will highlight approaches for fostering dynamic dialogue between the Christian traditions and youth and adults in living communities of faith.

2. **Deeper Understanding.** This series will engage this dialogue to deepen understanding of youth, theology, and youth ministry. Of particular interest is the wisdom emerging from a variety of underexplored sources that will be identified and interpreted, including the following:

   • the wisdom of youth

   • the wisdom of communities engaged in youth ministry

   • the contexts of youth, including their inner landscapes, communities, cultures, and physical environments

   • the resources of Christian tradition

3. **Transformative Practices.** From these conversations and the wisdom gleaned from youth, communities, and their contexts, this series will especially highlight a range of practices for engaging youth in ministry, such as:

   • doing theology and ministry with youth

   • taking youth seriously—their wounds, blessings, and gifts

   • mobilizing and enhancing youth agency and vocation

   • enhancing formation and transformation of youth as they journey in faith

   • articulating clear approaches to youth ministry

   • discerning a congregation's unique youth ministry

In *Finding God in the Graffiti*, Frank Rogers Jr. reveals the fruit of over a decade of practical and theoretical research with young people exploring effective teaching approaches. Bear in mind that this book is not just another exercise in speculation by an academic. Frank Rogers Jr. knows this subject inside and out; and he knows it as theory born of practice and as practice provoked by theory. In this postmodern climate in which foundational ideas and centralized power are suspect, the power of story is being rediscovered by philosophers, social theorists, and theologians. Yet religious educators, schoolteachers, spiritual guides, and hallowed keepers of cultural heritage have long known the power of story in communicating a lesson or passing on wisdom. Religious formation is not primarily a matter of adopting a set of ideas; it is more akin to appreciating and responding to a beautiful story. And in responding to religious story it matters who gets to tell the story of our lives, since not only is social power at stake, but also such things as spirituality, agency, and community.

Reclaiming the power of narrative is especially important for contemporary youth and young adults. Social critics from Christian Smith to Jeffrey Arnett are claiming that young people have lost a sense of purpose in this culture. Some decry young people's loss of theological language as a means of characterizing their lives, while others observe that the sea of burgeoning options and the expanding world of information are leaving many young people paralyzed, without a sense of how to choose. To a large extent, meaning and identity are a function of the stories we tell ourselves about ourselves and our world—that is, how we "put things together." Clearly it is a religious and social imperative that religious institutions engage young people, as Walter Brueggemann suggests, in "telling the odd stories of their lives through the stories of the Bible and the odd stories of the Bible through the stories of their lives." For Christians the medium of story makes sense only because story tells an "incarnate" truth clothed by rich detail of earthy elements and human passion.

Frank Rogers Jr. provides a helpful typology of approaches that covers the full range of narrative pedagogies available—to nurture theological reflection, spiritual growth, and social empowerment. Rogers illuminates powerful new and old narrative approaches as a means of helping young people to establish a sense of their identity in context, to pass on a community's sacred stories, to identify a culture's destructive plotlines, and to spark a sense of personal power for social change. Rogers claims that these represent alternate ways of experiencing God.

True to the underlying philosophy of this book and its commitment to the power of story, Rogers makes these approaches come alive by embedding them in stories of youth. In themselves these stories will evoke the Holy, but they also hold promise for the renewal of youth ministry and the church's ministry of education.

We are proud to present this book in this series. It represents a lively and well crafted interpretation of an important movement in Christian formation and youth ministry. We are pleased to present *Finding God in the Graffiti.*

DAVID F. WHITE AND FAITH KIRKHAM HAWKINS
Series editors, Youth Ministry Alternatives

Series editors David F. White and Faith Kirkham Hawkins are respectively C. Ellis and Nancy Gribble Nelson Associate Professor of Christian Education at Austin Presbyterian Theological Seminary in Austin, Texas, and Director of the Youth Theological Initiative and Assistant Professor of Youth and Education at Candler School of Theology at Emory University in Atlanta.

Acknowledgments

This book began with a simple love for stories. A host of people taught me that stories are not only lovable, they are liberative. I attribute to them my transformation from storyteller to narrative educator.

My Teachers: Dave Miller, my youth minister some thirty years ago, first awakened me to the power of stories; I still remember many that you told us. Steve Greenstein, Augusto Boal, Marie-Claire Picher, Fran Montano, William Alderson, and, above all, Daniel Judah Sklar trained me in the use of narrative and the stage as a liberating pedagogical space for young people.

My Colleagues: Dean Jack Fitzmier at the Claremont School of Theology insisted that research into narrative pedagogy belonged at a graduate school. Scott Cormode helped craft the argument for funding such research and remained a most generative dialogue partner throughout its duration. Other faculty colleagues have sharpened and sustained my narrative research through their ever-present collaborative encouragement—Elizabeth Conde-Frazier, Jack Coogan, Andy Dreitcer, Carol Lakey Hess, Sheryl Kujawa-Holbrook, Ellen Marshall, and Marvin Sweeney. In addition, David White, both as director of the Youth Discipleship Project and as a leading scholar of Youth Ministry, has unfalteringly believed in this work—I am grateful for all that you have taught me.

My Financial Supporters: The Narrative Pedagogies Project was first established by a grant from the Lilly Endowment. Craig Dykstra and Chris Coble, in particular, have been steadfast supporters of my research in ways that transcend the financial. Ralph "Doc" Roberts was an early advocate for both the power of narrative in young people's lives and in a graduate school educational model that brought seminary students into the lives of marginalized teenagers. The professorial chair he endowed will sustain liberative youth pedagogy for years to come.

My Project Assistants: The Narrative Pedagogies Project organized numerous opportunities for young people to participate in story-based programs. The project staff for the summer-based drama program, Acting 4 Change, and the yearlong programs in local venues were heaven-sent. Bethany Carpenter, Desiree Keim, Eric Kyle, Brian Parcel, Sun Young Park, Judy Simon, and Joe Taylor—you more than assisted; you cocreated. I celebrate the ways you befriended teens, empowered them into becoming storytellers, and even acted in their productions. JC Aevaliotis—your brilliant improvisational gifts were transformative.

My Students: Through the years of research that inform this book, I taught classes to CST students about various dimensions of story-based education. Each course included a laboratory setting in which CST students assisted in a narrative program with a group of marginalized young people; the students, then, facilitated their own projects in contexts important to them. Quite literally, hundreds of CST students and young people participated in these projects scattered throughout Southern California. Their creativity, compassion, and commitment deepened the research immeasurably.

My Research Assistant: Eric Kyle worked on this project with such depth—as a program assistant, a field-based student, a site host, a stage technician, a library researcher, a dialogue partner, and an editorial consultant—he deserves a writing credit for this manuscript.

My Friends: Frank Alton, Andy Dreitcer, Doug Frank, and Mark Yaconelli—friends of fairy-tale proportions—have walked with me through this research for so long they could write the stories themselves.

My Teenage Companions: Without a doubt, this book would have been grossly ungrounded and academic if not for the hundreds of young people who participated in the Narrative Pedagogies Project. Participants from the Westmont Community Center in Pomona, Acting 4 Change, the Youth Discipleship Project, the McKinley

Boys' Home, the Leroy Haynes Center for Boys, Willard Elementary School in Long Beach, Peppertree Elementary School, and Rosary Catholic High School in Fullerton—your stories have not only taught me, they have inspired me.

My Publishing Midwives: The staff at The Pilgrim Press have been unwavering in their support for this manuscript. David White and Faith Kirkham Hawkins have graced me not only with their enthusiasm for my work but with including it in the groundbreaking series, Youth Ministry Alternatives. And Ulrike Guthrie—editor extraordinaire and a literary agent writers would covet—you set the bar for birthing a book to print.

My Family: My sons and boys—Justin Rogers, Michael Daugherty, Sammy Daugherty, Steven Cope, David Falkinburg, Steven Otto, and Raza Rasheed—stories have surrounded us from the inception; I savor how interlaced yours are with mine. And Alane—my love, my wife, my spiritual companion—you are the happy ending, in a story that stretches forever.

Introduction

A bare concrete wall stands at the center of the stage. A teenage boy walks up with a spray can and paints graffiti-style, "Drugs." He sits on a crate, faces the audience, and asks, "Where is God?" A teenage girl follows him. She walks to the wall, spray paints "Divorce," and repeats the question, "Where is God?" Another teen, then another, paints the wall, sits on a crate, and beseeches the audience. The words "Suicide," "Anorexia," and "Depression" litter the wall. A last girl writes "Death." Then she too sits down, faces the audience, and asks the question, "Where is God?"

For several moments, they sit in silence. Then another young lady, a stranger, walks into the scene. Surprised to see the crowd she asks, "What's going on?"

"We've seen a lot of stuff," a teen answers. "And we want to know, where is God in the middle of it all?"

"You've come to the right place," the young lady responds. "I'm looking for God too, and I heard He was coming here."

"You're kidding," another teen says. "When?"

"I don't know. I just heard He was coming here."

"So we just wait?" another asks.

"Yes. We just wait."

The teens ponder this. Then they settle in. Bundling themselves against the cold, they stare silently at the ground.

And they wait for God.

The twelve teenagers participating in Acting 4 Change, a three-week summer drama program, did not sign up knowing they were looking for God. Ryan had a crush on Katrina; Katrina was looking for something to do during the long dry spell of summer vacation;

1

Francine and Paula were Katrina's best friends and would have hung out in detention to be with her. Not Emily. At one time close, she and Katrina had a falling out but they shared the same youth leader who talked up the program. Only Lauren had an explicit interest in drama. She was a budding thespian at her high school until she dropped out when her father moved out of the state. The teens were unsure of what they were in for. The program's invitation was simple. Through storytelling, creative writing, and improvisational role-playing, the teens were to create an original dramatic piece—and to perform it for their community—that told the story of teen-agers' real-life experience. Given the tenuous motives that drew them, they were game.

The program harbored deeper hopes. Just one of the story-based experiments sponsored by the Narrative Pedagogies Project, Acting 4 Change was created around the belief that story can be a uniquely transformative means of educational ministry with young people. Story has the ability to reveal the most vital longings that pulsate in people's lives and souls, to communicate the cherished wisdom of our religious and cultural communities, to foster reflection on how the narratives of our lives intermingle with the narratives that ground our faith, and to inspire people to journey toward hope as empowered agents of healing in our world. In short, the drama program hoped the teens *would* find God—that within the tangle of plotlines playing out in young people's lives, the movements of God would be discerned, along with the sacred story God aches to craft within the stories of our lives.

But where to begin?

The drama program began by surfacing the stories the teens were already dying to tell. Like an old-time oil speculator poking holes in the ground until a geyser erupts, the adult leader used improv games and writing exercises to identify the narrative themes that would generate the explosion of energy betraying the young people's subterranean concerns. Once identified, the themes could be con-cretized into dramatic scenes. Projected onto the safe space of the stage and personified by fictitious characters, the teens could shape stories that incarnated simmerings within their souls, stories no less real for being pretend.

For example, the Acting 4 Change teens participated in a writing exercise in which each person chose an object from a pile of dozens of props, then wrote a monologue of a teen in crisis struggling with something the object represented. Lauren was drawn to a pair of Walkman headphones. As she wrote, a character listening to gangster rap emerged who developed into a young lady named Chloe struggling with her father's recent death. The teens deepened their characters by elaborating on the character's significant relationships, their feelings toward God, their most deep-seated fears, and their greatest wishes.[1] Chloe became a young lady angry at God for killing her devoutly Christian father. Her deepest wish was to believe in God again; her deepest fear was that God could not care less about the pain her father's death caused her.

Once each teen had a character and a conflict, they fleshed out a scene for each character through improvisation. The group helped the writer create a setting where the character's crisis could be explored. Different options were brainstormed—perhaps Chloe goes to heaven and confronts God, or maybe she's in juvenile hall after vandalizing a church. In this case, the writer placed Chloe at an afternoon tea with her churchgoing aunt who confronts Chloe about her self-destructive behavior. Backstories, fears, and wishes were developed for the additional characters, and volunteers improvised the parts of the conflicting parties. The group discussed the improvisations and made suggestions to make it more realistic, to expose the underlying dynamics and motivations, and to express as truthfully and effectively as possible the experiences of the persons living through the identified situation. Invariably the teens drew on their own experience or those of persons they knew. The scene continued to be improvised and reflected upon until the writer and the troupe of teens were satisfied that the scene depicted the experience they wished to communicate. Eventually, the scenes were shaped for the final production.

〜

As the teens wait for God in front of the defaced wall, the young woman, the stranger, looks around at them and asks why they are looking for God. One teen responds, "I have this friend Bobby." As he speaks, the lights fade and the stage is rearranged. The lights come on, and a scene telling Bobby's story is played out for all to see.

Bobby walks into a vacant apartment with his girlfriend Lindsay. His parents having died when he was four, Bobby struggles with depression and suicidality. Increasingly, he has found solace in a drug habit that he thinks he has successfully hidden from Lindsay. Bobby loves Lindsay and has found this apartment for the two of them to move in together. When he reveals this surprise, Lindsay is shocked and hesitant. Bobby presses her until Lindsay confronts Bobby about his drug use. Bobby denies it, but Lindsay pulls out drug paraphernalia from his car. Bobby is indignant; the drugs keep him from killing himself. Lindsay begs Bobby to seek help. Bobby says he will, but only if Lindsay moves in with him first. Lindsay fears that Bobby is merely placating her; she's seen it before in a brother who overdosed. She insists he get help first. Bobby gets enraged; if Lindsay loved him she'd move in with him anyway. Lindsay is rattled, but she holds firm. Bobby screams at her to leave. Lindsay is scared of losing Bobby but scared of giving in as well. Bobby yells again. Lindsay tells him he's killing their relationship and himself along with it, then walks out. Bobby fumes around, then scrounges through his pockets for enough drugs to overdose on. He studies them, then walks off-stage as well. The lights fade, then return once the set has been cleared. The teen says that Bobby hasn't been seen since. He asks, where is God in the midst of such hopelessness?

The crowd takes in the story. Then the stranger asks another teen why she is looking for God. The teen introduces another scene that is likewise staged before the crowd. Jessica sits in a softball dugout after a game. To her disgust, her mom walks up and sits down beside her. Once quite close, they haven't spoken civilly to each other in weeks. Jessica's mother is divorcing Jessica's father. The father has confided in Jessica that he doesn't want the divorce and that the mother is planning to move to New York to follow her dream of becoming an interior designer. Jessica has felt betrayed ever since, both by her mother's decisions and by her mother's continued secrecy about her plans to move. Jessica and the mother launch into a fight that has already seen many rounds. Jessica pleads for her mother to stay with her father. The mother defends the divorce. Jessica demands to know why. The mother demurs. Jessica pushes, insisting that she deserves the truth. The mother merely says it is complicated. Jessica bemoans the unfairness of having her life destroyed while her mother refuses to be honest with her. The mother simply shakes her head but continues to withhold her secret. Jessica tells her to leave. The mother hesitates. Jessica walks off herself. In her wake she spits, "You realize that you're divorcing me, too."

When the lights return to the original scene, the teen asks the stranger, where is God in the midst of such brokenness?

The crowd takes in this story. Then another scene is introduced and played out for the group, and several more after that. The last teen introduces Chloe's story. Chloe's father was killed in a storm-related traffic accident. She and her father were faithful churchgoers, the father a devout Christian and Chloe's religious confidant and role-model. Now Chloe has lost her faith. She hangs out with a gang, listens to gangster rap, and shuns the church she once worshipped at with her father. Her aunt, a minister's spouse, has asked Chloe over for tea. Chloe, with a defiant attitude, shows up. The aunt expresses her concern for Chloe and invites her back to church. Chloe says she hates God for killing her father. The aunt says that God didn't kill him. "Then why didn't God stop it?" Chloe wants to know. "God has a plan," the aunt responds. "God's plans should not be so hurtful," Chloe retorts. The aunt suggests that God is giving Chloe a chance to be a powerful witness for Christ as one who praises God even in the midst of tragedy. Chloe is indignant. She wants nothing to do with a God who would ask for such praise. The aunt, worried sick over Chloe's behavior, is at her wit's end. "What would your father think of you now?" she asks. The remark hits Chloe like a slap in the face. "My father is dead," Chloe answers. "As dead as the God I once believed in." The lights go out. In front of the wall, the crowd reappears with the light. This last teen looks at the stranger. Where is God in the midst of such anguish?

The crowd remains quiet as the stories settle. Then one of the teens asks the stranger if she has a story, too.

"Oh yes," the stranger says. "I have a story, too."

"Can we hear it?"

"Sure." She starts to speak but is interrupted by shouts offstage demanding that the crowd be dispersed. "I'll tell you tomorrow," she says. "Meet me back here at dawn."

The teens and the stranger disperse.

Act 1 is over.

To be sure, God can be known in the intrinsically valuable process of youth telling their own story and claiming the artistic freedom to express that story honestly and truthfully. In creating mirrors of teen experience in their community, they invite others to see their world and to empathize with the stories that compose their lives. In the spirit of feminist theologian Nelle Morton, they have been empowered into speech, claiming their voices in the process.

Yet youth ministry through narrative offers a further invitation. It invites young people to envision themselves as agents of change within the narratives of their social situations. This goes beyond teens naming realities they experience as thrust upon them; it invites them to explore how they might be intentional actors within them, shaping the storylines in life-giving directions. To facilitate this, the Acting 4 Change teens explored each scene in turn where they discussed underlying causes, considered promising resources, critiqued the messages of culture, reflected theologically, and envisioned possible responses. In the midst of such reflection, each person in the group was asked to sketch her or his own idea for how the story ended, some resolution to the dramatic tension within each scene's identified crisis. With twelve teens and four adults, each scene had sixteen possible endings. Often they were wildly diverse—some despairingly dark, others sentimentally utopian, still others fantastically wild. The various possibilities forced exploration about both what is life-giving within painful realities and what the teens wanted to communicate to their community. Through discussing each idea and improvising the most promising, various pieces rang true. Writing collaboratively, the teens wove these pieces together and crafted endings for each of the problematized situations.

The Acting 4 Change participants decided they wanted to communicate that hope could be found in even the darkest of crises. They explored what it would take for a young person to beat a drug habit and reconcile with a loved one, and what communication between a teen and a parent could look like. Katrina and Emily, improvising a parent and teen estranged, stilled the room when they stumbled into mutual apologies that echoed their own alienation. Chloe's struggle with theodicy generated particularly intense reflection. What kind of a God could inspire faith in the midst of tragic suffering, and how could such faith be kindled? All manner of scenarios were considered. The group imagined healing for Chloe through a caring surrogate father, but some felt that outcome trivialized her feelings for her real father. They envisioned Chloe suffering the consequences of her choices and being slain in a gang shooting, but that scenario seemed nihilistic and implicitly condemning of her justified anger. They improvised religious friends defending God's goodness with appeals to humanity's free will and the paradoxes of God's omnipotence, but that felt abstract and anemic in the face of Chloe's pain. Even a theophany from a whirlwind was imagined, an epiphany of transcendent reassurance, but it felt forced and untrue to experience. Scenario after scenario was improvised and scrutinized, each idea paling as Chloe's suffering critiqued the trite. They felt keenly the acid test articulated by the post-Holocaust theologian Rabbi Irving Greenberg: "Let no statement, theological or otherwise, ever be uttered that is not credible in the sight of burning children."[2] It took the group two weeks of wrestling before something credible finally rang true.

Act 2 opens with the young woman, the stranger, rushing onto the empty stage. The graffiti wall has been vandalized, busted in half, with a slab strewn on either side of the stage centerpiece. Where it once stood, a single vacant bench stands draped by a used sheet as if it once bedded a homeless person.

"What has happened?" the woman shrieks in obvious distress. "Where is God in the midst of *this*?"

As she struggles to make sense of the horror, the teens run in one by one, each enthusiastically proclaiming, "You're not going to believe it! The most amazing thing has happened!" Soon eight youths are jumping up and down around the stranger in cacophonous exuberance. "Bobby's been found!" "Jessica's reconciled with her mother!" "Chloe found faith in the most unexpected way!"

"Wait," the stranger shouts quieting the crowd, "One at a time. What happened?"

Each teen in turn introduces their scenes of resolution, the lights fading then swelling for the scene to be enacted as if happening in real time.

Bobby's girlfriend sits in Bobby's room considering a bottle of sleeping pills. She has reason to believe that Bobby, distraught that she did not love him, overdosed and died. Despairing at his death and second-guessing what she could have done differently, she considers swallowing the pills. Bobby rushes in and explains to her that a friend, a recovering addict himself, found him strung out and took him to a rehab center. Bobby has not only been clean and sober for two weeks but he's enrolling in college to become a rehab counselor like his friend. "I'm going to make it, Lindsay, I know it." He apologizes for the impossible situation he put her in and assures her that her tough-love line in the sand was the best thing she could have done. "I love you, Lindsay. And I'm getting help. Will you marry me?" The lights fade.

Jessica is in her bedroom writing a letter to her mother describing how much she misses her and how hurt she is that her mother has withdrawn so severely from her. As she is writing, her mother comes into her room. The mother has agonized over moving to New York and has been terrified to tell Jessica for fear that Jessica will feel rejected. She now realizes that her silence was not fair and that Jessica feels rejected already. She apologizes and tells her the truth about considering a move. Jessica weeps; she is so grateful that her mother has been honest with her, and she begins to see how agonizing her mother's situation has been. The mother expresses her fear about how Jessica would respond to such a move. Jessica admits such a move terrifies her but that losing an honest relationship with her mom terrifies her even more. The two embrace, and they mean it when they do. "What are we going to do now?" Jessica asks. "I don't know," the mother responds, "but we're going to work through it together." The lights fade.

Chloe has a dream that her father is alive and waiting for her at their church. Knowing it is simply a sleep fantasy, she reluctantly decides to go to Mass anyway. Only out of habit, she takes along the Bible her father gave her at her sixteenth birthday. As she walks in, the priest is consecrating the Eucharistic elements. He stares at Chloe as he says, "This is my body broken with yours." Chloe is stunned by the words. She had never thought of it before. Christ knows what it's like to be broken. He knows exactly how she feels—abandoned by God and torn up by grief. She opens her Bible and reads out loud the inscription she has not read since her father gave her the Bible. "My darling Chloe, I am giving you this Bible with the prayer that you will always know how much God loves you. No matter how hard things may get, Jesus will always be with you. Just as surely as I am with you, too—always watching out for you from wherever I may happen to be." She closes the Bible and stares at the body and blood of Christ. "Yes," she says, "Jesus is with me, the Jesus who knows what it means to be broken." Holding her head in her hands, she weeps.

After all the stories have been told, the stranger shakes her head with marvel. "It's amazing," she says. "Your stories were so sad, and now there's so much hope."

One of the teens notices the sorrow in her voice. "What about you?" the teen asks. "Didn't you say that you had a story, too?"

"I do," she says sadly. "But it does not end with the hope that yours do."

Once more, these teens are tasting something of the sacred. They are empowered to resist passive acquiescence to death-dealing storylines; they are emboldened to become agents of change within self-constructed narratives that promote their liberation; they are looking for hope and are determined to embody it. And in the joyous power that spills over, the Spirit of life bubbles through them.

Youth ministry through narrative holds further transforming promise. Religious communities believe that God is known within the constitutive narratives of their faith tradition. Indeed, community's identities are structured around the tradition's founding stories. God is encountered when these sacred stories are engaged with critical wrestling and contemplative appreciation. And faith is crafted when personal experience is constructed by and interpreted through these paradigmatic stories. Narrative approaches to youth ministry expose teens to these sacred stories. They engage teens imaginatively with these stories' symbolic worlds, and they explore with teens how experience is deepened, meaning is generated, and personal identity is ennobled when their own life stories are contextualized within the extended horizon of God's story stretching throughout history. The Acting 4 Change teens glimpsed the transforming possibilities of this additional process.

The adult leaders brainstormed faith stories that might resonate meaningfully with the teens' identified life stories. The Gospel of Mark emerged with interpretive promise—specifically the scenes where Jesus and his followers experienced the tragic crises of the crucifixion, the burial at the tomb, and the cryptic disappearance of Jesus' body on Sunday morning. For teens to interpret their experience through Mark's passion story, the story first had to be learned. Narrative exercises were crafted that simultaneously built community, unleashed creativity, and nurtured an acquaintance with the details of the story's symbolic world. The teens rewrote Mark's passion as newspaper journalists reporting for the *Jerusalem Tribune*, and they crafted a skit transforming the story into a contemporary whodunit complete with a Holmesian sleuth. With the story internalized, the teens were ready for a more poignant encounter.

Bibliodrama techniques were used to imaginatively reconstruct the decidedly somber missing-body scene on Easter morning.[3] The teens named the various characters mentioned in the text as present on that morning—Mary Magdalene, Mary the mother of James, Salome, and the mysterious young man. They brainstormed others who also could have been there—Peter, aching for forgiveness, may have been hiding in the bushes; a Roman soldier, drunk from a Saturday night party, may have been sleeping one off in front of the tomb; Pilate, unable to sleep after the week's unsettling events, may have been strolling in the shadows. After filling out the cast, they created a still-life human sculpture of the scene around a crate that served as the vacant tomb. Jesus' mother knelt with her head in her hands and wept at her son's disappearance. Mary Magdalene scoured the tomb with horror. Peter wrenched his clothes at being denied a last chance to plead for forgiveness. The hungover guard rubbed the sleep from his eyes. His superior bent over him enraged at the guard's incompetence. Salome was poised to spit on them both. Pilate smoldered in the shadows. Various disciples were sprinkled in confusion. The mysterious young man was horrified at the misunderstanding of Jesus' friends. The lack of joy at Jesus' resurrection was brutally palpable. All everyone knew was that the body was missing. Horror and confusion permeated the scene.

The pathos deepened as the teens animated the still-life sculpture. All the teens spoke a single line from their pose to express what they were feeling. Jesus' mother sobbed, "I just wanted to say good-bye."

Mary Magdalene frantically shouted, "He's got to be here somewhere." Salome spit, "The bastards stole him." The drunken guard stammered, "I don't know what happened." His superior threatened, "There'll be hell to pay." Pilate worried in the shadows, "This is not going to be good." A disciple glared at the guard, "Where did you take him?" Another despaired by the empty crate, "Where is God?" The mysterious young man implored, "You don't understand, he's really alive." A skeptical follower summed it all up, "You've got to be kidding."

The teens held the pose as the poignancy settled within them. Then they came to life and improvised the rest of the scene. The mysterious young man insisted that Jesus was really alive. The followers disbelieved him—some deemed it impossible, another demanded proof, someone else accused him of being paid off by the guards. None of them found it within them to shout a hosanna or jump for joy. It was all too cryptic and uncertain. Off to the side, the supervising officer scolded the guard for letting this happen. Finally Pilate intervened. He warned that this would turn against the Romans and ordered the guard to disperse the crowd. The guard, backed by the executionary threat of Pilate, commanded everyone to leave. The followers looked at each other. The guard raised his sword. They looked at the mysterious young man. He begged them to believe him. The guard charged. Confused and directionless, the followers scattered. Indeed, they were very afraid.

The conversation that followed was both provocative and animated as the teens brought their own experience to the disturbing story. They had never experienced the resurrection story as anything less than a triumphant appearance by the incontrovertibly glorious presence of Christ. We explored various options as to why a writer would end a gospel like that.

"But isn't that the way life is?" one teen observed. "We don't ever see Jesus actually in front of us. We have to take it on faith."

"But some people saw him. The Bible says so."

"We have to take that on faith, too."

"So where does one find the risen Christ today?"

"That's the question, isn't it?"

The young woman, the stranger, steps out to tell her story. "I had a friend, too. Though we were poor, he lived with us in our neighborhood. He was the kindest person I ever met. He cared for the sick, he befriended the people nobody liked, he taught us to love, to stand up for what is right, to believe we deserved a better life than the one we are living now. He was a holy man—sent from God. Some even thought he was the Messiah. I did. Until the Romans killed him. They buried his body right here. The wall you painted—that was his tomb."

She points to the concrete slabs sprayed with graffiti. The teens realize, the walls, dripping with the words "Drugs," "Anorexia," "Suicide," and "Death," once housed the body of Christ.

But the walls are now broken and the tomb is empty.

"So where is his body now?" a teen asks.

"I don't know," the stranger says. "I came this morning to anoint it, but somebody has broken in and stolen it."

"Who would do that?"

She sighs. "He had a lot of enemies."

The teens are startled to see a young man appear from behind the tomb. "What are you doing here?" he asks.

"We are looking for God," a teen responds.

"He's not here," the man says. "He's alive. Jesus has risen from the dead."

The teens look at one another bewildered. "You got to be kidding," one says.

"No. He really is alive. Jesus has risen."

"So where is he?" one asks, then another, "Yeah, where is God?"

"He's out in the world," the man responds.

"Where in the world?" they want to know.

The man eyes the followers. "He's wherever hope rises out of despair, kindness in the midst of cruelty, solidarity in the face of affliction. That's Jesus—risen from the dead. That's where you find God."

The teens take this in as the man disappears from view. Then it dawns on them.

"So God was with Bobby when his friend sponsored him and gave him the courage to fight his drug addiction."

"And God was with Jessica and her mother when they finally started communicating with one another."

"And God was with Chloe when she realized that God knows the same brokenness she does."

They look at one another as their fledgling insight takes hold.

"I have to say," the young woman ponders. "It's not what I expected. So where is God now?" she asks.

"Like the man said," a teen responds. "He's out in the world."

They look offstage. "There's a lot of suffering out in that world," the young woman says soberly.

"Yes," a teen says. "But God can be found within it."

"We're going to go look for him," another teen says. "Do you want to go with us?"

"The young woman considers. "Yeah," she says. "Let's go find God."

The lights fade as the teens hasten offstage.

The Acting 4 Change teenagers had the courage to tell raw stories of teen experience. They faced unflinchingly the pain of adolescent life in their communities—they named it, they felt it, they let it gut through them to the point of artistically representing it with truthful intensity. And as they dwelt within these painful realities, they looked for the presence of God, that spiritual impulse that births life and hope in the midst of the world's woundedness. Like the Gospel of Mark, they did not find God in triumphalistic epiphanies that secure fairy-tale endings. They found only glimpses, allusions as veiled as a cryptic stranger's unsubstantiated insistence that an absent body means resurrected life. Acts of solidarity and truth telling, a mother's apology, a father's gift, moments of kindness, friendship, and Eucharistic pathos for one's shared brokenness—these were the glimpses of God found in the graffiti of teen experience. Sobered by the suffering yet heartened by their hope, this was the story these teenagers told.

But in telling their story, they also reframed it. Interpreting their experience in dialogue with a paradigmatic narrative of the Christian tradition, these teens in essence wrote their own gospel. They did not so much retell the Gospel of Mark in which Jesus dies and then rises in veiled allusion. They told the gospel of their experience in which teenagers of today's world faced their own suffering in the Gethsemane of adolescence and ached for a God that seemed

to abandon them. Sharing this story within the narrative framework of Mark's Gospel transvalued their experience and opened
them to new possibilities of meaning. The ravages of drug addiction
and teenage depression became ways in which they experience the
agony and death of Jesus. Stepping out on one's recovery and sober
solidarity within a common suffering became ways of knowing the
same life-giving Spirit that raised Jesus from the dead. What began
as a wounded story of teens looking for God within the stories of
their lives ends with the stories of teen lives participating in God's
story of birthing new life within a wounded world. From the tombs
of adolescent suffering, this gospel proclaims, empowered young
people rise envisioning themselves as agents of hope and change
within a story that continues the liberative work of the Christ who
inaugurated it. Through crafting this story, these teens are learning to narrate their lives with meaning and purpose. And through
story—their own, their community's, the gospel's—they are indeed
finding God.

This book is an invitation to explore more deeply how.

Religious educators, schoolteachers, spiritual guides, and hallowed
keepers of cultural heritage have long known the power of story
in communicating a lesson or passing on wisdom. This recognition reaches back to our religious and cultural roots. Our earliest ancestors clarified customs, instilled values, and described the
origins of the world and its creatures through sharing myths and
folktales around the campfire. Jesus, the central figure in the Christian context that frames this book, taught through parables drawn
from everyday life. Indeed, the Gospel writers themselves, of all the
modes available to them, chose a narrative form to communicate
who Jesus was and what he taught. Good teachers are good storytellers. They know the magic words to intone when the eyes of their
students glaze over. "Let me tell you a story . . . ," and at once, interest is recaptured, attention is engaged, and energy is kindled as the
spell of the story descends. The tale is planted deep, and it remains
lodged within the memory long after didactic content is forgotten.

The educational power of story, however, is not limited to spicing up a presentation. As seen in the drama program above, contemplative engagement of sacred stories can connect persons to the pools of presence from which faith emerges. Awakening the storyteller within can kindle creative vitality. Telling one's life story strengthens personal power, and interpreting it through a community's myths deepens life's meaning. Crafting liberating plotlines to live bestows social agency. The power of narrative is so educationally compelling that teachers within a multitude of contexts have created story-based curricula as energizing as they are imaginative. African American religious educators are teaching Christian faith and cultural pride through blending biblical stories with black biographies. Inner-city educators are creating storytelling circles and drama troupes to enhance classroom learning. Liturgy councils are internalizing texts through Bibliodrama and performing them during worship, while feminist educators are empowering abused women through accessing their stories of personal truth. Popular educators are using the stage to dramatize social conditions and mobilize the oppressed as change-bearing actors within their communities. Seniors at a community center are writing spiritual autobiographies, at-risk boys are resisting gangs by mythologizing their lives around the hero's journey, and church drama groups are uniting generations by writing gospel musicals. Truly, the educational possibilities of narrative seem boundless.

Inspired by this vitality, the Narrative Pedagogies Project was created to explore how the variety of story-based educational methods could be adapted for Christian ministry with young people. Our mandate was specific: to surface the full range of narrative pedagogies available—namely, any educational method that intentionally uses the narrative arts of storytelling, drama, and creative writing to nurture theological reflection, spiritual growth, and social empowerment—and to commission youth ministers, seminary students, and program staff to employ these methods with young people to discern their generativity. Over ten years, hundreds of youth throughout Southern California—as diverse as the region itself—have participated in these narrative experiments. This book tells a few of their stories: the confirmation class in South Central Los Angeles that brought the church down with its freedom ride through black Christian history; the African American junior high misfit who soared with personal power as he reframed his identity through a recontextualized ugly-duckling story; the teenage church drama troupe in the months following September 11, 2001, who dared craft a play where terrorists and their victims encountered one another in heaven; the Korean American young women who critiqued the patriarchy within both Korean folk-tales and Christian texts of terror; the abused boys at a residential treatment facility who, inspired by Job, explored theodicy by putting God on trial; the belittled Pakistani young lady who found her voice and claimed it through writing and telling a story; the social justice group at a parochial high school whose dramatization of a drunk-driving incident leveraged the adoption of disciplinary procedures that embody restorative justice. Each of these young people participated in some form of narrative pedagogy, and through these pedagogies each of them experienced something of the sacred.

But they did not experience the sacred in quite the same way.

While the seemingly boundless variety of narrative pedagogies are united in their celebration of story's educational power, these pedagogies embody quite different assumptions. What is the purpose of narrative education—to pass on a community's sacred stories, to spark critique of destructive cultural plotlines, to unleash the creativity of a budding storyteller? What stories are engaged within the narrative pedagogy—a religious tradition's wisdom stories, an individual's personal stories, the storied nature of social change? And what is the locus of narrative's transforming power—the inspired nature of the story itself, the narrative structure of human identity transposed by a meaningful myth, the spiritual vitality of artistic creation, or the collective empowerment of social agency? To be sure, God is at work in these life-giving pedagogies, but the participants experience this God in rather divergent ways. In short, the field of narrative pedagogy is analytically entangled, a graffitied wall, if you will, where different narrative understandings, like spray-painted monikers and fluorescent taglines, are jumbled over, through, and within one another often in the same educational program. These tangled narrative strands need to be teased out. With the care of a city activist exegeting a graffitied wall to identify a neighborhood's players, the distinctive types of narrative pedagogies need to be identified as well so they can be engaged with intentionally.

The purpose of this book, then, is threefold. First, it brings conceptual clarity to the field of narrative pedagogy, classifying the various pedagogies into identifiable types systematized around each type's distinctive assumptions about story, its purpose, and its liberatory power. Second, it illuminates the life-giving impulse within each educational type, the unique claim to the sacred's presence implied in each transforming pedagogy. Third, through stories and practiced methods, the book describes how each type has been and can be adapted for Christian educational ministry with young people.

The book is organized around six chapters, one exploring each of the six distinctive types of narrative pedagogy. While, for the sake of conceptual clarity, each type is presented in a somewhat pure form, practitioners often combine a number of types in any given program. Indeed the summer drama program described to open this introduction employed all six pedagogical types. To orient the reader, the types are named here, with allusions to their embodiment in the Acting 4 Change program above.

First, narrative pedagogies can teach for *religious literacy*. Grounded in the awareness that certain stories are constitutive of any given faith community, these pedagogies teach for a basic familiarity with that community's essential narratives. To know a faith tradition is to know its stories, stories often considered inspired and therefore intrinsically salutary. Religious literacy pedagogies are operative when African Americans learn the constitutive narratives of their black Christian heritage, when intergenerational drama groups learn biblical texts by setting them to music, or in the case of Acting 4 Change, when teens rewrite Mark's passion account as newspaper reporters simply to learn the story's features, features that live within the teens long after the summer program is over.

Second, narrative pedagogies can teach for *personal identity*. Informed by the insight that identity is narratively constructed, these pedagogies help teens reimagine their personal life stories through the interpretive lenses of cultural or religious narratives that promise to be both meaningful and liberative. This approach is embodied when at-risk boys construct their identity around a classical heroes' journey mythology, when a junior high misfit transforms his self-understanding as a modern-day ugly duckling, or in the case of Acting 4 Change, when a group of teens reframes their experience of claiming hope in the midst of despair as a way of participating with the Spirit of God that raised Jesus from the dead.

Third, narrative pedagogies can teach for *contemplative encounter*. Recognizing that some narrative texts have the power to mediate the presence of God, these pedagogies cultivate a profound indwelling of a story in the hope of experiencing the sacred reality embedded within it. Whether prayerfully interior or reverently communal, these approaches engage the imagination to meditate upon a text until it becomes palpably alive and pregnant with presence. When it happens, the participants know it—like the abused boys who so embodied Job's prosecution of God, God issued forth from the trial itself, or like the teens in Acting 4 Change whose still-life sculpture of Mark's missing-body scene created a hush as real as the anguish on Easter morning.

Fourth, narrative pedagogies can teach for *critical reflection*. Disturbed at the death-dealing storylines that infiltrate culture, these pedagogies awaken a critical consciousness toward stories, often already internalized, that squelch life and inhibit human dignity. Such critical reflection is nurtured when Korean American women critique patriarchal folktales, when post-9/11 teens resist storylines of vengeance toward terrorists, or when, in Acting 4 Change, a teenager grieving the death of her father realizes the feeble salve of gangster rap.

Fifth, narrative pedagogies can teach for *creative vitality*. Recognizing that artistic expression is intrinsically rejuvenating—a healing journey for some, a spiritual path for others—these pedagogies fan the narrative creativity flickering within each person. As people make up stories for telling, write their own fiction, or stage original plays, free expression is praised, the art forms themselves are celebrated, and the mysteriously revitalizing process of creativity is trusted to work its magic. This magic bubbled through both the Pakistani young lady emboldened as she told the story of claiming her name, and the Acting 4 Change teens taking their bows as the audience applauded their theater piece.

Sixth, narrative pedagogies can teach for *social empowerment*. Building on narrative's power in mobilizing social change, these pedagogies use story and the stage to problematize forms of oppression and empower the oppressed's collective agency to work toward liberation. Not only are social conditions transformed but the self-understandings of the participants as well—from passive spectators before massive social forces to empowered actors capable of creating social change. This approach is embodied when a high school social justice group uses drama to inspire more just disciplinary procedures, and when the Acting 4 Change teens envision a future of hope, identify concrete actions to attain it, and use the stage to rehearse their way into it.

As hinted in these brief synopses, each form of narrative pedagogy, while analytically distinct, is an established means of educational generativity. Also, each offers a unique promise in mediating the sacred to young people. This is good news, for our youth live in a world where plotlines of destruction and plotlines of hope are often difficult to distinguish; a world where drug-damaged love and hard-fought recovery, family estrangement and tender understanding, tragic loss and compassion's balm are all bewilderingly interlaced; and the ways of death and the ways of life are near impossible to untangle. In illuminating the healing possibilities of narrative through precise descriptions of its various pedagogies, this book hopes to help young people discover the divine presence pulsating toward peace within this complex world. In short, in finding God within the graffiti of narrative pedagogies, this book hopes to help teens find God within the graffiti of their lives.

One

How do stories transmit a faith tradition?

Narrative pedagogy and religious literacy

The Reverend Doctor Joshua Caleb Helton III was pastor of Bethel African Methodist Episcopal for thirty-two years. An original freedom rider as a seminary student, Pastor Helton was a seasoned field operative in the civil rights movement before migrating west to shepherd a church in the heart of South Central Los Angeles. The church was besieged: riots had decimated the community; poverty and nihilism were rampant. And yet, with the prophetic force of Moses, and Aaron's administrative acumen, Pastor Helton transformed a ragtag remnant of the faithful into a beacon of power and hope. The rec hall soon housed a career center, a college preparatory program, and an office for social ministries; the church formed a children's school, then a leadership academy; forged an affordable housing alliance, then established an economic justice coalition; even the cultural arts were acclaimed as the congregation's gospel choir started selling CDs and selling out church halls all across the town. In three decades, Bethel AME became both a thriving congregation and a fixture in the African American community. And ever dressed in his three-piece suits, his shoes polished, handkerchief creased, and his tie knot crisp and cinched with a pin, Pastor Helton stood tall at the helm. He was the congregation's captain. He was beloved. And now, hastened by heart surgery, he was stepping down.

The congregation knew that nothing but the perfect farewell tribute would do, and they knew where to start—with Pastor Helton's unwavering commitment to youth. For three decades, Pastor Helton had conducted each year's confirmation process. His teaching strategy was simple: he told stories—stories of his days in the civil rights movement, stories of forebears who fought through slavery, stories reaching back to biblical ancestors. Pastor Helton believed young people needed to know their heritage: who they were, where they came from, and the people who make one proud to be an African American Christian. The young people absorbed the stories, and they researched others. As part of the process, each teen had to find one historical figure she particularly admired, study that person, distill his or her legacy, and identify that person's most ennobling qualities. Then on Confirmation Sunday, as each teenager confirmed her faith and claimed the community as her own, the young person named her patron role model and claimed her or him as her guide as she navigated the bayous of adulthood.

With Pastor Helton derailed by ill health, Yolanda Jones was commissioned to take over the confirmation class. Once again, the teens would learn stories from their heritage and choose one historical figure to study in more detail. But in addition, they gathered stories from the congregation. They consulted with the choir and studied Negro spirituals. Then they crafted a play that both confirmed their faith and commemorated the genius of Pastor Helton's legacy. It promised to be a Confirmation Sunday unlike any other.

Decked out in his standard-issue tailored suit and accessories, the guest of honor made his first congregational appearance since the surgery that sidelined him. Buoyed as much by the rousing applause as the two canes he clung to, Pastor Helton walked the aisle and sat in the front row. The cheering crowd stood until a teen took center stage and introduced the afternoon's program: a freedom ride through African American history.

As the curtains part, the stage reveals a vandalized bus turned over on its side—charred, slashed, and ripped. Around it, trash bins are upended and rubble is piled. Sounds of a riot shriek offstage—police sirens, gunshots, glass being shattered by baseball bats. Backdrop to the wreckage, a gauze veil is draped in wide strips. Beyond that, darkness.

Cautiously, a group of teenagers crawls out and surveys the damage.

"Whoa, look what they did to our ride," one youth wails at the overturned bus.

"It's trashed, man," bemoans another.

A third teen fingers the splayed wires. "This is gonna take some work."

"Forget about it," Torrance sneers, a tall teen whose anger gets people's attention.

"But we gotta find a way out."

"There *is* no way out," Torrance continues. "You just gotta eat the Jim Crow . . . and hide good when the bullets fly."

One teen counts the group. "Say, where's Sonny?"

They glance around. "They got him already," Torrance despairs. "I'm telling you, it's hopeless." Shots fire again, sirens squeal. The teens, all but Torrance, scurry to the bus's undercarriage and cower. "Yep," Torrance sums up, "it's all plain hopeless."

As the youth crouch in fear, a plaintive voice carries from back-stage. Against the veiled backdrop, a train's silhouette eases by. Its lone passenger is singing:

This train is bound for glory, this train.
This train is bound for glory, this train.
This train is bound for glory, hop on board and hear the story,
This train is bound for glory, this train.

Only one of the teens hears the song, a young woman who slips away and gravitates toward it. As she nears the backdrop, the train stops. The passenger, an elderly woman dressed in a nineteenth-century frock and shawl, slips through the veil. She cups the teen's face, gazes into her eyes, and whispers intently. Smiling, she slips off her shawl and drapes it around the young woman's shoulders. She reboards the train, and as the train eases off-stage, she continues her mournful refrain. Somewhat mystified, the teen returns to the others huddled against the bus. One of them notices her shawl.

"Where d'ya get that?"

"It's the weirdest thing," the young woman contemplates. "Harriett Tubman just came to me, like in a vision. I think she came to help us."

"Who's Harriett Tubman?" one teen asks.

The young woman mulls it over. Then she tells Tubman's story: how Tubman escaped from slavery and organized the network of safe houses that comprised the Underground Railroad; how she returned to the South and rescued her sister and nieces, then returned many times more, teaching spirituals that hid codes to follow, evading captors through wading in the waters, keeping an eye on the north star, and like Moses before her, freeing her people from slavery. A forty-thousand-dollar reward was put on her head, but in nineteen trips, she was never caught, liberating over three hundred herself and inspiring countless more.

The others take in her story. But once its spell recedes, confusion descends. "How's that going to help us here?" someone asks.

"I don't know," the young woman concedes. "But I think she's telling us, if she could do it, we can . . . we can make a train to freedom."

"We tried that once," Torrance quips while digging through debris. "Look where it got us. Anyone's who tired of bedtime stories help me look for Sonny."

"Well, I've got to try," says the teen in Tubman's shawl. She walks to the back side of the bus. "Anyone gonna help me?"

The teens sit in indecision. Shots decide it for them: the teens race around and bury themselves in the trash piles. The teen in Tubman's shawl stands tall. Oblivious to the gunfire pings, she pushes, determined to right the bus herself. Behind the veil, the song returns, a duet now, a man and woman singing in mournful tandem as the train eases across the backdrop.

"This train is bound for glory, this train. . . ."

One teen hears the song and rises to explore. Harriett Tubman is still on the train, with another figure behind her. As the teen nears the veil, this new figure slips away from the train. He cups the young man's face, whispers to him, then disrobes his nineteenth-century gentleman's coat and slips it on the youth. His work done, the figure returns to the train, resumes the song, and eases across the stage. The other teens notice the young man's new coat and the questions return, "Where d'ya get that?" "Frederick Douglass came in a dream." "Who's Frederick Douglass?" And the teen tells the story—how Frederick Douglass escaped the plantation and became an eloquent self-taught lecturer; how he wrote a book, then started a journal, the *North Star*, that united and guided the abolitionists' movement; how he traveled to Washington and convinced Abraham Lincoln to outlaw slavery once and for all through the Emancipation Proclamation.

Again, the teens are spellbound by the story, then befuddled as to its meaning. "Don't you see?" the newly cloaked teen proclaims. "It's like Frederick Douglass is here, telling us we can stand up to slavery of any kind. From plantation masters or ghetto violence, it doesn't matter—we can claim our own emancipation and ride the train to freedom." He joins the teen in Tubman's shawl and shoulders the bus to right it. It refuses to budge. More shots ring out. The other teens furrow in terror as Torrance keeps searching for Sonny.

And the Freedom Train backstage eases by again; then it does so again, and does so yet again. One by one the passengers swell, the singing swelling as well, as historical dignitaries pass their stories and bestow their mantles onto the teens that they commission. A youth draped in an African head wrap remembers Sojourner Truth—how she escaped from slavery; how she traveled the land and proclaimed the truth that all God's people are equal; how she boldly became the original freedom rider when she integrated a carriage by planting herself on its comfortable seats, then reciting the law into the driver's ears as he tried to dislodge her. She got her ride, then made darn sure the driver lost his job.

A teen draped in a judge's cloak tells Thurgood Marshall's story— how he survived impoverished schools and worked his way through a law degree; how he challenged racist statutes and ended up on the Supreme Court. Another teen tells of Rosa Parks; another of Ruby Bridges. One by one, the stories come out; one by one, the Freedom Train's song grows louder; one by one, the group with their shoulders to the overturned bus gains strength in a concerted effort to right it. But the school bus does not budge. And neither does Torrance. Until his shout ends the momentum.

"I found him!" Peeling off debris from a pile, Torrance lays bare a
teenager's body. "It's Sonny." The others rush over. "And he's alive!"
As the teens tend him, Torrance fumes to the side. He's so angry,
he's beside himself. "See!" he exclaims. "They're trying to kill us
and all you can do is tell stories." He kicks an overturned trash can,
grabs a length of pipe, and takes a swing at the bus. Behind the
veiled backdrop, the Freedom Train returns. It is filled with all the
characters who have appeared already—with one more. This time,
Torrance hears it, and he skeptically nears the veil. A tall lean man
with an intellectual's glasses slips through and whispers to him.
Torrance shakes his head. The man speaks with quiet authority.
Torrance turns away. The man turns Torrance back and stares at
him with smoldering intensity. Their common rage fuses and Torrance nods. The man places his glasses on Torrance's eyes. Torrance sees; the man returns to the train, and with it, eases off stage.
As Torrance returns to the group, he is still puzzling over what just
happened.

"Malcolm came to me. He wants me to tell his story." Torrance
does, confusedly at first, then increasingly inspired. He tells of the
death of Malcolm's father when Malcolm was but six and his subsequent life of drugs and delinquency; how he turned from crime,
became a Black Muslim, and turned his rage into a militant black
pride; how he hated any whisper of racism, demanded freedom at
any cost, and insisted on a self-respect that defied even an assassin's
aim. The story takes Torrance to a fever pitch. "You guys are right,"
he blazes, "we can refuse oppression. We can ride away to a Mecca
of dignity. Let's get this bus back on its tracks."

His words inspire the others. They lean into the vehicle and shove.
It does not move. They shove again. Still no movement. They shove
harder, then harder still. As their shoving continues to no avail, the
Freedom Train rolls again behind the opaque veil. Sonny is revived
by its music and hobbles toward the curtain. A new figure is at the
end, one who slips through the veil and cups Sonny's face, then fits
Sonny with his suit jacket and a Nobel medal around Sonny's neck.

The train rolls on, and Sonny walks dazedly to the still-straining group. They notice him and rush over.

"You're okay," they exclaim.

"And somebody came from the train."

"Yeah," Sonny replies bewildered.

"Who?"

"It was Dr. Martin Luther King."

"What did he say?" they ask.

"He told me a story. It happened in Birmingham, when they went there to integrate it. He was at a church to preach to the demonstrators and just as he stepped to the podium, this one white man in the front row lunges, knocking King onto the floor and beating up on him. The place went crazy. A mob jumped up, grabbed the man, and was muscling him toward the door when King stood up and shocked the crowd by yelling over everyone, '*Stop!*' He walked up to that man, and put his arm around his shoulder. Then he looked at the crowd and said,

> What do you want to do with this man? Beat him? Kill him? Do unto him what he's done unto us? That's not our job here. Our job here is to step into his shoes and ask ourselves, "What would we be like if we were taught since we could walk that the Negro was a thing?" Our job is to see his hatred and refuse to mirror it back, to understand him, to appeal to his humanity, and to welcome him into the Beloved Community that welcomes each one of us.

"That was his dream—that one day we'll live in a world where *all* God's children are one. We can live it now. We can resist violence and love our oppressors into goodness. We can right this bus, and ride it all the way to the Beloved Community Martin Luther King dared imagine. Let's go."

The others, inspired, bolt to the bus. This time, they feel it. This time, they have the power. This time, the bus, like their burgeoning personhood, is standing up and driving them to freedom. They shove. It budges. They shove harder. It lifts ever so slightly. With the force of history, they shove even harder. The bus inches higher. A foot off the ground, it hovers for a second. A second longer. Then it crashes back down with a leaden thump. With all their strength, they simply cannot do it. Torrance kicks the ground and storms, "It's pointless. It's just too heavy for us."

"I don't get it," says one teen. "It seemed so possible. Look at us. We've got all these stories. I thought for sure they would do it."

"That's just it," Torrance spits. "They're just stories. They're nothing in the face of real tribulation. They pump you up, then let you down. They're just a bunch of lame old stories."

Without a spark to contradict him, the teens gaze at the ground. Their stories seem dead in the dust.

Then it comes. From the back of the auditorium, a lone plaintive baritone voice bellows as if singing from the grave.

> When Israel was in Egypt's land,
> Let my people go.
> Oppressed so hard they could not stand,
> Let my people go.
> Go down, Moses,
> Way down in Egypt land.
> Tell old Pharaoh,
> "Let my people go."

The soloist walks up the aisle. All turn to see a teenager dressed to the nines—a tailored three-piece suit, polished shoes, tie crisply knotted and cinched with a pin. Everyone gets it instantly. Pastor Helton has entered the building. And he's singing his signature song.

The spiritual wails as the teenage pastor walks the aisle and mounts the stage's steps. When the music fades, the pastor inquires, "What's going on?"

"Man, we're stuck in this ghetto and our bus has been trashed. We can't get it back on its feet."

"What're you using for muscle?"

"That's just it," Torrance says. "All we got are stories."

"Well," Pastor Helton considers, "stories can be a mighty powerful thing. I rode on a bus much like this one, through some pretty mean places, too. And all I had were the stories that people passed on to me."

"But what good were they?" Torrance pushes.

"I'll tell you what good they were. We came into a place as bad as this. And we took those stories and we built ourselves a train. A Freedom Train, right here in the ghetto. And you know who was on that train? Harriett Tubman was on that train. Now she didn't go by Ms. Harriett Tubman, no. Her name was Martha Simpson." (As he mentions her name, the real Martha Simpson—a middle-aged woman from the church—walks on stage humming "This train is bound for glory, this train.") But I tell you what, when gangs were enslaving our neighborhood with fear, she built us an Underground Railroad—a community watch so our children could walk to school in safety.

"You know who else was on that train? Frederick Douglass was on that train. Now here, he goes by Steven Jackson." (The real Steven Jackson walks out humming and stands alongside Martha Simpson.) "But when the mayor zoned a toxic waste dump in our neighborhood, he marched on up to city hall and talked that mayor down. We had Sojourner Truth on that train, and Thurgood Marshall, Rosa Parks, and Malcolm X." As he names each heroic figure, their real-life counterpart walks on stage humming in chorus with the others—the single mother who started the Sojourner Truth Shelter for Women, the janitor who studied law by night and now is a superior court judge, the X-ray nurse who refused to leave when unjustly dismissed from her job, and the schoolteacher who stayed in South Central to teach Black Studies at the church youth academy. By now the youthful Pastor Helton is all but preaching over the music. "Do you see them? They're standing in our midst. Those stories are life. Those stories are who we are. Those stories are who we can become if we see ourselves with the eyes of faith."

"But they're still just stories," Torrance protests. "How do they help us lift up a bus?"

"The stories are your strength," Pastor Helton proclaims, the music still humming as he scans the young people. "Look around you. You've got Harriett Tubman shouldering that bus." He points at the teen in the shawl. "You've got Frederick Douglass here, Ruby Bridges, why you've got both Malcolm and Martin. If they can't raise this bus, nobody can."

The teens' sheepishness betrays their shame. "But you've got us all wrong," the teen with the shawl reveals. "I'm not really Harriett Tubman." She takes the shawl off. "I'm just Tiffany. I'm in the ninth grade."

"And I'm not Martin, I'm Sonny."

"And I'm Diana. We're not the people you think we are."

Pastor Helton eyes Tiffany as he walks up to her, puts Harriett Tubman's shawl back onto her shoulders, and says, "Oh . . . but you *are* Harriett Tubman. Her blood runs through your veins. And you, you *are* Sojourner Truth, and you *are* Malcolm X. They dwell in your soul, they feed your dreams, their strength rushes through you like a river toward freedom."

The teens look at each other, and then at the bus. The humming behind them turns into a whispering chorus—"This train is bound for glory, this train." The music quickens their fledgling hope. Emboldened, they shoulder the bus once more. As the music mounts, they heave. The bus nudges. The music gets louder. The bus inches upward. The music breaks free. And in a mighty burst of power, the bus stands up and the teens cheer.

But the cheer is short-lived. The bus is in no condition to be driven. Yet the teens are undaunted. Buoyed by the music, they get to work. Pastor Helton directs the adult choir to positions around the bus and, slowly, they swivel it around. As the front pivots out of sight, the teens get busy with the cleanup operation. The audience cannot see the bus, nor what the teens are doing with the scrap they are retrieving from the bins and piles on the stage. But they see the result. By the time the bus comes full circle, a miracle of restoration has occurred. The bus looks like a cross between an electric trolley car and a blues band's luxury coach: the seats are new and plush, the sides are bright as if freshly painted, marquee lights trim the edges, and the teenager's historical props—the shawls and coats, glasses and gowns—now span the wall in a muraled tribute to the liberative heritage that sustains them. The sign across the top titles it well: FREEDOM TRAIN BOUND FOR GLORY.

The youth are ecstatic and take their seats within. The chorus recedes to the back. Pastor Helton watches from the side as proud as the Maker beholding the first day of creation.

"Come on," one teen yells. "We're ready to go." Pastor Helton nods knowingly. "What's the matter? We need to get out of here." She points to the conspicuously empty conductor's seat.

"I'm not coming with you," Pastor Helton reveals.

"What do you mean? You're our driver. You're the only one who knows the way."

"No," the pastor says. "You don't need me anymore. You've got everything you need right here."

"But what will you do? You can't stay here."

Pastor Helton smiles. "Do not worry. All is taken care of." From backstage, the song begins again, its mournful tone in contrast to the jubilation just moments before. Behind the veil, the Freedom Train eases into view, filled with history's heroes.

"Look," one teen exclaims with hope. "Another story is coming to help."

"No," Pastor Helton assures. "No one else is coming. The train is here for me."

"No," the teens protest. "You can't mean . . ." But Pastor Helton is right. As the teens watch aghast, the pastor eases across the stage, slips through the opaque veil, and takes his place at the end of the waiting train. The train resumes its journey. To the chorus that has sung throughout history, the long line of legends eases out of sight.

The teens gaze wistfully at the train's wake. Shots snap their sorrow short. As panic returns, they search each other out. The conductor's seat remains empty. "Quick," one teen yells. "We gotta get outta here. Who's gonna drive the bus?"

Like an eager recruit clueless to danger, a five-year-old cries out from the audience, "*I'll drive it!*" The crowd chuckles, but the boy is dead serious. Standing on his daddy's lap, he has seen it all and is ready for action. Sonny improvises.

"You will, will you?"

"Sure I will."

"Well . . . do you know the song?"

Without waiting to be asked again, the precocious child starts right in, "This train is bound for glory, this train." Other children join the chorus. With Sonny's wave, the whole spontaneous choir rushes the stage. Soon children are hanging from the bus's side, piling on the teenagers' laps, and cramming into the cab sharing the wheel with Sonny. With the bus jammed, Sonny returns to the script.

"Okay . . . , let's get out of here. Let's ride this train to freedom." The boy on his lap turns the key. Nothing happens. He turns it again. Nothing still. Shots fire from offstage. The violence is getting closer.

"Quick," one teen screams. "We've got to get out of here."

Another turn of the key. Still nothing. Sonny dashes out to the engine. He lifts up a handful of wires. "I hate to say it, but this bus is too far gone." Just then, a young man with a pipe runs onto stage. When he sees Sonny, he wields it like a baseball bat. A handful of teens leap off the bus and surround the would-be assailant. The thug might get Sonny, but he wouldn't live to enjoy it.

"It's the guy that beat up Sonny," one yells. As Sonny recognizes him, rage fills his eyes. He raises the wires to use as whips. The two circle each other poised to attack.

Then Torrance steps off the bus, dragging the pipe he salvaged earlier. "I get it now," he says. "Why the bus won't start. We're not supposed to flee to the promised land. We're supposed to build the promised land right here." He worms through the crowd and addresses it from within. "Look," he says, pointing to the thug, "he's just like us—scared, poor, so beaten down he can only fight back. Someone's got to stop it. Someone's got to remember that we're brothers and sisters clawing for the same thing—peace, dignity, a tableful of food, and a family to enjoy it with." He looks at the thug as he lays his pipe on the ground. "This isn't the way," he continues. He sidles over to Sonny, takes the wires from Sonny's hands, and tosses them onto the ground as well. "We just want to be free—free from violence, free from fear, free to be the family God created us to be."

The thug ponders with his pipe still poised. Torrance approaches him. Like coaxing a gun from a toddler, he cautiously reaches up and disarms him of the pipe. Then he bends to the ground and, using the wires as binding, fits the pipes to form a cross. "We're starting a church," he tells the thug. "What d'ya say? Ride with us to freedom." He opens his arms and embraces him. The thug is tentative, his eyes peeled on Sonny. Sonny watches as Torrance releases the thug and steps aside. Then too, Sonny relents.

"Yeah," he says, "ride with us to freedom." Setting their hostility aside, the two embrace with conviction. As they hold each other tight, a spotlight shines through the veil. Looking down from his perch as if an angel on high, the teenage Pastor Helton watches on approvingly. Then he sings. As the spiritual meanders through the scene, Torrance hands a teen on the bus the cross stitched from weapons. The teen plants it front and center, then fastens an addendum. FREEDOM TRAIN BOUND FOR GLORY now has a name . . . BETHEL AME CHURCH. They sing their proclamation, and their prayer:

"This train is bound for glory, join with us and live the story, This train is bound for glory, this train."

Theoretical underpinnings

For Pastor Helton, faith is a freedom ride. Being an African American Christian means being part of a history, a movement that has traveled through time. Born of dignified origins, a people has labored toward a promised land of peace and prosperity. Repeatedly, they have found themselves pummeled and enslaved by oppressors. But oppression has not vanquished them. Along the way, luminaries have arisen, reminding them of their original dignity, restoring for them their guiding hope, and pounding through oppression's mire with the relentless drive of a locomotive. This movement through history defines the African American Christian. To be one of them, to claim their faith as one's own, is to join them on the train—to journey through the same lands, to be guided by the same stars, and to be bound for the same promised glory. One cannot hop on board, however, unless one sees the train, unless one knows the story.

Pastor Helton and Yolanda Jones exemplify a *religious literacy* approach to narrative pedagogy. Their primary purpose is to teach African American young people an appreciative awareness of their religious and cultural heritage—to be fluent in the core symbols and images through which their community interprets experience.[1] When Bethel AME has a "dream" that its neighborhood flourish with justice and peace, its leaders want their youth to know the nuances of meaning and the constellation of values this dream entails by virtue of its roots in the one Martin Luther King proclaimed, and the Israelite's vision of the promised land before him. Such literacy is essential for full communal participation, otherwise the convictions and themes that define a community have no meaning, and the guiding images that inspire the community have no power. One cannot fully join a community whose language one does not speak.

If recent studies are correct, today's young people are urgently in need of religious literacy.[2] Christian Smith and Melinda Lundquist Denton, after conducting the largest-ever study of teens and religion, find that the vast majority of North American young people are "*incredibly inarticulate* about their faith . . . and its meaning or place in their lives."[3] Teenagers are seldom cognizant of their faith community's core convictions, let alone conversant with how to embody them within their world. This is especially unfortunate in that adolescence is usually the time when young people are invited to affirm their religious heritage and claim their faith community as their own. Communal rites of passage such as confirmation and bar and bat mitzvah are occasions on which teens are expected to learn their religious tradition more fully and to make some form of a mature public profession of their faith. Yet affirming one's faith implies knowing its contours; and claiming one's community implies knowing that community's identity.

Pastor Helton and Yolanda Jones show that narrative has a unique promise in nurturing religious literacy. At its most basic level, given their engaging nature, stories are an unusually effective way to communicate a religious heritage, for stories remain with people long after didactic content has dissipated. More than that, the process by which a community's faith tradition is known and owned is intrinsically narrative in structure. Knowing a community entails learning that community's story, and joining a community entails making that story one's own.

Why are stories so effective for teaching religious literacy?

First, *religious communities profess that some stories are intrinsically transformative.* Like precious jewels whose sparkling beauty bestows delight, certain stories are treasured by a faith community. Beholding them renews the soul, kindles the spirit, and quickens the hope that sustains a people. Pastor Helton did not tell random folktales or amusing fables out of some simple love for storytelling. He told stories that are uniquely liberative within his religious culture, stories that can lift the bus of the human spirit resisting racial oppression.

Narrative theologian Gabriel Fackre calls these "canonical stories," narratives that have paradigmatic authority for a community's sense of identity, integrity, and purpose. They are the community's functionally sacred stories—the ones to which the community returns to remember who they are, the ones that inform the community's vision of the good and beautiful life, indeed, the ones through which God is known and understood. The death and resurrection of Jesus, his birth, the parables he told—the Good Samaritan and the Prodigal Son—the story of Creation, the exodus, Daniel's faith in the lion's den are all such sacred stories treasured within the Christian tradition.

As the tradition grows, and God continues to be known, other stories are added that function with communal authority. James McClendon, a narrative ethicist, underscores this capacity in Christian biographies, specifically the stories of exemplars whose lives embody Christian convictions in truthful and inspiring ways.[4] Their stories are sources of renewal and reflection for religious communities. For Bethel AME, the biographies of Harriett Tubman, Rosa Parks, and Martin Luther King embody authentic faith and spark a similar faith in the present. Stories of resistance and emancipation during slavery are sacred, as are those of the Montgomery bus boycott, the march on Selma, and the triumph of love in the face of hatred within the boiling cauldron of Birmingham. These stories settle into the soul like spiritual leaven. When they are remembered, one's dignity as a people is reclaimed, faith in a God of justice is renewed, and the resolve to fight for freedom is emboldened. Surely, religious literacy is incomplete unless these canonical stories are known, and their beauty beheld.

Second, stories are so effective in conveying religious literacy because *the content of religious faith is narratively constituted.* The canonical stories through which God is known form the substantive core that grounds religious faith. People do not place their faith in a system of doctrine or a set of ethical commands; they place their faith in God, a specific God, who has acted concretely in history and is only known through the particularity of these concrete actions. The content of faith is a story, the story of how a particular God has related with God's world, the hope toward which that God is inviting all of creation, and the ways this cosmic storyline is playing out today. Doctrine alone deadens; narrative, however, enlivens, for God is not known in theological abstractions but in the blood and marrow of living events.

Likewise, Christian theological reflection on this is unmoored speculation unless it is grounded in the story of how God was saving the world through the historical events of Jesus and his Jewish ancestors before him. To the extent that Christian communities continue to experience God's saving work, an articulated doctrine of salvation must ring true with these stories as well. Bethel AME experiences a God who saved an ancient people from slavery, who inspired an Underground Railroad when slavery appeared again, who empowered a weary seamstress, emboldened an elementary school kid, and commissioned a Baptist preacher to fight for the civil rights of the oppressed. These stories have authority. The community *knows* them to be true. Their doctrine of salvation, therefore, will be derivative of and will elaborate upon these sacred narratives. More than simply the salvaging of a soul, for example, salvation for Bethel AME includes a people's liberation from oppression, their claiming of human dignity, and their dream that God will restore the bonds that racism has rent asunder.[5] Teaching a theological concept divorced from these taproot narratives not only deadens the pedagogy but it obscures the essential meaning found only within the stories.

Similarly, moral precepts are narrative dependent.[6] What grounds the ancient Israelite ethical command to show hospitality to the stranger? Political expediency? Geographical necessity? No. The command emerges from and only has meaning within the narrative of God's hospitality when the Israelites were strangers in Egypt (see Ex. 23:9). Ethical deliberation entails determining what actions are "fitting" within the story a community is called to live. The teens of Bethel AME engaged in precisely this type of reflection. How should they respond to the thug who threatens them? To be sure, they have relevant moral precepts—like the Sermon on the Mount admonition for followers to love their enemies; yet this precept's substance and power are only known in the stories in which it is enfleshed—for example, in Martin Luther King's redemptive response to the thug who threatened him, the dream of radical inclusion that inspired it, and the example of Jesus that grounded it.

In sum, the contents of faith—the doctrines, commandments, even its ritual practices—are all narratively constituted. A faith tradition is not known when its theological doctrines can be articulated, nor when its ethical precepts can be distilled. A faith tradition is known when its canonical stories are absorbed, when these stories become the soil from which theological reflection springs forth, and when they provide the narrative framework that defines faithful behavior. In short, the core of religious literacy is the narrative core of religious faith.

The third theoretical underpinning supporting the narrative structure of religious literacy goes beyond religious communities treasuring sacred stories, and beyond these stories grounding the substantive content of religious faith. More than that, *religious communities themselves are narratively constituted.* The very glue that binds a people's collective identity is the story of their common journey toward a shared goal. In essence, communities *are* stories. Consequently, religious literacy—fluency with the language a community shares—includes knowing the narratives by which that particular community's core identity is constituted.

George Stroup reminds us that a community, as opposed to a mob or crowd, is a group of people united around a shared sense of a common past through which they interpret the present, and a common future toward which they are journeying together. For Christian communities, this narrative identity has both cosmic and particular dimensions. On a cosmic level, Christians see history as unfolding along a grand narrative arc that begins with Creation; meanders through the decisive events of the fall, the exodus, exile and restoration, the coming of Jesus, the founding of the church; and streams through the centuries toward the promised coming of the Kin-dom of God.[7] This grand cosmic storyline is understood as God's story playing out in history. What makes a community "Christian" is not the doctrines it espouses nor the precepts it advocates; it is the shared self-understanding—nurtured by ritual, proclamation, and educational reflection—that this group of people is part of this grand story, and that together they are seeking to participate with that story ever more faithfully.[8]

On a particular level, groups of Christian people gather together in specific communities that seek to live faithfully to this cosmic story within a particular historical location. Their particular communal identity is the story of how they as a specific group of people began with some form of call from God to be a church, the vision of the Kin-dom of God on Earth they have sought to embody, and the peaks and valleys along the way as they have quested toward that vision. This "communal story" is what unites them as a people. In the same way that a community is "Christian" to the extent that the cosmic story of God in Christ frames their self-understanding, an assembly of persons has a specific congregational identity—the Hillside Church of God, for example, or the Santa Ana Catholic Worker—to the extent that they share a common story of living as God's people in that particular historical location.

Bethel AME is a community where story defines its life together. Its people share a common cosmic narrative arc. As Christians and African Americans, they look to the same origins and roots—the chosen ones of Israel, the church called by Jesus, the African home-land from which they were exiled; they plot their people's decisive events along a common cosmic storyline—exodus, slavery, emancipation, segregation, civil rights; and they quest for a common sense of the Good—a promised land, a dream, of freedom and dignity, prosperity and peaceful coexistence.

The people of Bethel AME are also united around a shared communal narrative. They are the people who were called into being by a charismatic civil rights pastor, who have continually discerned what the promised land looks like in contemporary South Central LA, and who have wrestled together to embody their dream guided by the luminaries who have lit up their past. They are the story of Martha Simpson laying the rails of Harriett Tubman within the slavery of gang violence, of Steven Jackson treading the track of Frederick Douglass within a biased city government, of Pastor Helton extending the ride of Martin and Malcolm through an urban ghetto, and of all the other present-day parishioners who are not so much woodenly mimicking their ancestral companions as joining them on the same campaign those ancestors pioneered. Bethel AME is a Freedom Train. And its core communal identity is the story of how this train has sometimes lumbered and sometimes raced toward the land promised by God.

The genius of Bethel's confirmation process lies in its recognition of their narrative communal identity. They know that embracing a community and the faith it proclaims involves knowing the stories by which that community is constituted. Their youth need a sense of the cosmic narrative arc—God's Freedom Train through history—that shapes the identity of African American Christians, and they need to know how Bethel AME in particular has participated in this narrative arc within its own specific context.

The genius of their process goes further still. The youth are not merely learning the community's narrative identity; they are being invited to make that identity their own. At Bethel AME, knowing one's tradition goes beyond absorbing that tradition's stories to joining the story's journey: fixing one's own eyes on the northern stars that glitter with the dream of freedom, donning the mantle of exemplars who have laid track in their promising light, and stepping into the narrative adventure of sustaining that track's redemptive direction. In short, religious literacy means more than noticing the Freedom Train that rolls through history. It means claiming one's seat upon it, and with the chorus that sustains it, singing it toward glory.

Educational movements

Given the power of story to teach a tradition, religious literacy approaches to narrative pedagogy seek to do three things:

1. They help people learn the core stories that form the heritage and identity of their particular faith tradition.

2. They enable theological and ethical reflection grounded in these stories. That is, they involve others in the ongoing discernment of what these stories reveal about God, God's relationship with the world, and what it means for a people of faith to live true to their narrative vision.

3. They encourage people to join the story—to internalize these stories as their own, to interpret the world through these stories' lenses, and to respond in ways that participate with the stories' faithful unfolding.

Religious educators have long recognized the centrality of stories in passing along a community's heritage. From the earliest ancestors of the Jewish tradition, for example, a narrative recital is woven into the heart of Passover; when children inquire about the ritual's meaning, elders for centuries simply reply by recounting the exodus story. Nevertheless, recent years have seen a heightened attention to story's promise in nurturing religious literacy. [9]

One representative educator, youth minister Sarah Arthur, specifically addresses narrative's contribution to the religious literacy of Christian adolescents.[10] Arthur is convinced that postmodernism, with its obliteration of communal metanarratives and its corrosive radical relativity, is leaving teenagers starved for transcendence while skeptical toward religious traditions they in fact know little about. With nothing else feeding them, teens flock with religious devotion to such transcendent epics as *The Matrix* and *The Lord of the Rings*. Arthur wants "to impart Biblical and theological content to young people"[11] in ways that captivate their imagination. She recognizes that not only is Christianity a storied tradition, but story is the way any community transmits what really matters to the next generation. Observing that media-saturated teens think more in images than concepts and that a good story has the power to entrance even the most overstimulated junior high-schooler, Arthur calls for youth ministers to claim their role as *bards*, "poets charged with the task of keeping and imparting the stories, language, values, and beliefs of a culture"[12] in ways that invite youth into the storytelling tradition of Christianity. Toward that end, Arthur invites leaders of youth to tell stories, lots of them, with the passion of people who love and believe them—rather than with the enthusiasm of "one reciting a telephone directory."[13] And she lifts up confirmation as the opportune time to teach young people the cosmic storyline of the Bible as a whole—as "the narrative portrait of who God is"[14]—and also how that narrative arc continues throughout the Christian tradition.

The five educational movements of religious literacy narrative pedagogy

So how do you use story to teach religious literacy? Whether embodied in Sarah Arthur's immersion of postmodern teens into Christian metanarratives or Pastor Helton's tutorial for African American teens on their cultural and religious heritage, the essential method of a religious literacy approach to narrative pedagogy has five distinctive educational movements. These movements need not be followed in rigid order. More like movements in a symphony, the individual melody lines can intermingle within one another. Nor does every practitioner explicitly name all five movements in their pedagogical descriptions. However, the full symphonic richness of this approach to narrative pedagogy is heightened to the extent that each movement is given its due attention.

The first movement is *to discern which stories teens will engage in any given session or program.* It is logistically impossible to teach teens every significant narrative within a community's tradition. To choose which stories one will teach, the youth leader should consider the audience for which the event or program is designed, the specific purposes therein, and the particular collection of stories that are most important for their community, drawing from *canonical stories* (exemplary biographies, revelatory moments within the tradition, along with specific narratives within the community's sacred writings); *cosmic stories* (metanarrative arcs that frame history as an ongoing storyline whether spanning the Bible as a whole, the development of the Christian tradition, or the historical movement of a particular religious culture like African American Christianity); and *communal stories* (those local narratives that shape the identity of a particular congregation or religious community).

Sometimes, the story selection will be guided by the educational event's designated theme or topic. For example, in a session on salvation, a narrative educator would seek authoritative stories that illuminate various aspects of the saving work of God. Other times, the straightforward purpose of narrative literacy will be determinative, the stories selected being those most decisive in knowing deeply one's faith tradition. In either case, the stories may be selected by the educator (presumably in consultation with some curricular oversight body) or by the learners encouraged to discover such stories for themselves. At Bethel AME, both occurred. Pastor Helton carried a satchel of stories from which he shared some decisive ones, and yet he also empowered the confirmands to research others that inform African American Christian identity. Either way, educators should be reflective about what stories teens are encouraged to engage.

The second educational movement is *to help youth experience the story as a story.* Obviously, once selected, religious narratives must be presented to the learners. Too often, however, a narrative aesthetic is neglected when religious stories are communicated—a Bible story is mumbled a few verses at a time by volunteers around the circle, or a historical tradition is dissected on a transparency in an outline of names and dates. Part of the power of stories to seep into the soul's memory and lay claim to one's identity is their ability to entrance—to transport people into their narrative world where characters are palpable, settings are tangible, and experiences are brought to life. A gospel account in the hands of a storyteller can arouse twenty thousand teens at a youth rally to a spontaneous standing ovation. A civil rights memory in the hands of Pastor Helton can hush a handful of breathtaken teens. In any context, when a story is shared *as a story*, the experience and the story are both unforgettable.

Narrative pedagogy's invitation to youth educators is to expose youth to religious stories in aesthetically compelling ways so that the youth can experience the power of the story come to life. Educators can craft biblical accounts and biographical vignettes for contemporary retelling, and they can cultivate their storytelling skills.[15] Other narrative art forms are available as well. Films like *The Prince of Egypt* or *Godspell* engagingly dramatize religious narratives, while others like *Bonhoeffer* or *Eyes on the Prize* compellingly portray liberative historical moments. Literature, for those who love to read, can also recount sacred stories in narratively compelling ways, as seen, for example, in Walt Wangerin's *The Book of God*, Anita Diamant's *The Red Tent*, or Alex Haley's *The Autobiography of Malcolm X*.[16] Mark Miller advocates extended simulations of biblical stories in which the youth "relive" such narrative episodes as the Creation, the Sermon on the Mount, the Last Supper, or the death and resurrection of Jesus.[17] Reader's Theater, scripted skits, poetry, mime, and graphic novels—the possibilities are limited only by the educator's imagination and his or her particular narrative gifts. Yet the central invitation is clear: share the story with all of its captivating power.

The third educational movement is *to nurture intentional reflection on the story*. This third educational movement reminds us that experience alone is not education. Merely experiencing the enthralling power of a good story is not mining that story's educational potential—not illuminating that story's insights about God, faith, and life; understanding the layers those insights embody;

and connecting them with the insights gleaned from one's own life experience. Without the cauldron container of intentional reflection, the flash fire of experience flames out, the moment passes, and its potential to mobilize passion dissipates. In short, reflection is what separates education from entertainment.

Reflection can be nurtured in formal and informal settings. Formally, after sharing a story or viewing a movie, discussion groups or writing prompts can stimulate deeper engagement with the narrative. Informally, casual conversation during coffee hour after worship or while painting scenery for a confirmation play can be opportunities to reflect on a shared narrative experience. One can imagine Pastor Helton, for example, as he's buttoning his robes on Confirmation Sunday, looking over at the teen rehearsing her biographical statement and inquiring, "Tell me again, what is it about Rosa Parks you so admire?"

So, whether we do it formally or informally, we aim to cultivate four types of reflection:[18]

- *Reflection that deepens understanding of the story.* After telling the story of the Good Samaritan, Jesus asked his listener, "Which of the three do you think proved to be a neighbor to the man who fell into the bandit's hand?" (Lk. 10:36). Jesus wanted to ensure that the lawyer not only *heard* the story, he *understood* its narrative world. This type of reflection cements details, explores motivations, and ensures that the story's nuances are noticed. Pastor Helton, after telling the story of Martin Luther King's response to the assailant in Birmingham, may have nurtured this reflection with such questions as, "What do you think the assailant was feeling?" "What was going on in the black mob's instinct to lynch?" or "Why did Dr. King respond as he did?" Such questions encourage a comprehension of the story on its own terms.

- *Reflection that surfaces one's personal connections with the story.* This type of reflection is oriented around a listener's unique experience of the story—the feelings generated, the desires kindled, and the characters with whom one specifically identifies. Such reflection deepens the organic way the story is already seeping into the listener's psyche, and it stimulates the buds of meaning the story is spontaneously germinating. To facilitate this, Pastor Helton might ask, "With whom in the story do you most sympathize?" "How did the assailant's attack make you feel?" or "What would you have done if you were attacked like Martin Luther King was?" Such questions surface and strengthen the unique responses flickering within the listener.

◆ *Reflection that draws out the story's conceptual possibilities.* As detailed earlier, religious narratives provide the substantive ground from which theological convictions and ethical norms emerge. One component of narrative pedagogy is nurturing the capacities to link second-order conceptualization with first-order narrative experience. These capacities include discerning and articulating theological and ethical insights that are embedded within authoritative stories, understanding how abstract concepts and moral principles are incarnated in narrative experience, and relating conceptual insights from different authoritative stories. Pastor Helton would illustrate such reflection by asking questions like, "Where is God in this story?" "What does this story reveal about human brokenness and sin, or the nature of love, or the complexities of forgiveness?" or "How is Dr. King's response like or unlike Jesus' response to those who assaulted him?" Such questions draw out theological insights and encourage grounded conceptual reflection.

◆ *Reflection that interprets contemporary experience through the story's lenses.* As discussed above, faith from the perspective of narrative pedagogy is not so much an adherence to doctrine or an allegiance to ethical principles. Rather, it is participating in the narrative journey of a particular faith tradition. As such, growing in faith entails less the mechanical application of distilled precepts and more the interpretive practice of seeing and responding to the world from within the symbolic framework of a community's constitutive stories. When

Martha Simpson encounters gang violence in her neighborhood, she and the rest of Pastor Helton's parishioners do not
discern a faithful response through calculating the cold principles of justice, love, or even communal empowerment; they
frame the experience through liberative storylines bestowed
on them. The oppressive fear of gang violence becomes a contemporary form of slavery in which an Underground Railroad
can be blazed anew. Such narrative interpretation kindles the
spirit, ignites the imagination, galvanizes a people, and unlocks
hidden resources for response. Harriet Tubman's strength
emerges, along with her courage and savvy, and soon a network of community safe houses protects their children's path.
This interpretive reflection can be nurtured. After his story
of Dr. King in Birmingham, Pastor Helton might have asked,
"Where is such violent assault happening in our world, and
where are we tempted to lynch?" or "What would it look like to
dream King's dream and respond in a way similarly inspired?"
Through such reflection, the eyes of narrative faith are formed,
and teens learn to see God aching to bend the world toward
justice.

The fourth educational movement is *to deepen knowledge of the
story by helping the young person retell it as a story of their own
creation.* An activity that is energizing for a leader to craft will not
necessarily be equally energizing for youth to take part in. The
educational value of an activity lies more in the *creating* of it than
in its *execution.* Education is deepened when a learner becomes
active and their own creativity is accessed: material becomes more
intensively internalized, the learner's own connections emerge, and
insights are generated from the depths within rather than skimmed
from the surface without. Consequently, one learns a tradition's stories best when one makes that story one's own through creatively
retelling it.

Pastor Helton recognized this insight. He not only exposed
his youth to liberative stories, he invited them to research and
re-present one such story, an exemplar's biography, with which
the teen particularly connected. Yolanda Jones took this one step

further when she invited the confirmation class to craft an original play that portrayed the heritage their pastor so deeply cherished. As ideas flashed and plotlines solidified, insights were generated and the stories were internalized. "Hey," one teen must have exclaimed along the way, "let's frame the whole thing as a Freedom Ride— that's what it is anyway." "I've got an idea," another teen may have blurted. "The choir's singing can help us lift the bus." "Wait," and on it goes, "we can end it with Bethel becoming the Freedom Train— wouldn't that be cool?" To be sure, energy swells, meaning is generated, and stories are internalized ever more deeply by writing a play rather than merely by watching someone else's.

You can nurture this in a variety of ways, some simple, some elaborate, some amusing, some profound.[19] For example:

- *Storytelling:* Invite youth to retell stories in various ways and contexts. This can be as straightforward as sharing a biblical tale at worship like a storyteller of old, or as playful and creative as a camp activity retelling a story from the point of view of a different character (the Prodigal Son parable from the perspective of the dad, or the brother, or the swine), placing it in a different setting (in high school, outer space, Middle-earth), crafting it in a different genre (as a newspaper article, a Michael Moore documentary, an episode from *24*), or extending the story a frame further (what happened the morning after the party?).[20] Not only are such activities fun, they demand an engagement with the biblical story in ways that cannot help but internalize it.

- *Drama:* This can be as simple as the role-play of a parable in a youth group meeting to an original feature-length production of *Christ's Passion in the 21st Century*, or *The Complete Bible: The Director's Cut*, or indeed, *God's Freedom Ride through African American History*. Of course, such productions require research, the results of which are internalized when crafted into a narrative portrayal.[21]

- *Film:* Borrow a parent's video camera and invite teens to make a movie instead of an original play, or film an oral history of parishioners remembering the sacred stories that frame the community's identity. In both cases, have a community-wide world premiere.

- *Songs*: Invite the teens to rewrite the Jonah story to the tune of *Gilligan's Island*, or as a Christian rap; or let the musicians form a band and compose a concert on the history of their heritage through music.

- *Experiential Multisensory Immersions:* As alluded to above, Mark Miller has demonstrated the promise and power of simulation events in which teens "relive" biblical narratives.[22] As powerful as these experiences are, their educational value can be enhanced when the teens are invited to create these immersions rather then merely experience them. Recruit them onto the design team, perhaps after an initial experience, and craft a new simulation experience for junior high schoolers, parents, or other youth groups.

So certainly expose young people to paradigmatic stories and nurture their reflection upon them. But then also invite teens to retell the stories. The stories become intensified through internalization.

The fifth educational movement is *to encourage young people to live the story within their particular context.* Pastor Helton yearned for more from his confirmands than that they encounter his community's stories, reflect intentionally upon them, internalize them through a narrative retelling, and then simply lock them away like narrative relics in the climate-controlled display cases of their minds. These stories are sacred; they pulsate with spirit, throb with hope, and crackle with the power to launch a pilgrimage to the promised land of God. Pastor Helton longs for his teens to be captured by these stories' power, and to embody their liberative vision. "Where is God calling you to be Harriet Tubman today?" is the thrust of his teaching. "What cattle car of teen experience needs hitching to the Freedom Train through history?" "What is our invitation in laying down the rails?" Pastor Helton knows: these stories are not fully learned until their storylines are lived.

Religious literacy, then, is incomplete without stepping into the storyline's trajectory and extending it into the arena of the world in which youth live. After they have reflected upon and internalized their community's constitutive stories, encourage young people to explore their own contexts and engage them in ways that embody these stories' vision. How might the youth perpetuate the story they have joined? Here, they did it by imagining how the Freedom Train is seeking to roll through today, and by stepping into the personages of those who have kept that train rolling throughout history. These youth were invited to *be* the story they have internalized.

Yet this narrative embodiment is not an act of historical reincarnation in which past events and personages are mimicked in contemporary contexts but an act of heroic actualization in which the spirit that empowered the saints of old is known anew and embodied freshly in today's world. Youth are not to lose their identities through costuming themselves in their ancestors' garments; they are to find their own identity taking form from within the roles their ancestors played before them. For the faith claim is this: the more one steps into the power of these stories, the more these stories unleash the power within. "You *are* Harriet Tubman," Pastor Helton insists, not because this teenager, Tiffany, has channeled a nineteenth-century legend, but because some of that legend's gifts really do live within the soul of this particular teenager. And as Tiffany involves herself in the same story Tubman lived—as she dreams the same dreams, grieves the same hardships, feeds from the same hopes, and fights for the same cause of freedom—she will discover a spirit within her, like Tubman did before, that can liberate the oppressed through her own unique gifts and character. In being Harriet Tubman, and Rosa Parks, and Martin Luther King, and Jeremiah, Hagar, Miriam, and Moses, youth will find their own place in the ongoing story that God is living in the world. And they will, indeed, be religiously literate, in the full, embodied sense of the term.

Knowing God's stories is one way in which the sacred can become a living reality within a young person's life. Because faith traditions and the communities that embody them are fundamentally composed by stories, they mediate the presence of God. This is the promise of religious literacy: In coming to know one's narrative heritage, and becoming conversant with it, one is swept up into the transforming movements of God. The Freedom Train not only materializes, it inspires a people to construct a railcar out of the world's debris; it moves them to pack it full with young and old, black and white, friend and foe together; then, like Pastor Helton after work well done, it carries that people back home.

Two

How do stories shape one's sense of self?

Narrative pedagogy and personal identity

In the brutal pecking order of junior high, Spencer was low bird in the barnyard. African American in a predominantly Anglo school, burdened with a Pillsbury doughboy physique, and a special needs child mainstreamed into a school class several years past his intellectual development, Spencer was the continual target of his classmates' ridicule. If it bothered him, however, he hid it well. His head bobbing like a bobblehead doll, he ambled down lockered hallways and across crowded cafeterias with a perpetual smile and a Magoo-like obliviousness to the rolled eyes and stifled chuckles that followed in his wake. Deep within, he had an indomitable spirit. And he brought that spirit with him to the storytelling unit I led in his seventh-grade English class.

The unit was designed to celebrate storytelling from around the world. Each session, I shared a narrative from a different culture and taught techniques in the oral tradition of storytelling. The students chose a culture not their own and researched its myths and folktales. They picked one story, crafted it, then honed their skills to tell it. On the final day of the unit, the celebration came. Each student told his tale in a festival of cultural diversity. Spencer told one, too. But he had a different design. Something in him wanted to tell his own story.

Early in the series, when the class trekked to the library for source material, I found Spencer ignoring the books and doodling in the corner. His buoyant spirit decidedly more sober, he drew a dead bird lying in the playground. Holing up beside him, I asked him if the bird had a story. It did.

"The bird lived with a bunch of other birds, but he was different. He looked different; and he couldn't fly as fast or as high as the others. So the other birds teased him, and flew all around him making faces and saying mean things. So the bird started practicing in secret, to try to learn how to fly as good as the other birds. One day, the other birds saw him, and they told him they didn't want him to learn to fly better, that they didn't want him around at all. So they threw rocks at him until they broke his wings. Then he fell from the sky and landed in the playground dead. That's where I found him."

We talked about the story, about how bad the bird must have felt, and how sad it was that it fell from the sky and died. Then I told Spencer that his story reminded me of another, a Danish tale about a duckling who was told he was ugly because he was so different, only that story ended differently. The folktale kindled his imagination. We went on the hunt for other tales that were variations on the same theme. One in particular seemed to have his name written all over it. He tinkered with it, wrote it out, and rehearsed it so many times he could recite it in his sleep. Then, at the year-end storytelling festival, he surprised us all with his compelling rendition. As radiant as one borne aloft, he beamed and bobbled through his original adaptation of "The Ugly Chicken."

There was a farmer who had a whole barnyard of chickens—white hens for as far as the eye can see. But for some reason, nobody was buying his chickens and he was losing money fast. He told his friend the problem and his friend said, "I know how you can make some money."

"Yeah, how?"

"I was up in the mountains the other day and I saw this eagle—the most beautiful creature you ever did see. You could catch that eagle, put it in a cage, and people'll come from all over the land just to see that eagle. A buck a throw, you'd be rich in no time."

So the farmer hiked the mountain, set a trap, and caught him that eagle. But when he got back to the barnyard, that eagle fought back—he scratched and clawed at that farmer until the farmer gave up, got himself a gun, and shot that eagle dead.

When his friend came by, the farmer told his friend the problem. The friend listened and said, "I see what you mean. The problem is, that eagle knows what it's like to be free. There's no way it will stand for being in a cage. But I know what you can do. That eagle had a nest up in those mountains. And there was an eagle egg in that nest. If you go get that egg, put one of your best sitting hens on top of it, why that egg'll hatch and an eagle will be born. But it won't know it's an eagle. It'll think it's a chicken. Why, people'll come from all over the land to get a good look at that eagle. You'll be rich in no time."

So the farmer did it. He found that egg, brought it to the barn, and set his best hen on it. The egg hatched and out came a tiny baby eagle. But when the baby eagle hobbled out into the barnyard, all those chickens, with their beautiful white feathers, just teased that eagle and made fun of how ridiculous he looked.

"You're the saddest-looking chicken we've ever seen," they said. "Look at your ugly brown feathers; look at how they stick out on top of your head; look at how you walk on those scrawny-looking claws. You belong in the corner by yourself or back in the henhouse."

So the eagle tried to make himself look like a chicken. He rolled around in some flour to make his feathers look white, he took some wire and tied down his head feathers, and he pried open his claws to make it easier to walk. But when he walked back into the barnyard, all those chickens just laughed all the harder.

"Look at you," they said, "you're even uglier than you were before."

So the eagle walked off by himself to the corner of the barnyard and played by himself. And as he played there, he looked up into the sky and he saw this tiny speck circling around. The speck got bigger and bigger, closer and closer, until it became an old grandfatherly eagle flying all the way down, then landing on a tree branch. The old eagle looked at the baby and said, "What're you doing down there?"

"What do you mean, 'what am I doing'? I'm a chicken."

"You're not a chicken," the old eagle said "You're an eagle. You belong in the sky where you can fly."

"Fly?" the baby eagle said. "I can't fly. I'm a chicken."

"Boy," the old eagle said, "someone's done a number on you." And just to show him, the old eagle grabbed the baby by the shoulder with his claws and flew to the top of the sky. "This is how eagles teach their young how to fly," said the old eagle. "I'm going to drop you, and when you fall, you stick out your wings and the wind will lift you up."

So the eagle dropped the baby, and the baby fell just like a rock—straight down, getting closer and closer to the ground, and just before he crashed himself dead, the old eagle swooshed down and caught the baby by the shoulders.

"Now we're going to do that again," said the eagle.

"Please don't," begged the baby. "I'm going to die. I can't fly. I'm a chicken."

But the old eagle dropped him anyway, and boy did that baby fall, just like a rock—straight down. And just before he crashed into the ground the old eagle swooshed down and grabbed the baby.

"Now we're going to try this one more time," said the old eagle. "And this time, as you're falling, I want you to stick out your wings, lift up your head, and say, 'I am an eagle.'"

"Please don't," the baby squealed. "I'm going to die. I'm just a . . ."

But the old eagle dropped him anyway. And the baby fell, just like a rock—straight down. But this time, as he was falling, the baby stretched out his wings, lifted its head, and cackled, "I-I-I-I-I-I-I . . . a-a-a-am-m-m-m . . . a-a-a-n-n-n EAGLE."

And just then, the wind caught hold and the baby swooshed up into the sky. The baby couldn't believe it. He was flying. And all day he just flew all over the land, until he was tired and he and the old eagle landed on the branch by the barnyard.

"Wow," the baby said. "I really can fly."

"Of course you can fly," said the old eagle. "You're an eagle."

"But why am I so ugly then?" said the baby. "I've got these ugly brown feathers, this hair that sticks up, and these claws that are all scrawny."

"Are you kidding?" the old eagle said. ""Brown is the color of royalty; your head feathers are your crown; your claws are meant for hunting not for waddling; you're the king of the sky."

Just about that time, a bunch of chickens waddled over looking for the baby to make fun of him. When they saw him up in the tree, they said, "What're you doing up there?"

"I flew up here," said the baby. "I'm an eagle."

And the chickens just laughed and laughed. "Now that ugly chicken thinks he's an eagle."

And while they were laughing, the old eagle looked at the baby and said, "Are you ready to get out of here?"

"Yeah, I'm ready."

And to the amazement of all those chickens, the two eagles stretched their wings and flew away.

And they never did come back.

As Spencer told his story, he stood tall and shined. He wasn't just telling a story he found; he was telling his story. Right before our eyes, he became an eagle. He was the king of the skies.

I saw Spencer the following year. He strode by me in the hallway with his toothy grin.

"Hey, Spencer," I hollered. "How you doing?"

He just shuffled by and smiled. "I'm still flying," he said. "I'm still flying."

And that he was.

Theoretical underpinnings

Spencer was in search of a vital sense of self that would sustain him through the cackling barnyards and threatening skies of his life. Harassed and ostracized, he saw himself as a misfit—an ugly chicken, a broken-winged bird without the juice to keep himself aloft. Yet as he engaged an alternative narrative that reframed his experience, his sense of self was transformed. Spencer was no longer a deformed farm animal, he was an eagle, a sky-king in disguise. He wore the color of royalty, he bore the crown of his destiny, he had hidden gifts aching to be unleashed. As if hatching from an egg, this new sense of self was birthed within him. With it, Spencer was free to shed the lies he was fed, to discover his power, to claim his voice. When he spread his wings and flew away from his barnyard prison, his identity soared as well; he was liberated into a truer, more emboldened vision of himself.

Spencer exemplifies the aims and movements of a *personal identity* approach to narrative pedagogy. A coherent sense of self is fundamental to being alive. Human beings need to know who they are, what they stand for, where they've come from, where they're going, who their people are, what their place is, what their strengths and worth are, what their challenges and needs are. Without a coherent sense of identity, life loses meaning, experience becomes fragmented, personal vitality is stifled, and social bonds become frayed. Adolescence, as Erikson has classically documented, is a uniquely significant time when the crisis of identity becomes acute and the contours of one's identity begin to cohere.[1] Youth ministers and teachers of teens have long tended to this adolescent need for identity formation.

Narrative educators, however, along with narrative therapists and psychologists, recognize the importance and power of story in forming and transforming one's sense of personal identity. Identity is inherently narrative in structure. The self is a story—each of us, in essence, the central protagonist in the novel of our life. Further, this narrative sense of identity is informed, sometimes for good, sometimes for ill, by the narratives of one's community. Destructive narratives erode a vital sense of self, while life-giving narratives can heal and restore. Spencer poignantly demonstrates this. His fractured sense of self was captured in the narrative of the broken-winged outcast whose attempts to fly were bullied to the point of depletion, a narrative informed by the life-squelching stories of himself with which others harassed him. The hope for a new life-restoring self-narrative, however, was lodged deep within him. Being exposed to healing and liberative cultural narratives birthed that hope into being. Such is the essence of a personal identity approach to narrative pedagogy. Its fundamental purpose is to help persons access the stories they are living, reflect on the extent to which these stories are life-giving or life-denying, and reimagine their self-narratives in dialogue with the healing and restoring narratives of their cultural and religious traditions. In short, it invites young people to narrate their own lives, with stories that promise to make them soar.

Why are stories so effective for shaping and restoring personal identity?

First, *personal identity is narratively constructed.*[2] The power of narrative in teaching and ministry is not that we all love a good story; it's that we all *are* a good story. Narrative is the form through which we constellate our experience into meaningful patterns. It is no accident that, when asked to tell about ourselves, we share a story.[3] We do not merely list the raw data and vital statistics of our past, reciting a list of dates and places as if reading the entries on a timeline. Nor do we narrate every single occurrence we have ever experienced. Rather, we engage in the interpretive and constructive process of telling our story. We highlight certain events and ignore others; we assign purpose, sequence, and motivation oriented toward a particular goal; we cast some moments as setbacks and others as times of triumph; we identify allies and enemies, peaks and valleys, gifts and liabilities we've discovered along the way. In short, we transform the innumerable random occurrences on the canvas of our past into a life narrative that has coherence and meaning.

This core life narrative is the enduring identity that grounds our sense of self. It clusters into a cohesive whole all of the particulars of our personal identity. It provides us with a past that has resonance and stability; it propels us toward a future with an identifiable goal; it gives us a sense of character that remains constant within the variety of contexts we may find our self in; it defines our values, identifies our people, and mobilizes us to act in the world with purpose and significance.[4] In essence, it answers the essential question of our identity. Who am I? I am the son of an immigrant trying to make it in America; I am the overlooked stepdaughter longing for love; I am the survivor of abuse staving off depression; I am the ghetto kid fighting the dopey drag of poverty and gangland violence. Who I am is the story I am living. And everything we experience—whether a surprise in our day or someone we encounter along the way—is interpreted through and given meaning by the self-narrative we are living.[5]

Narrative ethicist Stanley Hauerwas suggests that this storied structure of identity is rooted in the essence of what constitutes a self. For Hauerwas, a self has agency; it acts in the world with purpose and intentionality. Without a self we would be merely tossed about by life's circumstances like a cork blown about by the stormy seas. It is the self that responds *actively* to life's events rather than succumbing passively to them. To act implies a direction—a goal toward which one strives and for which one longs. This is the essence of narrative—an agent setting out with an objective.[6] Along the way, things happen. We discover wounds that hamper us, blind spots that threaten us, strengths that empower us; we meet allies who support us, teachers who guide us, enemies who threaten us; we experience barriers that defeat us, challenges that strengthen us, successes that propel us all of which shape, deepen, and redirect the agent on the journey. To be a self, by definition, is to be a story. No wonder we tell stories when we want to be known. To know people's stories is to know their dreams and hopes, the quests that drive them, the demons that threaten them, the friends they most trust and hold dear. It is to know much more than the facts and dates that constitute their past. It is to know their essential self.

To be sure, while personal identity is narratively constituted, not all self-stories are life-giving or liberative. People often construct personal narratives that reinforce hopelessness, shame, or victimization. "I am an imposter desperately disguising the sham that I am," "I am a manic-depressive powerless before the grip of despair," or even, "I am an inferior outcast broken-winged by the bullies who beat me." Narrative therapists seek to surface such stories and transform them into ones that promote the flourishing of life.[7] Richard Gardner, for example, invites children of divorce to make up a story for his make-believe television program, then he offers a story of his own. In the mutuality between them, a new, more hopeful story emerges. A weary dragon, for example, who has lost her fire after a storm has ravaged her island becomes a dragon warrior who discovers a fire within and takes on the bewitching powers holding her true self captive. Dan McAdams notices similarly that "low generative" adults are crippled by stories that sabotage their vitality, most notably the self-defeating narrative that no matter what good may happen in one's lives, something bad will always follow.[8] With such a self-story, the ugly chicken cowers in the barnyard, the young eaglet gets stoned beyond repair, the baby dragon sleeps in the cave, and the despondent adult refuses to raise his hopes too high. "Some plots save us and others damn us," Robert Stone succinctly observes.[9] They can send us soaring into the skies, or they can plummet us straight into the ground. The aim of narrative pedagogy is to surface whatever stories form a person's identity, then empower that person to author stories that narrate her life with power and purpose.

A second dimension of narrative's effectiveness in shaping personal identity is that *religious and cultural narratives transform meaning within identity-bestowing self-stories.* Personal development is not a private enterprise. We construct identity within a story-saturated social context.[10] The communal narratives that permeate a social context—with their array of images, visions, character types, and storylines—not only inform the construction of personal self-stories, these narratives introduce symbolic worlds that expand the horizon, deepen the meaning, and heighten the significance of our self-stories. This transformation of meaning, in essence, transforms our experience.

The power of narrative to transform experience is illustrated in the anecdote of three laborers who were laying brick. A passerby sees them and asks the first one, "What are you doing?" "I am laying brick," the laborer gruffly responds. The passerby asks the same of the second laborer. This worker is a bit more forthcoming and says, "I am building a wall." The passerby then asks the same of the third laborer. This bricklayer stands tall and smiles with satisfaction. "I," the laborer says emboldened with purpose, "am building a cathedral."

Life is experienced differently when interpreted through a wider horizon of narrative meaning. The single activity of mortaring brick, experienced as mundane labor by one, is given heightened purpose when experienced through the more exalted cultural narrative of building cathedrals. A cathedral builder stands in a tradition of artisans. They are vital within a vast team of carpenters, glass-cutters, and other skilled craftspeople oriented around a single religious purpose. Their work has importance. A house of worship is being built. God is being glorified and will be for generations. The cathedral builder, existentially, lives in a different world than the disheartened layer of brick.

Similarly, experience is transformed by the religious and cultural narratives that constitute one's faith community. Martin Luther

King Jr. transvalued the meaning of the civil rights movement when he interpreted it within the narrative religious framework of the exodus story. Fighting for integration became part of a larger historical movement dating back to Jewish captivity under Pharaoh when a people destined for greatness marched their way toward freedom. An activist's dream became a promised land. The Red Seas of racism could be encountered with faith in their eventual parting. Sitting at the front of a bus was more than merely resisting an unjust municipal ordinance; it was participating with God in the liberation of God's people. Interpreting experience within such a larger narrative framework grants a sense of belonging to a historical and divinely sanctioned movement; it orients one toward a defining vision, it solidifies resolve, and it connects one with a people and the rituals and practices that sustain that people's narrative journey. In short, religious narratives expand the horizon on which one's life takes place. A single historical moment in Montgomery is linked to the cosmic arc of justice toward which the entire universe is bending.

The third dimension of narrative's contribution to identity formation flows directly from the last theoretical coordinate. For personal identity models of narrative pedagogy, *the essence of Christian faith is living one's self-story within the interpretive landscape of the Christian narrative world.*[11] Christian faith is more than pledging allegiance to a catalog of doctrinally orthodox belief statements, and more than putting into practice a list of ethical commands. To the extent that beliefs, actions, and, indeed, all of experience are rooted in the narratives that give our lives meaning, Christian faith entails living intentionally and self-consciously within the narratives that constitute the Christian tradition.

Interpreting one's life through Christian narrative categories opens one up to a fundamentally different way of being in the world than, say, navigating one's life by the Horatio Alger mythology of lifting yourself up by your bootstraps, earning your worth the hard way, and outwitting hostile competitors for your slice of the American pie. Entering into the symbolic world of Christian narratives invites one to see the world as the arena of God's activity and discovering oneself as a player within that history; to interpret oneself through new images—the lost sheep who was sought and restored, the wandering prodigal lavishly welcomed; to interpret others with new eyes as well—as brothers and sisters in Christ, children of the same Source that beholds all with a mother's embrace; to experience life events through the arc of gospel storylines—born anew from the womb of compassion, baptized as beloved, living for peace, dying for truth yet knowing that death will not be overcome; and to live toward the vision that grounds Christian hope—the kin-dom of God where enemies are reconciled, justice is restored, wounds are healed, and all will be well. In essence, Christian faith entails navigating our lives by these narrative coordinates, synthesizing our personal self-stories with the stories that constitute the Christian narrative horizon until we discover that the story of our lives bears the very story of God's transforming love.

This invitation of faith to live into an identity-bestowing Christian narrative is exemplified in a story about my son, Justin. When he was three or four years old, Justin loved to play pretend. In fact, he pretended his way through the entire day. He pretended to shave with me in the morning; he pretended to drive from his car seat to and from preschool; he pretended to cook dinner with blocks in the kitchen. He pretended so much, and with such absorption, I wondered at times if he really knew the difference between pretend and reality. My concern skyrocketed when he pretended to be Peter Pan.

To say that Justin "pretended" is misstating the reality. Justin did not *pretend* to be Peter Pan; he *became* Peter Pan. For six solid months, he refused to respond to his own name. If the food was at the table and I called out, "Justin . . . dinner time," he quite simply ignored me for his swordplay with Captain Hook. When I corrected myself and cried out, *"Peter* . . . dinner time," he would parley a final thrust, then skip to the table singing, "I get to sit next to Wendy."

I lost my son to a Disney character.

Several months into this period, I walked through the living room and overheard Justin scolding a doll with the words, "Gaston, you are positively primeval." Recognizing a line from *Beauty and the Beast*, I stopped and asked him what he was doing. Justin replied that Gaston was quite the rascal and needed a talking-to, maybe even a time-out. I asked him, "If that is Gaston, who are you?" He said, "Why, I'm Belle, of course." Before I could celebrate the developmental milestone, however, Justin clarified. "But Dad, I'm only *pretending* to be Belle. I'm *really* Peter Pan."

Then he went even further. He pretended to be a Catholic priest.

We came home from Mass one Sunday and settled in the backyard to savor the sunny afternoon. I sat in a lawn chair reading the paper while Justin played in his sandbox. He was filling teacups from a pitcher when suddenly he had a great idea. He scurried into the house, scrambled up the stairs, bolted into his bedroom, then returned to the sandbox, his arms bulging with the teddy bears that typically sat upon his bookcase. He placed each one along one side of the sandbox, then dashed back into the house, up the stairs, and into the family room, lugging back an armful of rag dolls from his toy box. These, too, were placed along the sandbox, then back into the house he went. He searched everywhere—in the closets, under the bed, behind the couch—gathering every stuffed animal, puppet toy, and action figure he could find until all four sides of the sandbox were crowded to capacity.

Then he climbed into the center, draped his blankie over his back like a Superman cape, and, with all the pomposity of a high-priest in full regalia, he administered the Eucharist. He poured sand from his pitcher into a teacup, placed it on the rail in front of a teddy bear, and intoned, "The Body of Christ." He filled another teacup, placed it before the next stuffed figure, and repeated, "The Body of Christ." On he went, filling cups and pots, buckets and bowls, and setting them before those gathered along one side of the sandbox rail, down along the second side, and getting halfway through the third when something horrible happened.

He ran out of Eucharist.

He did not run out of sand. He ran out of containers to pour the sand into. And he knew. Something was profoundly wrong. He stood in mid-celebration, his head low, his shoulders bent, his eyes as dull as a storm cloud shadowing the afternoon sun. I watched from my chair and tossed out, "What are you going to do now?" He shook his head. He had no idea.

Then in a flash, his eyes brightened, his head rose, he stood up straight and exclaimed, "I got it. We'll share."

With the deftness of a seasoned dinner host, he clustered all the celebrants into groups of three and four, then placed within each group a single container of sand. There may not have been enough cups and bowls for every *individual* to have their own Eucharist, but there was Eucharist in abundance if each *small group* shared from a common cup.

And it dawned on me.

Justin was not pretending anymore. He played his way right into the heart of what Eucharist is really all about. The meal is for everyone. You gather all the people you can find. You sit each one at the table. You serve all the food that you have. And if you run low before everyone is fed, well, you share what you've got until more comes.

In his developmental task of constructing a personal identity, Justin is trying on the stories of his religious and cultural communities. He is Peter Pan for a while—the swashbuckling hero who can take on Captain Hook; he is the kindhearted beauty who bestows care on beasts and talks down rapscallion villains; and now he is a well-fed disciple, feeding the world's hungry as he dreams of the feast of life. This is the essence of Christian faith—to play oneself into the good news s§Utories that promise enduring meaning, the flourishing of life, and the spirit-stirring epiphany of participating with the sacred restoring and healing our world. Justin played his way into the story of God's cosmic banquet; Martin Luther King played his way into the story of God's march for justice; we play our way into the story when the plotlines that mark our core identity bear the ever-unfolding plotlines of God's activity birthing creation out of love, sustaining creation through times of distress, and propelling creation toward that day when every story finds its way back home. Such is the aim of narrative pedagogy from a personal identity perspective—to help us all find our story held within the restoring story of God.

Educational movements

Given narrative's power to shape a liberative sense of self, personal identity approaches to narrative pedagogy seek to do three things:

1. They help people access the often subliminal stories that constitute their sense of self-identity.

2. They expose people to the healing and liberative communal stories of their religious and cultural traditions.

3. Through a critical and creative synthesis of self-stories and communal stories, they assist people in constructing a coherent sense of narrative identity that is meaningful, healing, and life-giving.

Various types of educators recognize the power of narrative in nurturing a liberative sense of personal identity. Teachers of personal mythology, for example, invite persons to compose grand narratives that encompass their entire lives and capture such core identity components as the chapters that frame one's past, the future toward which one lives, and the essential people, events, conflicts, and themes that give shape to one's personal biography.[12] Proponents of spiritual autobiography likewise invite persons to reflect on the arc of one's entire life, in this case composing narratives that explore the ways one's life story has sought for, eclipsed, and participated with some sense of the sacred.[13] Peter Morgan's "Story-Weaving" method of congregational education finds connections between personal experiences and various biblical narratives for example, connecting moments of communal crisis with conflicts in the early church.[14] Dori Grinenko Baker's "Girlfriend Theology" invites young women to share stories from their lives and then, through the lens of scriptural narratives and rich theological images, to discover the presence of God within them in ways that create fresh meaning.[15]

One representative religious educator, Anne Streaty Wimberly, connects African Americans' self-stories with narratives from both the Bible and their African American heritage.[16] In a society that insidiously conspires with racial self-denigration, Wimberly seeks to empower African American young people with a sense of self that has dignity and purpose. For her, identity is embodied in the two components of liberation and vocation. *Liberation* entails seeing oneself through the eyes of God—as gift and as beloved—and responding to God's invitation toward lives of personal, relational, social, and economic wholeness. *Vocation* entails living in the world with meaning and purpose, called by God to work toward a beloved community of justice and equality.

Wimberly observes that the struggle for liberation and vocation is fought within the concrete territory of everyday life experience. Therefore, her educational method begins by inviting young people to tell stories from their everyday lives, for example, a time when they felt racially denigrated and how they responded. Wimberley then shares stories from the Bible—God calling Jesus "beloved," perhaps—and stories from their African American heritage—say, Howard Thurman's account of his grandmother insisting her grandson was not a slave but a child of God. These stories become mirrors through which young people reflect on their own stories and discern ways that liberation and vocation are either nurtured or hindered within them. Through this story-linking process, liberative stories transform young peoples' self-stories in ways that promote an identity of dignity and purpose.

The five educational movements of personal identity narrative pedagogy

So how can we use narratives to shape personal identity? Whether embodied in Anne Wimberly's African American story-linking process, groups that compose spiritual autobiographies, or junior high students reimagining their lives around liberative folktales, the essential method of a personal identity approach to narrative pedagogy has five distinctive educational movements. While a certain logic informs the order in which they are discussed, some of the movements are interchangeable. For example, the heartbeat of this approach involves bringing personal self-stories and liberative narratives from a communal tradition into generative connection with one another. Some methods start with personal self-stories while others begin with stories from a liberative tradition. The order is not critical. What *is* important, however, is that each of the five movements be nurtured somewhere in the process.

The first educational movement is *to help teens access the personal self-stories by which they live.* At some point early in the process, teens are invited to articulate the stories that implicitly or explicitly form their personal identity. These self-stories can be accessed in one of three ways. First, teens can share "life experience" stories related to the topic of a session. For example, in the discussion of Anne Wimberly's work above, the topic was claiming dignity in the midst of racism; consequently, the teens were invited to share a recent experience in which they felt denigrated by virtue of their ethnicity. If the topic was our questions about God in the midst of suffering, the invitation might be to share a story of a person a teen knows who has experienced some form of suffering. Though the story is not their own, the person whose story they are moved to share will reveal, though indirectly, their own questions. Case studies of life stories— say how a group responded to epithets in a bathroom—can also inspire self-stories when teens are invited to share how their own experience has been similar or dissimilar to that in the case presented.

A second way to access self-stories is through the structural themes that constitute identity. Teachers of personal mythology and spiritual autobiography invite stories that depict, among other things, one's earliest memory, a peak experience, particularly low moments, key relationships, influential heroes and heroines, gifts one has, challenges one has faced, or moments that embody one's longings, hopes, and fears. Each of these is a single snapshot of the fuller mosaic that composes one's sense of identity.

A third way to access self-stories is through creative writing exercises. Though more subtle, fiction reveals clues of self-identity through the characters, conflicts, and resolutions conjured by the imagination. Spencer, for example, unwittingly opened a window into his essential self through the story of the broken-winged bird.

The second educational movement is *to nurture critical reflection on these self-stories.* In this approach, the purpose of critical reflection is to surface and make conscious the life-giving or life-denying dynamics embedded within the stories we are living. Without reflecting upon them, these dynamics remain buried, sweeping us away like a subterranean riptide. Spencer was unconsciously caught in the current of a story that contributed to his self-diminishment. Simple questions about his central character's feelings and deepest desires, the strategies it employed toward satisfying its longings, and how satisfying the results turned out to be helped Spencer reveal his own longings to soar with the crowd, his desperate efforts to fit in on their terms, and the spiritual death to which these efforts led.

Anne Wimberly provokes critical reflection straightforwardly. In response to the stories of their everyday experience, she asks teens to identify where life is being nurtured or celebrated, and where life is being blocked or sabotaged. She then pushes deeper by prompting reflection on the causes underlying these dynamics—the structures, policies, cultural assumptions, and social mores that contribute to demeaning conditions and those that sustain the flourishing of life. She helps the teens see ways—both subtle and blatant—that society encourages and reinforces self-defeating self-stories, and she helps teens see the seeds of stories subversive to the dominant order— stories that whisper of another way but are drowned out by those that discourage life.

One fruitful method for prompting reflection on self-stories comes from processes of composing spiritual autobiographies. Dan McAdams suggests that all personal identity stories are structured around one of four narrative arcs—a good past flows into a good present (silver-spoon stories), a good past deteriorates into a bad present (fall-from-grace stories), a bad past gives rise to a good present (rags-to-riches stories), or a bad past disintegrates into a bad present (hopelessly tragic stories).[17] After presenting this typology, he invites persons to discern what arc their own life stories follows, what contributes to the sustaining of these arcs, and how satisfying these arcs have become. Common to each of these examples are questions that surface the basic trajectory within one's self-story, the extent to which it bears or sabotages life, and the reasons that life is either nurtured or denied. Such reflection makes possible the awareness required in narrating one's life with purpose and intentionality.

The third educational movement is *to expose teens to liberative stories from their religious and cultural traditions.* The transformative power of this approach to narrative pedagogy lies in reinterpreting our self-stories through the lens of liberative stories within our cultural and religious traditions. Obviously, for such reinterpretation to take place, teens need to be exposed to these paradigmatic stories. The techniques for presenting such stories have already been discussed in the previous chapter. These same techniques can be employed here.

For the purpose of transforming personal identity, two categories of paradigmatic stories are most helpful to introduce to teens. First, teens should be exposed to an array of *individual narratives*—in other words, the stories, myths, and biographical anecdotes that permeate our traditions. These include parables from the Gospels, for example; folktales and wisdom stories; and episodes in the lives of biblical characters and saints, heroes and heroines. Sharing with Spencer the story of the ugly duckling and other tales of hidden dignity being discovered is an example of exposing such stories to teens. Likewise, Anne Wimberly embodies this when she shares a gospel story of Jesus being called "beloved," or an anecdote from the life of Howard Thurman. Her criteria for selecting such stories are instructive: the stories should be relevant to the theme of the session, and the stories should truly bear liberative assumptions.

The second category of stories to which teens should be exposed are *grand narrative arcs* that cluster many individual stories into an overarching horizon of meaning that structures one's past, present, and future into a coherent identity. The exodus story of Jewish liberation, so brilliantly employed by Martin Luther King Jr., is one such grand narrative arc. It paints the past of a chosen people called by God, a fall into slavery, and the calling of a liberator; it frames a present with its encounters with despots, its mobilizing campaigns for freedom, improbable partings of impossible waters, times of wandering in the wilderness, and miraculous manna to sustain the journey; and it points toward a future, the unseen yet certain arrival at a promised land. Personal identity can be enriched by plotting one's life events along such a liberative trajectory.[18]

Similarly, the Narrative Pedagogies Project invited teens to write their life stories as gospels. We laid out the narrative arc from divinely ordained birth through temptations in the wilderness, encounters with deadly powers, moments of crucifixion, and ending with hints of resurrection. Then we asked teens to chart significant moments in their life stories along this gospel trajectory and write the "good news" story, along with Jesus, of how God was working in their particular life. Joseph Campbell's "mono-myth" has been used this way as well. Here, teens imagine their lives as a hero's journey through the arc of a call to adventure, a separation from home, a season of tests and trial, a sacred vision or encounter, and a triumphant return freshly emboldened with gifts and powers discovered on the way.[19] In each of these examples, personal identity is created and interpreted within a cosmic narrative horizon that bestows dignity and deepened meaning.

Introducing teens to liberative stories need not be the *third* "step" in the process of nurturing a narrative identity. It can just as easily be the starting point. One can begin a session by sharing a liberative story or laying out a narrative arc, then asking teens to identify where they see themselves within that framework, and to tell a story that exemplifies this. Peter Morgan, for example, offers a rich exercise in which persons are asked to think of their favorite Bible character, reflect on the characteristics they admire in that person, then share a story in their own life where they either resemble that character or are subtly aspiring to bear some of that character's qualities.[20] Though the order is reversed, stories from personal lives and liberative traditions are accessed and linked together.

The fourth educational movement is *to engage in a mutually illuminating dialogue between our self-stories and the liberative stories of our religious and cultural traditions.* Having accessed teens' self-stories, and having presented some of their traditions' liberative stories, the opportunity is available to engage in an interpretive dialogue between them. As discussed above, liberative narrative identity develops when these two sets of stories are brought into generative encounter with one another. Simply presenting religious and cultural stories alongside personal stories is insufficient. Self-stories need to be enhanced, critiqued, recontextualized, and transformed by traditions' liberative stories. Spencer needed more than a few moments of inspirational entertainment from a folktale that promised flight. He needed to free the eagle within him, the one that was caged in a debilitating story.

Such interpretive dialogue can be nurtured through various layers. First, teens can be invited to try on the liberative story, to enter into its narrative world, so to speak, and examine the terrain within it. This can be done through rewriting the story in their own words, dramatizing the story, or role-playing it much like Justin did with the Eucharistic narrative he heard at Mass. Anne Wimberly often invites teens to paraphrase biblical stories into modern parlance, contemporizing, for example, Psalm 139, which celebrates the dignity of persons tended by God even in the womb. Second, teens can be invited to reflect on the themes within the liberative story. Wimberly might ask the teens to write themselves a letter from the God who called Jesus "beloved" or the grandmother who reminded Thurman he was a child of God regardless of a racist society communicating otherwise.

This movement of generative dialogue is nurtured in spiritual autobiography exercises as well. After understanding the narrative arc, teens can reflect on how their story embodies a hero's journey—how they have left home, what foreign land they are wandering in, what quest drives them, what dragons they are facing, what guides are equipping them along the way. Similarly, teens can be asked to locate themselves within the gospel trajectory and describe the demons that tempt them, the gardens of Gethsemane they endure, the deaths they have known, and the resurrection for which they long. Through such critical and imaginative reflection, insights are generated and horizons of meaning take hold.

The fifth and final educational movement in this approach is *to help teens envision and commit to liberative action within the unfolding story of their lives.* For narrative ethicists like Stanley Hauerwas, and narrative religious educators like Anne Wimberly, the final aim of the narrative reframing of identity is not merely a shift in our self-understanding but a transformation of how we live concretely in the world.[21] Consequently, the process culminates in young people envisioning how an identity informed by liberative narratives might be embodied in the next chapter of their lives. Spencer engaged in this process through narrative. He wrote a story that embodied a newly empowered identity, then claimed that identity by performing it within his community, soaring as an eagle in our midst. Anne Wimberly concludes her educational process with teens making specific decisions for ethical living. She invites the teens to reflect on how the stories of their experience might end differently if they embodied liberative storylines. The teens brainstorm, for example, alternative responses to dehumanizing behavior and constructive actions that bring change—nonviolent resistance to verbal abuse, perhaps, or a campaign against racial slurs in their community. As they step into the power of a restored identity, that identity takes hold, and they find themselves participating in the story of God healing and transforming their world.

An unlikely selection as keynote speakers, a group of teens from the Narrative Pedagogies Project was asked to share their stories at a clergy conference in Palm Springs, California. From Los Angeles, the only way to the resort oasis is on the lone interstate that bisects the otherwise barren desert. Jazzed at the chance to share their material, they packed their props into a battered Volkswagen bus and were midway through the arid wasteland when they sprung a flat tire. Determined to make the gig on time, they ransacked the van only to discover that the jack had long since disappeared. Without AAA, before the era of cell phones, and with maybe two bucks in change between them, they sat on the side of the road and stuck out their thumbs like hippies who had lost their way from Woodstock.

Within minutes, a bishop in the district drove by, but he was lost in his thoughts on his way to the conference. A while later, the senior rector of the parish renowned for its justice programs came along, but he too zipped by on his fast track to get to the retreat center.

And following him was a denominational representative for youth ministry, whipping by as if the teens were unseen residue along the side of the road. For sixty minutes, the teens remained stranded while dozens of motorists passed them by, many of them clergy, some of them diocesan officials; even the archbishop flew by as if late for a forgotten guest appearance. Only after all hope for a timely arrival was abandoned did someone take pity. A sputtering pickup truck, missing the hood and a headlight, both cab and bed bulging with migrant workers, pulled over. Unable to string together a complete sentence in English, the Mexicans whipped out a jack, hoisted the car, and changed the tire in minutes. The teens thanked them in the only Spanish they knew, offered them two bucks of change (which was ardently refused), then sped to the conference to salvage what they could of the evening.

They arrived ninety minutes late. The group of clergy, long weary of the coordinator's insistence that the teens were surely on their way, had broken into a spontaneous exchange about the state of youth today, their aversion to responsibility, their absorption in mind-numbing activities, and their epidemic disillusionment with the church, the likely cause for these teens' tardiness. After an hour and a half, the clergy were sure: if they showed up at all, the teens would be either sheep-faced and apologetic or oblivious and unrepentant.

The teens were neither. They entered the conference room, set down their props, then introduced themselves with a story. "You will never believe what happened on our way to this retreat." Rolled eyes and muffled sighs quickly gave way to the sounds of embarrassed backsides shuffling in their seats. The teens had a parable to share. Strangers in need, hurrying clerics, Samaritans in the form of illegal immigrants—the gospel allusions were painfully self-evident. At the story's end, an awkward pause filled the room. Then the archbishop stood up. "Mea culpa, mea culpa, mea culpa," he proclaimed. "We thought we invited storytellers. Little did we know, we invited prophets who brought us the Word."

Such is the power of the narrative transformation of identity. Stories can turn worlds upside-down. Ridiculed farm animals become eagles of the sky, slaves become children of God, playing children become hosts of the heavenly banquet, and broken down teenagers become teachers of the gospel. Narratives transform experience. They invite us to see ourselves and others in new ways, and they open us up to fresh possibilities for being in the world with compassion and a commitment to justice. As we step into the world of liberative narrative horizons, we change. Our sense of self changes. Our relationships with others change. Even our relationship with God changes. For as surely as a disrupted freeway road trip can become a gospel parable, God can be known in the stories of our everyday experience. Indeed, it is precisely in these stories, woven into the story of God healing our wounded world, that clipped wings of all kinds are restored, and broken spirits take flight.

Three

How do stories mediate a profound experience of the sacred?

Narrative pedagogy and contemplative encounter

The eleven teenagers sitting in a semicircle before me were skeptical. They lived in St. Joseph's, a Catholic residential treatment center for abused boys, and had signed up for an after-school drama program that offered one credit of a religion requirement. The program promised them the opportunity to tell and stage their own story— one absolutely true to their own experience, religious or otherwise. Their rolled eyes said it all. They were sure to be censored.

I began by sharing a story about an abused boy I befriended in seminary who later killed himself. We speculated about the stories he may have wished to tell but were silenced with his death. The conversation quickly turned to my seminary context. One of the boys voiced that he did not believe in God because there is too much suffering in the world. A good God would not make a world with evil in it, and would do something about it if evil came. The boy's comments hit a nerve, and an impassioned discussion broke out about God's involvement with the suffering the boys knew so well. I suggested that stories and plays have been written on this very topic, some of them in the Bible. The boys were intrigued.

The following week, I shared the story of Elie Wiesel's play, *The Trial of God*, in which a group of Russian Jews, in the tradition of Job, put God on trial for allowing evil to flourish in their sixteenth-century village. A passionate Jewish innkeeper serves as the prosecutor and lays out in graphic detail the arguments that suggest

God's culpability for the world's evil. No one is willing to serve as the defense attorney until a stranger slips into the scene warning the Jews of a pogrom coming their way. The trial continues as the danger mounts. The stranger recites the traditional defenses for God—that God's ways are inscrutable, for example, and that suffering is redemptive in the end. One by one, the prosecuting innkeeper rebuffs the defenses and refuses to be appeased by God's seeming indifference or impotence. The play crescendos as the pogrom reaches the inn. The prosecutor insists that God is guilty. And with the murderous shrieks piercing through the pounding doors, he demands to know the stranger's identity. Who is this person who dares defend God in the face of evil? The stranger removes his mask. It is Satan.

The story ignited the boys passion to write their own play putting God on trial. I suggested that we start with Elie Wiesel's biblical inspiration—the book of Job. We got no further than the second chapter. Satan, with God's permission, had just inflicted Job with boils after annihilating his livelihood and slaughtering his children when theological indignation erupted. "Sucks to be righteous," one boy exclaimed. "Yeah," another added, "God couldn't care less." "Forget a trial," yet another concluded. "God deserves to be executed."

Clearly the story had the potential of surfacing deep emotion. I suggested we perform a Bibliodrama of the text—a technique designed to explore in a structured and contained environment the emotional realities embodied within a scriptural passage and the emotional realities triggered within the reader. I began by inviting the boys to name all the characters present within the story. "God!" one boy sneered. "Satan," sniped another. "Job." "Servants." "Job's wife." On it went. After the obvious had been named, I invited the boys to use their imaginations and think up persons who *could* have been present even though they were not necessarily mentioned in the biblical text.

"How about the angels who watched God do this and didn't say a thing?" one boy started, sparking the others' imaginations.

"How about the servants who had to dig out the bodies from the house that caved in on the children?"

"How about the body of a dead child still buried in the rubble?"

"I got it, how about the ghosts of the dead children crying out to God?"

"Yeah, how about the ghosts of *all* the dead children God's let Satan kill?"

"That's good," a few others enthused.

Following the energy, I asked, "Who would some of these ghosts be, these innocent children whom God let die?"

"Children murdered for one."

"Or shot by gangs."

"Or shot by their fathers."

"Or just beat by their fathers but they might as well be dead anyway."

"There was this one girl I knew," a boy who had yet to speak confided. "Her father did her every night. No one believed her. Then she killed herself with razor blades. Her ghost would be there."

"Yeah, it would," I said. It sure would.

"Okay," I nudged the process along. "Now let's take these characters and create a still-life snapshot of one moment in Job's story with some of these people in it." We cleared a space on the stage, then created the portrait one character at a time. Each boy chose the character he most connected with, took a pose that expressed what that character was experiencing in the scene, and held the pose until all the characters were present. First, we needed Job. One boy leaped up knowing *exactly* what Job would look like. He boldly stood at the edge of the stage and faced the black-curtained backdrop at the stage's rear; both his arms reached out, each hand holding a defiant middle-finger salute to God, the world, or anyone else who dared to look on. Satan came next. He stood to the side in cross-armed satisfaction at the rise he got out of Job. Another boy had an idea as one of Job's victimized children. He lay as if in a coffin on the floor between Job and the backdrop curtain; he was as stiff as a plank, dead, but his head was tilted up in anguished confusion as he stared into the empty space from where God should have been watching. Several others liked this idea and laid down beside him, creating a cemetery row of casualties all looking back at the curtain in anguished confusion.

"Who is missing from the scene?" I asked the remaining boys. One stood up. "We're missing God," he announced. He stepped through the bodies and placed himself in front of the curtain facing off at Job with the row of corpse-ghosts between them like macabre railroad tracks. He stretched his arms as if a crucified Jesus and stared at Job straight on. Job's eyes met his. Neither one flinched.

The tension was palpable, as was the truth the scene expressed. I let it hang. And I thought we were done when one boy sensed something missing. "I'm God, too," he told us. Like the ghost victims, he laid on the floor coffin-style. But he lay at the base of the curtain behind the outstretched God. He filled the grave the crucified God would fall back into once the suffering on the cross was complete.

Now it was finished. The boys held their poses. The pathos increased as the silence deepened. Some profound truth had been revealed, yet we were not sure what it was. I asked each character to sustain the pose and think of one line their character would say that captured precisely what that character was experiencing. I started with the ghosts. The first coffinlike victim looked up at the outstretched God and simply asked, "Why?" The rest of the row followed suit. "You don't deserve to be God." "You should feel what it's like." "Where were you when I really needed you?" "You're going to pay for this."

Satan spoke next. His self-satisfaction had long since dissipated. His face betrayed a sense that the whole thing had gotten way out of hand. He too looked at God. His voice sounded regretful: "It's on you. You did this. Not me."

Job spoke next. His eyes were still locked with God's. His hands were still stretched in obscene defiance. He spit his words and meant it. "It sucks. Every bit of it."

God spoke back. His outstretched arms were a mirror to Job's. His words were as well. He got it. But he couldn't do a thing about it. "It sucks," he acknowledged. "Every bit of it."

The words hung. The stares held, too. Then the dead God spoke, the one at the foot of the crucified Jesus. He lifted his head from his coffin burial long enough to catch Satan's stare. Then he summed up the scene. "You win." His head fell back. Silence returned. As did God's death.

The effect was chilling. For thirty seconds, we all felt it. This was Job's experience. It was theirs, too. Life sucks. God gets it. But he's dead.

From this pregnant germ of a portrait, the boys composed their play. For ten weeks, they wrote monologues, brainstormed story-lines, and improvised scenes. Then they staged a performance for the other youth and staff at the treatment facility. The play was titled *The Night That God Got Nailed*.

In the courtroom setting, an imposing judge's throne stood at the stage's center. Angled on either side were podiums for the prosecution and defense. Witness chairs lined one side, and in the back corner, God watched over the proceedings. God was a large face, constructed out of butcher paper and brushed paint, mounted on a wooden plywood frame. The face was a cross between the majestic head in the Wizard of Oz and the long-haired Jesus pasturing sheep. The characters, all played by the boys, consisted of a judge who resembled an abusive, alcoholic father; a defense attorney; and a series of prosecuting witnesses.

The plot pivoted around the prosecutors who, one by one, took a turn at telling their story to the judge as evidence of God's indifference in the midst of increasingly horrific cruelty. After each monologue, the defense attorney made a feeble response, in part defending God and in part blaming the victims. The judge, however, grew impatient. Pulling out a giant foam-rubber hammer from behind his throne, he leaped from his seat and bludgeoned the witness to death in the middle of the courtroom. The same scene played out with each successive prosecutor—a story was told, the defense pontificated, and the judge beat the witness to death. And throughout, God watched from the corner completely unmoved, the growing mound of bodies on the floor only underscoring God's impotent apathy.

When the judge bludgeoned the last witness, the defense attorney snapped with rage. He grabbed the hammer from the judge and beat the judge to death, the judge's body falling upon the mound of bodies now piled on the stage. Then the attorney looked at the impassive God. For a moment, the attorney seethed. Then his rage broke again. Screaming, "Why don't you do something?!!" he hacked away at God with the hammer. As God's face was bludgeoned, the butcher paper was shredded to pieces. Underneath the paper, a large mirror was revealed splintered as if hit with stones. Written in red and dripping like blood were the words, "Keine Juden," "Colored Only," and "Spare the rod, spoil the child." The defense attorney stepped back from the mirror and, with horror, gazed at his reflection within the mirror's stains. Then, in disgusted self-loathing, he took the hammer and pummeled his own body until it joined the heap of others lying motionless on the floor.

After a most pregnant pause, a boy dressed in black emerged silently from behind the black-curtained backdrop. He positioned himself behind the mirrored face of God. Then he slowly swept the mirror from one end of the audience to the other, giving each person in the seats the opportunity to see themselves in the mirror of God's bloody face. When it reached the end of the audience, the mirror continued to pivot until its back was completely turned. The boy held the moment, his outstretched arms grasping the backside of God's face. Then the boy pushed the face through the black curtains behind the stage until it disappeared altogether. With God's vanishing, the play was over.

For weeks, the boys worked on their play. Throughout, I asked them to reflect on how dark the play had become. "Where is the hope?" I continually pushed them. We brainstormed possibilities and improvised alternative endings in search of the most authentic truth we could uncover. We tried God sending an angel to raise the litter of bodies back to life; we tried God giving a final monologue on love and forgiveness; we tried a final scene in heaven where God welcomes the suffering home. But none of the endings rang as prophetically true as the ending the boys first envisioned.

The play was an extraordinary success. The boys gave two shows. Each show ended the same way. After God's broken face swept across the audience and departed, a profound silence permeated the auditorium. Some sacred truth had been told. The audience knew it. They felt it. And then they broke into a spontaneous thunder of applause.

As I stood with the beaming boys on the stage taking their bows before the second standing ovation, the boy who pivoted the silent face of God looked up at me and said, "You've been wanting to know where the hope is, Frank." And he pointed to the applauding crowd of abused boys and well-meaning caregivers. The combination of tears and catcalls made it clear. The audience saw themselves not only in the marred mirror of God's face; they saw themselves in the marred mirror of the boys' story, their own story told and held in a grace that gets it.

"There," he said. "There is the hope."

Theoretical underpinnings

The boys at St. Joseph's had little interest in becoming literate in their tradition's narratives or in reflecting upon the self-stories that shaped their personal identity. They yearned for an authentic encounter with truth, an encounter that resonated with their own experience, no matter how dark their experience might be. For them, stories were mirrors. Whether the biblical account of the book of Job, Elie Wiesel's *The Trial of God*, or the testimony of a teenager succumbing to the seductions of suicide, stories surfaced and reflected their own angers and agonies, their own doubts and despair, their own darkness and pain only deepened by the sense that God has abandoned them within it. They knew suffering in their bones. Forsakenness was real. The questions they posed to God and the world were far from academic, and the only truth worth considering was the one that would meet them in the palpable depths of their raw and naked experience.

Paradoxically, the truthful encounter for which they yearned was mediated through their imagination. A dramatic immersion into Job's narrative world brought the raw realities embedded within the story so vividly alive it stunned us into silence. The despair, the heartache, the tortured protest at God all became palpably real as the boys lived into the scene. The biblical narrative took on flesh and coursed with the blood of the victim whose suffering inspired it. Truly, the boys came to *know* this story, the way one knows an elegy that has pierced to the bone.

This immersion into the biblical story was far from historically objective. The teens were not imagining the "true life" that Job was necessarily experiencing, nor were they concerned about the textual accuracy of their interpretations. Rather, they surfaced their own experience and flooded it into the various characters to which they were unconsciously drawn. Job's middle-fingered defiance boiled with the rage of the teen who portrayed him; the Satan who gloated for a while then got grossed out bore the repulsion of the boy who stepped into the accuser's skin; and the ghosts haunting the stage, the abandoned corpses whose suffering was met by divine immobility, each one incarnated the anguish and desertedness of the children who assumed their death-stare posture. In essence, the imaginative dramatization of Job's narrative created a liminal space where emotional depths implied in the story could be evoked, but more, emotional depths within the boys could be evoked and explored. The characters the boys created served as symbolic containers for the boys' own emotional experience. The soul of the story became exposed, yes; but it laid bare the soul of the boys as well.

This liminal space of the imagination, as the boys were to discover, is a place where the sacred resides. As the soulful realities of Job's world surfaced and mirrored that of the boys, a palpable presence emerged in that wordless space where truth has been told. Like a marred mirror that takes it all in, God's presence may not wipe clean the world's suffering, but it sees every story that knows it. Hope is not the absence of despair; it is the truth of despair being held.

The boys of St. Joseph journeyed through a *contemplative encounter* approach to narrative pedagogy. Contemplative encounter narrative pedagogy facilitates an existential experience of the underlying realities embedded within a sacred story. Disillusioned by Bible studies, for example, that nurture a mere cognitive familiarity with a story or a deepened intellectual understanding of that story's context and meaning, contemplative encounter narrative educators help young people feel the soulful realities from which the sacred stories were first written; infuse them with the soulful realities of their own experience; and through the synergistic interplay of textual images and personal experience, encounter the sacred presence with which these narratives are saturated. For these educators, sacred stories are rich imaginative worlds into which readers are invited to plunge, worlds where they can feel the anguish of Jesus at Gethsemane, say, or rejoice at the Prodigal's return. Such plunges become journeys of self-discovery, for inevitably one's own anguish is surfaced from a private Gethsemane, one's own shame embraced at the Prodigal's reception. They also become journeys of sacred encounter. The God that dwells within these stories swells in palpable presence. A compassionate Jesus companions us in the garden of our anguish; welcoming arms embrace our shame when coming home to the divine; a pregnant silence fills a stage gone dark, and we know our truth has been told and heard. The mirror of the textual narrative reveals us to ourselves, and in that reflection we catch a glimpse of that sacred mirroring presence that holds and heals our every experience. Contemplative encounter narrative educators aim for the very center. They seek to facilitate a glancing gaze at the looking glass of God.

Why are stories so effective for fostering such deep contemplative encounters?

First, *sacred stories and myths have the power to mediate an encounter with the numinous.* Myths, by definition, are stories about the gods, or if not the gods, the transcendent energies that pulsate in that sphere we delineate as Mystery, the numinous, or the sacred.[1] These transcendent energies go by many names—Athena, the Holy Spirit, the creative life force, the archetypes of the collective unconscious—but they are always "more than" the material world while affecting the world as surely as the tide affects the sea's ebb and flow. Myths describe how these sacred realities engage the natural sphere. Their scope includes the entire range of human experience—birth and death, the cycles of the seasons, family dysfunction, love and hatred, violence and peace—and their purpose is to reveal how our lives can live in relation to or in harmony with the deeper currents of spirit that flow from the divine.

Myths, however, are far more than instructional manuals for godly living. Like icons, they bear some of the reality to which they point. The numinous breathes through our sacred stories like an echoing whisper reminding us of and re-evoking the primal encounters that inspire our religious traditions. As Joseph Campbell puts it, "Myth is the secret opening through which the inexhaustible energies of the cosmos pour into human cultural manifestation."[2] Representing the Passion story of Christ's death and resurrection has the potential of connecting us to the sacred spirit giving rise to new life within death of any kind. Immersing ourselves in the travails of Job can open the ground for a sacred encounter that understands the indignity of innocent suffering. Myths have a mystical function. More than providing data on the divine to inform our doctrines and beliefs, myths pulsate with a sacred energy and bind us anew to the spiritual reality that breathes through all of creation.

Christians make similar claims about the sacred stories within the Scriptures. Theologian Karl Barth exhorts that the presence of God pounds through the Bible "like the tremors of an earthquake or like the ceaseless thundering of ocean waves against thin dikes."[3] He suggests that reading the Bible is like gazing out a window and spying a group of people—Paul, Miriam, Deborah, and Moses—waving their hands and gaping with awe at some sight in the sky obscured to us by the ceiling of the room from which we are observing them.[4] The purpose of reading sacred narratives is not to become well-versed in the words and actions of these biblical figures; it is, quite simply, to glimpse for ourselves the divine realities to which these figures are so passionately pointing. Sacred stories are portals to God. For Christians, they are inspired—not in the sense that their every word is crafted with literal precision but in the recognition that these stories have the power to mediate an encounter with God. Barth continues, "There is a river in the Bible that carries us away, once we have entrusted our destiny to it—away from ourselves to the sea."[5] Sacred stories ripple with the river of God's Spirit. Giving into their world not only takes us to the sea; it soaks us in the numinous waters of God's very presence.

Second, stories are effective in fostering contemplative encounters because *narrative knowing is existential,* a form of knowing distinct from and deeper than mere cognitive or intellectual reflection. This distinction was revealed to me in no uncertain terms.

My first semester in my midwestern college, I took the required course in Old Testament. The moment I saw the professor, I was inspired. A student of Howard Thurman and an organizer alongside Martin Luther King, the Reverend Doctor James Earl Massey was a mystic and a prophet. He had the presence of a Gothic cathedral at dusk—at once awesome and serene, massive and gentle. I was always reduced to a whispered reverence in his presence. He was also brilliant. His lectures were peppered with quotations from philosophers ancient and contemporary; he quoted great swaths of Scripture verbatim; and he retold biblical stories with the authority of one who had been there. With the impudence of a freshman hotshot from the coast, I was determined to impress the Sheol out of him.

Our final was an oral exam in his home, an intimate tête-à-tête in which he could quiz us on anything we had studied that semester. I was prepared. I scoured every textbook, filled binders with outlines and diagrams, then distilled them into dozens of note cards that I rifled through for days. When I advanced upon his house in the December twilight, I was armed with enough knowledge to petition for a Ph.D.

Dr. Massey received me as if I were a minister making an evening pastoral visit. He held the door with a warm smile, then ushered me into his elegant living room decorated with museum-quality artifacts and a grand piano in the corner. Opening a Bible, he began the exam by reading a verse from the Psalms, "Be still and know that I am God. . . ." He paused. "Tell me, what does this verse mean to you?"

I immediately assaulted him with my intellectual acumen. "Well, this is clearly an example of an eschatological hymn most likely written after the deliverance of . . ."

"No, no," he interrupted, "what does this mean to *you*, personally?"

"Well, the Hebrew word for 'know' is *yada*, which suggests a uniquely intimate form of know . . ."

"No, no," he interrupted again with the patience of a school marm beside a mentally challenged child. "I want to know what it means to *you*, personally."

I looked at him quizzically. "To *me*, you mean, personally?"

"Yes. I know you're working your way through college, your family's in California. Where are you finding stillness in your life right now?"

And for the next thirty minutes, we had a delightful chat about the busyness of college life, the elusiveness of stillness, and the whispers of God to be heard when the harriedness settles and your soul opens. It felt like a session with a spiritual director more than a final exam with a biblical scholar. Then he brought the chat to an end by saying, "Thank you, Frank, for coming by. This was a lovely conversation."

To be honest, I was incredulous. "You mean we're done?" I asked. He nodded. And then I got indignant. "But you hardly asked me anything. I mean I *studied* for this thing. I can *ace* this exam. Go ahead and test me. I *know* this stuff."

He looked at me with a quiet tenderness. Then he said with a smile, "You know, I'd like to give you a gift." He stood up and walked to the piano stationed in the corner. I learned later that he had studied to be a concert pianist, until he was called to the ministry. He sat on the stool, poised his hands on the keys, and bent his head; his eyes closed, and he went into himself as if listening for the source of music deep inside his soul. Then he played music unlike anything I had ever heard, unlike anything I could ever have imagined. A classical concerto floated through the room like a wispy spirit and soothed me into a stillness so quiet a whisper from God could be heard.

When he finished playing, the music lingering in our midst, Dr. Massey paused, then faced me with moist eyes. "I've been playing that piece for over fifty years," he said, "and I still do not know it fully. When you know the Bible like I'm trying to know this concerto, believe me, you will pass any exam in life that's important."

Knowing a psalm, like truly *knowing* any narrative, is far deeper and more existential than mere cognitive or critical reflection. One can be thoroughly knowledgeable of a story's details, have memorized its every intricacy, analyzed its historical context, and scrutinized its cultural usage as it was redacted throughout a religious tradition, and never be moved, never be touched to one's core, never encounter the sacred presence that pulsates in that story's depths. It is one thing, for example, to have heard the story of Jesus healing the hemorrhaging woman, and to learn that the woman was cultically unclean so Jesus' touch was an extravagant gesture of countercultural grace. Yet it is qualitatively another thing altogether to feel the shame of this woman ostracized by society, to access the part of yourself that similarly feels dirty and untouchable, and to experience in your soulful depths the presence of a compassionate Source holding and healing you in your shame. Only in such an existential encounter is the story truly known. As Carl Jung once wrote, "You can know all about the saints, sages, prophets, and other godly men, and all the great mothers of the world. But if they are mere images whose numinosity you have never experienced, it will be as if you were talking in a dream, for you will not know what you are talking about. The mere words you use will be empty."[6]

As scholars of religion and narrative observe, we engage stories with our full beings, not just with our minds.[7] We hear the story of Adam and Eve, for example, and we are powerfully stirred within. Our own sexual history, our embodiment as men or women, our relational wounds, how we feel about being single or partnered are triggered, often unconsciously, and impassion our encounter with the story. One woman folds her arms and scoffs, another mutters under her breath, one man storms off to the coffee pot, while another gets subtly aroused. These reactions are bodily, affective; like the reactions of the St. Joseph's boys to Job, they are rooted in unconscious wounds and desires.

Narrative knowing honors this dimension of engagement with a story. It recognizes that the power of stories lies in their ability to touch us in our depths and surface the yearnings and shames, the fears and rages that fester in the shadows and ache for the light of day.[8] When met with understanding and compassion, such surfacing is healing and life-giving—experience is validated, the power of our personal demons dissipates, suppressed psychic energies are integrated, and the Light of grace that holds and heals extends ever deeper into our being. As depth psychologists and scholars of mimesis understand, true healing only comes with reenactment. We need to *experience* our shame being held, not just profess it or write a scholarly paper about it.[9] Such imaginative reenactment is the means by which sacred stories are truly known, in ways in which we are known as well.

Walter Wink, the classically trained New Testament scholar, discovered the power of this existential knowing when asked, in a Bible study on Jesus' healing of the paralytic, to sculpt in clay the paralysis within himself.[10] Rolling his eyes at the silliness, especially when mindful of the exegetical work the Bible study sidestepped completely, he reluctantly played along. To his astonishment, the clay began to mold itself. Or rather, the deeply buried part of himself that felt crippled beyond repair took advantage of the opportunity to surface and be expressed. In holding that previously unknown part of him, the power of the story became real for the first time. The healing touch and grace of Jesus could come with the power to restore life. A text about which he was exceptionally learned took on an entirely new dimension. He *knew* the text existentially now. And he knew once more the divine reality to which that text attests.

The third reason stories are so effective in fostering contemplative encounters is that *the imagination is the medium through which the soul is accessed and engaged.* "The soul thinks in images," Aristotle famously observed.[11] Depth psychologists' similar insight is that the soul offers no direct access to it.[12] The soul is that unconscious region where our unmet yearnings and unhealed wounds, our untamed drives and unintegrated potentials, simmer in the shadows below our awareness. Like staring into the dark, we cannot know this unconscious content by direct reflection. It cowers and remains well hidden where it was buried in our struggle to survive and adapt through life. It can, however, be engaged indirectly. This content, along with its smoldering energy, gets expressed through images—in dreams, fantasies, and symbolic projections. These images offer an arena in which healing, integration, and transformation can occur.

The boys of St Joseph's demonstrated this precisely. If I had asked them what wounds were buried within them, what unvoiced truths yearned to be heard, what rages smoldered or sadness lingered or despair insidiously seduced them from the underbelly of their soul, they would have looked at me as if I were an alien asking about the spiritual vibrations to which our planet was attuned. Even a direct conversation about their fears and angers, their hopes and regrets, or even their feelings about God would have yielded a rather anemic discussion with little connection to the burning passions within them. The imagination, however, dramatically uncorked them. Narratives provided a safe and symbolic arena into which they could channel their own unconscious material. The story of a boy committing suicide, the image of God being put on trial, the characters they spontaneously created as they imagined who populated the world of Job—each of these served as a veritable narrative Rorschach blot onto which they could project their own rage at God, their own sense of abandonment, their own struggles to find life in the face of suffering. One boy interprets Job as a prosecutor impossible to appease, another sees Satan as a stooge filled with regret, one takes on the ghost of a daughter raped by her dad, another is a judge who can't tolerate backtalk. Each of these characters seem the playful product of their imaginative fancy. And yet, in ways perhaps never to be fully known, these characters were pitch-perfect embodiments of the boys' own powerful unconscious energies. Their particular creation was far from random. The boys' energy for these characters is testimony enough. They *know* these characters; they feel their passions and get their perspectives. These characters have become emotionally laden symbolic representations of some buried reality deep in their soul ready to be known and restored.

Walter Wink experienced this same function of the imagination in the Bible study described above. Though well-established as a highly accomplished biblical scholar, he had absolutely no awareness of something within him that felt immobilized and lifeless. No amount of direct reflection would have surfaced that wound deep within the shadows. The faceless paralytic of the Gospels, however, became a perfect image onto which this buried part of him could be projected. And through the exercise of sculpting a symbolic representation of this image, that part of him emerged with full force, ready to be held and transformed.

The power of contemplative encounter narrative pedagogy is that it provides an imaginative space to safely and symbolically access and engage the unresolved conflicts within our unconscious. The boys of St. Joseph had no idea. Neither did Walter Wink. They thought they had signed on for a playful engagement with some stories. In fact, they found themselves doing their soul work.

Educational movements

Given the power of stories to deeply touch our lives, contemplative encounter approaches to narrative pedagogy seek to do three things:

1. They help young people experience the emotional realities embedded within sacred stories.

2. They foster personal transformation through imaginative re-enactments of sacred stories infused with young people's emotional realities.

3. They facilitate an existential encounter with the Sacred through the interplay of the text and one's own imaginative capacities.

Various narrative educators promote a contemplative encounter approach to engaging sacred stories.[13] They share a dissatisfaction with nurturing a mere intellectual awareness of sacred stories or simply fostering interpretive connections between these stories and the stories of one's life. Rather, they seek to facilitate profound experiences that *feel* a story in service of personal transformation. Walter Wink, after experiencing the healing power of such encounters, considers this method as packed with explosives.[14] Believing the Bible is held captive by bankrupt academic methods of analysis, he advocates for the use of the arts—clay, poetry, music, in addition to storytelling, drama, and creative writing—for engaging sacred stories in ways that bring them more to life.

Peter Pitzele focuses on one narrative art form—dramatic role-play—and has crafted the most universally powerful form of Bible study for young people that I have ever worked with.[15] Pitzele grieves that the sacred stories of the Scriptures, for too long taught through abstract and academic educational methodologies, have become dead for a spiritually starving people. Bibliodrama is designed to "make the Bible come alive as living myth, relevant, disturbing, and still capable of taking your breath away."[16] Informed by Jewish Midrashic traditions, Pitzele considers sacred stories as burning with two types of fire, each capable of kindling the souls of the reader. The "black fire" refers to the black ink of the text itself—the actual words that name particular characters and chart the story's contours and trajectory. The "white fire" refers to the empty space between and around the explicitly black words of the text. This white space contains all of the possibilities not named in the text, like all of the characters who *could* have been present but simply were not mentioned. This white fire is fertile ground for the imagination. As the boys of St. Joseph's demonstrated, imaginative engagement with the white fire of a narrative not only makes the story crackle, it ignites passions within the reader that burn toward healing and life.

Contemplative encounters with a sacred story are not limited to the more public arena of group Bible study. They can be facilitated within the interior space of personal meditation. Ignatian contemplation, a prayer form developed by Ignatius of Loyola, invites people to imagine themselves within the setting of a particular sacred story.[17] Similar to Jungian active imagination, this imaginative immersion takes on a life of its own as the story unfolds with the participant within it. One becomes present, for example, at the sea of Galilee when Jesus walks across the water; whether cowering in the ship's hull in terror of the storm or boldly walking out to greet him, the participant encounters the presence of Christ precisely where they unknowingly ache for it most.

The five movements of contemplative encounter narrative pedagogy

So how can we use narratives to foster contemplative encounters? Whether embodied through Ignatian contemplation, Bibliodrama, or immersion exercises employing the arts, contemplative approaches to narrative pedagogy flow through five distinct educational movements.

The first movement is *to create a safe space in which such deep encounters can take place.* More than any other approach to narrative pedagogy, the cultivation of safe space is vitally important for facilitating contemplative encounters. The nature of the engagement is intimate—deep-seated emotions are accessed, sometimes inadvertently; parts of ourselves, deeply buried, are coaxed into expression; creative exercises like role-playing or pantomime may feel uncomfortably vulnerable. A safe and receptive environment nurtures and deepens authentic self-exploration, while a stale or even hostile environment stifles if not violates it. A safe space is nurtured in the following ways:

- *The Physical Space*: The physical environment can drastically enhance or sabotage a contemplative encounter. Sitting in a circle, or in a horseshoe with a space up front for role-play, is more inviting than chairs in rows or behind desks. Soft lighting, even candlelight during prayerful meditation, casts a more appealing glow than fluorescent lamps that glare with institutional anonymity. A quiet space can deepen a moment of wordless presence should it swell, while noise and chatter can stifle it altogether. Likewise, clutter can subvert inner quiet, while props or symbols can spark the imagination.

- *Ground Rules*: Whether laid out by the facilitator or generated by the group in a communal contract, ground rules are essential for the safety necessary to relax into this work. Crucial ground rules include:

  Confidentiality: What happens in the room stays in the room;

No Judgment: Nobody critiques or censors another's contribution;

Diversity Is Good: Multiple perspectives are welcome and do not imply that any particular one is better or worse, or right or wrong;

The Right to Sit Out: All participation is voluntary; art needs an audience as well as actors;

Physical Boundaries: Sexual or violent touch is always inappropriate, and all other forms of touch require the permission of all involved parties.

- ◆ *Centering*: It is often helpful to begin a contemplative encounter with a few moments to become present to the space, and one's hopes and feelings about being there. This can be nurtured through silence, meditative music, ritual, poetry, or a meditative reading of the story to be engaged.

The second educational movement is *to help youth warm up their imagination, their body, and their emotional availability.* If a contemplative encounter entails the crackling blaze ignited when images of a sacred story burn with the participants' emotional realities, then time must be taken to get the fire started and fan it into the initial flame of engaged participation. Warm-up exercises are playful ways to activate the imagination, become comfortable in one's body, access emotional fluidity, and build the sense of community that supports the deeper work to come. Most youth ministers have a large enough repertoire of icebreakers and yoga stretches, theater games and trust exercises to keep summer camps in business for years.[18]

Several exercises, borrowed from Bibliodrama, are illustrative of the warm-up helpful for narrative-based contemplative encounters. Their intent is to nurture an imaginative playfulness and to develop a facility for creating and embodying characters that will prove invaluable in subsequent activities. Tim Schramm invites youth to introduce themselves as an important element in their lives—a person, animal, or object to which they feel connected.[19] For example, a teen might become the mountain bike his real-life counterpart loves to race. Another exercise invites teens to brainstorm random objects from the Bible—Moses' staff, Noah's rainbow, Hagar's tears, Mary of Magdalene's anointing oil, and so on—then choose one to embody.[20] A partner then interviews the teen asking her where she came from, what is happening to her, how she feels about it, and any other question a late-night talk-show host might wish to pose. I often extend the exercise by asking the teens to line up against the wall, *without talking*, in chronological order of their appearance in the Bible. Then I randomly pair them up to discuss what difference it would have made if one of their objects had appeared in the other object's story.

Though of a different spirit, warm-up is also important for the more interior meditative encounter of Ignatian contemplation. In prayer, our bodies are our instruments. Stretching out, dislodging physical tension, abdominal breathing, and settling into a sustainable posture enhances the meditative experience. In addition, Ignatius suggests that we activate the imagination by internally journeying to the setting of the story we are meditating upon, then engaging the senses to bring that setting to life—the sights, sounds, smells, tastes, and sensations on the skin we can imagine are present in the story. This not only primes the pump of our imagination, it activates the process of giving oneself over to the narrative's world.

The third educational movement is *to facilitate an existential encounter with the sacred story*. With a receptive space created and the participants' imaginative capacities warmed up, the deepest movements of the pedagogy are prepared to unfold. Like an ocean expedition taking ever-deeper soundings of the sea, this unfolding takes place in layers.

Walter Wink, in his method of "Transforming Bible Study," uses Socratic questions to till the soil of the story's themes and their intersection with the participants' lives.[21] Such questions, first, unveil *critical* issues of the story's contextual meaning; for example, in the case of Jesus and the hemorrhaging woman, Wink might ask, "What social standing in first-century Palestine did women have during their menstrual cycle?" He then asks questions of *amplification,* which invite participants to live into the text so that it can become more vivid for them. An example might be, "What do you think the hemorrhaging woman felt after years of being so ostracized?" Finally, Wink asks questions of *application,* where participants explore their own lives for similar themes—for example, "Where in your life have you felt marginalized?" Essential to Wink's method is that this final exploration includes some artistic activity that deeply moves the participants and allows "the text to unearth that part of our personal and social existence which it calls forth to be healed, forgiven, transformed."[22] Such artistic activities include expressing the ostracized part of us in clay, or writing an imaginary dialogue between that part of us and Jesus.

Peter Pitzele's Bibliodrama also unveils a contemplative encounter in layers, though he focuses on theater exercises that engage the body and the imagination. After introducing the narrative—for example, Jesus and the hemorrhaging woman—Pitzele would have the group *cast the story* by imagining all the persons present within it (Jesus, the woman herself, etc.), including any imaginative characters who could have been present but were not actually mentioned (for example, her best friend, her child, Judas, and others). He would then facilitate a *group characterization* in which the participants, one character at a time, would voice various ways that character might be feeling in the story. Critical to this exercise is that the participants speak in the first person and in the present tense ("I am feeling depressed" as opposed to "the woman felt depressed"). This nurtures an internal connection with the characters that is deeper and more personal. Pitzele also invites multiple perspectives on the same character. To one participant, the woman may be feeling depressed, while others might sense her feeling angry, resigned, or resourceful. A group characterization is often followed up with the *interview game,* where each participant chooses one character to embody and then is interviewed by a partner, much like in the warm-up exercise previously.

Moving ever closer to the soul of the story, Pitzele would then invite the group to create a *group sculpture* of the scene, a still-life snapshot of the story's climactic moment—say, precisely when Jesus notices the woman's touch. One by one, the participants are invited to stand up and assume a posture that embodies precisely what that character is feeling and doing in the scene in relation to any other characters who may be already on stage. This exercise is most poignant when done in silence, the leader facilitating in whispered reverence. Once the sculpture is complete, the actors hold the moment while the audience observes. Then the sculpture can be *animated*—each actor, one at a time, speaks a single line that captures precisely what they are feeling at this moment of the story. The facilitator allows the last line to sink in, then ends the scene.

A powerful concluding exercise is the *empty chair*, in which the participants are asked to imagine that God is sitting in an empty chair on stage, then to pick a character from the story and assume a posture anywhere in the room that represents how close to or far from God the character feels and what his or her feelings toward God are. This too can be animated with a single line of dialogue or a written prayer to God from the character's standpoint.

Ignatian contemplation invites a similar imaginative immersion into a story but through the interior process of meditation. The person praying would imagine the various characters within the scene, and which character he is drawn to embody internally. He would sense the feelings that are emerging within him as he lives into this character; then he would allow the story to unfold around him. Perhaps Jesus turns to him after tending the hemorrhaging woman; or perhaps Jesus does not, and he is invited to hold whatever surfaces in the wake of Jesus' departure. Like a gentle fire ever inviting us into the heat of its healing warmth, these exercises draw us ever deeper into the story and the unique encounter waiting for us.

The fourth educational movement is *to de-role from the experience and debrief its significance.* Clearly such existential encounters can take a participant to a rather deep place. Care must be taken in coming back. Pitzele offers a helpful metaphor from diving. "You have taken the players down below the surface, and you must bring them back up. Deep-sea divers know that if they come up too fast, they get 'the bends,' cramps that come because the blood has not cleared itself of the nitrogen of the dive. Depending on the depth, it can take a diver quite a while to be ready to climb back into the boat."[23] Careful resurfacing first involves de-roling, stepping out of the character one has embodied and returning to the person one is in everyday life. Several activities can facilitate this: literally shaking off the role through physical movement, reconnecting with one's surroundings through the awareness of one's breathing or being back in one's body, or simply leaving some time for silence and journaling.

Once the participants have de-roled, they are available for debriefing the experience. Debriefing should take place on two levels. First, participants should reflect on their own personal encounters. What surfaced for them? What did they experience? What fresh insights do they have about themselves? What fresh insights do they have about God? Second, participants should reflect on the story itself. How do they see the story differently? How have their feelings for various characters changed? What significance do these insights have for them and their community? Debriefing is essential in that it solidifies insights and expands their significance. Debriefing, however, need not be verbal. After encounters that may be quite intimate and tender, participants may prefer to reflect in silence, or in the privacy of their personal journal.

The final educational movement is *to integrate these encounters into one's personal life.* The nature of contemplative encounters is that healing and insight occur in the liminal space of the imagination, whether in prayerful meditation, the playful dreamland of the stage, or the trance of artistic creativity. While these encounters are real and nurture profound subconscious shifts, they need to be integrated into the material world of everyday life.[24] Consequently, the participants should reflect on how they might embody their insight, sustain any healing, or claim, if only symbolically, the shifts they feel within them. Such integration can take various forms—a ritual of remembrance, a commitment to a course of action, or placing a symbol on one's bureau. What is essential is that it come from the participants themselves, that it is concrete and manageable, and that the integrative act resonates with the soulful shift within.

The untold story of *The Night That God Got Nailed* was that of Jason. The court sent Jason to St. Joseph's after he put a hand through a window at his school. He joined our program midway through. Without being part of the play's inspiration, he had trouble getting involved. I invited him to be a ghost who had a grievance against God, but he just wasn't interested. I found him one day horsing around with the props.

"What're you doing?" I asked, suspicious of vandalization.

He jolted as if caught in the act. "I've decided on a part to play," he quipped.

"Which one?" I asked.

"I want to be the mirror."

I was taken aback. "It's not really a part," I said. "It just sits there."

"I think it is," he answered. "Watch."

He took a scrap of mirror and tapped it with a hammer. It splintered into a spider web of shards. Then he told me to turn and face him. He held the mirror off to his side, then slowly slid his arm across to pass the mirror by my face. My gaze shifted—from his eyes that held both defiance and pain, to the cracked glass that mirrored my own, then back to his eyes, the mirror now gone.

It was chilling.

The mirror had eyes. And they saw as much as they begged to be seen. Such is the power of contemplative approaches to narrative pedagogy. Sacred stories become mirrors, looking glasses that reflect back to ourselves our wounds and our longings, our terrors and our demons. As we look closer, however, the mirrors become windows. The glass may be cracked, but through it, we glimpse eyes. Eyes that hold our own. Eyes that hold it all.

Four

How do stories
nurture a critical consciousness?

Narrative pedagogy and critical reflection

Can we conceive of an al-Qaeda terrorist in heaven?

This was the question that challenged Christian teens from "A Third Way," a dramatic arts program exploring nonviolent responses to the events of 9/11. The challenge came straight from Jesus. "You have heard that it was said, 'An eye for an eye and a tooth for a tooth.' But I say to you, Do not resist an evildoer. But if anyone strikes you on the right cheek, turn the other also. . . . You have heard that it was said, 'You shall love your neighbor and hate your enemy.' But I say to you, Love your enemies and pray for those that persecute you" (Matthew 5:38–39, 43–44). What does such a mandate look like in light of a terrorist attack on U.S. soil? Is it really possible to pray for a suicide bomber? Does God's redeeming love extend to even *these* enemies? During the summer after the attacks, these questions came with an urgency. A country was preparing for war. Was there an alternative to the violence of vengeance?

We began by admitting that an invitation to love our enemies is counterintuitive. Our enemies are those who mean us harm. When we are attacked—whether verbally, emotionally, or physically—our instinct is to retaliate. The problem is, such retaliation goads greater enmity, which only prompts further retaliation. I shared a Russian folktale that illustrates this familiar cycle of violence.

Two merchants have become bitter enemies. They spread malicious rumors about one another, they steal each other's customers, they sabotage one another's shops until, driven by their reciprocating rage, they square off in the middle of town. One shopkeeper bares his fists at the other. The second draws a knife. The first counters with a samurai's sword. The second pulls out a pistol. The first comes back with a rifle. The second whisks out a dynamite stick. The first barrels forth with a dynamite bundle and defiantly lights the fuse. Finally an angel, grieving the depth of vengeance and alarmed at the escalating violence, intervenes. She snuffs out the fuse of the first man, then parleys with him on the side. She tells him that she is prepared to grant him any wish in the world—extravagant riches, abundant children, a king's palace, anything he desires at all ... with one condition. Whatever he wishes for himself, she will also grant to his rival, twofold. The shopkeeper muses over the dilemma, desiring wealth yet bitter at the prospect of his rival's double share. Finally, he knows what he wants. He turns to the angel and confirms, "Whatever I wish for, my rival will receive twofold?" The angel nods. "Then what I want for myself is ... one blind eye."[1]

Not only is the invitation to love our enemies counterinstinctive, it runs counter to the cultural narratives that shaped national rhetoric immediately following 9/11. In the same way that narrative is the primary form through which individuals make meaning of their experience, communities and cultures interpret events through the lenses of their formative narratives. We may quest for true love, the American dream, the kin-dom of God, the blessing of Allah, global democracy, or multinational capitalistic domination, depending on the cultural narratives that shape us. Other people, communities, and cultures are interpreted as allies or enemies to the extent to which they promote or threaten such quests. How we engage those who threaten our pursuits, our "enemies" as it were, is also shaped by narrative. Stories form us toward either violent or nonviolent engagement with such people.

This is certainly true of North American culture. Walter Wink argues that violence, not Christianity, is the true religion of the United States.[2] This religion is sanctioned by an insidious but pervasive narrative, the myth of redemptive violence. The features of this myth are all too well-known: an irredeemable and unambiguous

"bad guy" threatens without provocation or cause a group of innocent people. Fortunately, an indestructible and unambiguous "good
guy," often a superhero of some sort, rallies to the cause. Using
violence—not diplomacy, negotiation, or persuasion—the "good
guy" completely annihilates the villain, ridding the world of evil in
doing so. When the villain is destroyed, order is restored . . . until
the sequel or next episode when an equally unambiguous villain
returns.

As the teens discovered, television and movie theaters are saturated with such narratives. I invited the group to list the most
popular movies they could think of—those still registering in their
consciousness—from the most immediate past, the months just
before and after the attack in September 2001. They had no trouble
listing the blockbusters: *Spider Man, Harry Potter, Die Another
Day* (James Bond), *X-Men, Lord of the Rings, Pearl Harbor, Mission
Impossible*, even *Jurassic Park* and *Men in Black II*. We then compared these to the essential features of Wink's myth of redemptive
violence—an explicit battle between good and evil, a clearly identified "good guy," an irredeemable "bad guy," a clear victory for good
accomplished through the violent annihilation of those embodying
evil. Clearly, the myth of redemptive violence was alive and well in
North American cinema.

We then compared this myth to the narratives used by U.S. governmental leaders as they shaped the public interpretation of the
events of 9/11. Al-Qaeda terrorists, unambiguously evil, attacked
an innocent community with neither provocation nor cause. The
terrorists, those countries that harbored them, and the people
who sympathized with them were equally unambiguous in their
evil, capriciously threatening freedom and the unequivocally good
American way of life. The only appropriate response was to use violence to obliterate the world of their presence, thus restoring order
and securing the cause of right. A simple matter of good against
evil. The similarities were self-evident.

The drama group then explored the alternative narrative implied
in Jesus' invitation to love our enemies—the myth of nonviolent
redemption. We explored Jesus' vision of the kin-dom of God with

its radical notion that all are welcome into a grace that forgives, heals, and invites restoration into right relationship. We humanized the persons involved in terrorist activities by reading stories of how they were radicalized by the systemic complexities of global greed, religious prejudice, and a pernicious poverty that ravaged the body and hardened the soul. We role-played the dynamics of turning the other cheek and discovered that the text, far from encouraging masochistic passivity before brutal violence, actually empowers dignity in the face of dehumanization and strengthens resistance to humiliation from an aggressor, however powerful. And we studied the stories of persons victimized by violence who healed into a radical forgiveness that invited perpetrators into an accountable reconciliation on the conditions of repentance and at least symbolic restitution.

Then we took on the task of writing a play that embodied this alternative nonviolent narrative.

The teens brainstormed various fictional characters who could have been involved in or touched by the tragedy—for example, a World Trade Center secretary, the daughter of a terrorist, an imagined terrorist himself. We developed several of them more fully by giving them a backstory—specific fears and hopes that motivated them, relationships important to them, defining moments in their lives, and an understandable purpose driving their actions. We also identified who the enemy might be for each character and developed their backstories. I then asked each teen to write the sketch of a play portraying the challenges and possibilities of one or another character responding to their enemy with nonviolent love. What would it look like, for example, for a U.S. citizen to love an al-Qaeda terrorist involved in a massive suicide bombing of a civilian population? Or alternatively, what would it take for a terrorist to find room in his heart for an American citizen he once attacked so viciously? A seventeen-year-old Lutheran young lady, a dancer and musician, wrote a sketch that captured the rest of the group. The others added characters of their own, then together they fleshed out the scenes. The play was titled *Terrorists in Heaven*. The teens performed it the summer before the March 2003 invasion of Iraq.

Center stage looks like a hall for a wedding reception. An Arab man and an Anglo man are contentedly playing flute and violin toward the rear. A half-dozen couples, including children, are dancing on a dance floor. Others cluster around tables, chattering and enjoying the music.

From either end, two men are escorted onstage by two angels. The first is a Christian, Joseph, who is praising God that his years of faithfulness have led him to heaven upon his death. The second man is an Arab, Hakeem, praising Allah for his arrival into heaven as well. Joseph hears the music and remembers how he was once a promising violinist before giving up his music to become a businessman. He asks the angel if heaven might afford him the opportunity to play again. The angel shrugs, signaling "perhaps." Hakeem hears the music as well and remembers how much he loved to play the flute as a child. He asks the angel if Allah might allow him to play once more, this time in Allah's court. The angel shrugs, "Perhaps'.

Joseph keeps strolling and expresses his excitement about being reunited with his dead daughter. The angel assures him that he will meet her soon. Hakeem likewise is eager to see his daughter, and is also assured of an imminent reception. Joseph becomes angry remembering how his daughter died at the hands of godless men during the World Trade Center attack. Hakeem becomes angry at how his daughter was killed by toxic poisoning from an oil plant under infidel control. The two shout in unison, "May the killers and their children and their children's children burn in hell forever. Praise be to Allah/Christ."

The angels stop and tell them that God is coming to greet them. Hakeem bows down awaiting Allah. He is surprised when he sees that Allah is a young Anglo girl. She welcomes him, then offers him one of the two flutes she is holding. Hakeem is delighted. He and the unconventional Allah play together with great joy. Across the stage, Joseph awaits the coming of Jesus with excitement. He is surprised to see that Jesus is a young Arab girl. She welcomes him and offers one of the two violins she is holding. He, too, is delighted to play with the unconventional Jesus.

With music, Allah and Jesus lead the two men to their dwelling place in heaven, a common table within the reception hall. As the two couples converge on the table, both men recognize their daughters with the other stranger. The daughters, delighted to see their fathers, drop their instruments and race into their father's arms where they are embraced with delight. The ballroom musicians keep playing as if serenading the reunion. The daughters lead their fathers by the hand toward the table the two will share. The men stop when they notice each other. Each of them asks what the other is doing there. "I refuse to share a home with that man," they both say.

"Yes," the daughters reply. "Hatred can turn even heaven into hell." Then they explain that the beauty of heaven is that the fathers get to live with their daughters, but only as long as the four live together, caring for one another as a family sitting around a common table.

The fathers are adamantly opposed and offended. Hakeem appeals to Allah, "How can you let this infidel into heaven?"

The young girl Allah turns to him and says, "The same way that I allow you." Hakeem is confused. "After all, I welcome you even after you killed me." Hakeem is aghast that he would ever kill his God. The young girl explains, "I was one of the children in the World Trade Center that you attacked with your airplane." Hakeem is horrified.

Joseph is indignant. He appeals to the young girl Jesus demanding to know how Jesus can let such a terrorist into heaven. She responds, "The same way that I allow you." Joseph is confused. "I was one of the children who worked in your oil refinery in the Persian Gulf. I died of toxic poisoning because you didn't see the need for safety precautions." Joseph is horrified.

Joseph turns on Hakeem, asserting that at least he is not a cold-blooded killer. Hakeem turns on Joseph, disparaging the unsafe plant conditions, the capitalist greed that fuels American business, and the imperialistic policies that killed his daughter and drove him into ter-rorism in the first place. The two scream at each other. They get louder and louder until simultaneously they slap each other in the face. The two ballroom musicians stop playing. The dancers stop dancing. All of heaven goes silent. Allah and Jesus comfort the downcast musicians, then lead them to a table with food and drink. Then they look at their fathers. The two men are horrified that they have silenced the music of heaven. The girls come, take each of their hands, and lead them to the vacant musician chairs. They hand the two men a flute and vio-lin. Hakeem and Joseph look at each other reluctantly. Jesus and Allah retrieve their own flute and violin and begin playing. Gradually, the fathers begin to play, then give themselves to the music. The dancers return to their dancing. The people return to their chattering.

Allah and Jesus quietly exit from opposite ends of the stage. The fathers continue to play. The dancers continue to dance. Two new strangers are escorted onstage from either side—a Palestinian and a Jew. Each carries a machine gun; each praises God to be in heaven after death; each expresses excitement at getting to see their dead daughters alive again. Which they will, the two angels affirm, any minute now.

Terrorists in Heaven embodies an alternative narrative to the myth of redemptive violence. This narrative dares envision a heaven where Muslim, Jew, and Christian are all welcome. American businesspersons and al-Qaeda terrorists are complex human beings. Each is capable of grief, love, and creative flourishing, as well as violence, self-deception, and complicity with evil actions. A complex web of international structures and practices contributes to violence even in its most harrowing forms. The "bad guy" is redeemable; the "good guy" has a shadow. Both are invited to participate in reconciled life, with the precondition that they help heal the violence to which they are both party.

In a world where enemies are not only hated, they are bombed without remorse, this alternative narrative rises from the rubble with a song. Its song sings for healing—for killer and killed alike.

Theoretical underpinnings

The teens of today are living in the midst of war. They have endured not only the wars in Iraq and Afghanistan thundering from halfway around the world; they are weathering a war of religious narratives. With the relentlessness of a carpet bombing, the myth of redemptive violence reverberates throughout the news media, the entertainment industry, the discourse at civic gatherings, and the rhetoric of governmental officials. Its creed is so ubiquitous, its truth seems self-evident. There are bad people out there; they do bad things for no good reason; good people would never dream of being so bad; the only good thing to do is for good people to rally, and rid the world of all the bad people who refuse to stop doing such terribly bad things. Good and bad are so clearly defined, we no longer grieve when the bad get their due.

Within this drumbeat of the seemingly gospel truth, the teens of "A Third Way" did a radical thing. They dared critique the dominant narrative by which their country went to war, indeed the underlying mythology by which all war is waged. And they sought an alternative narrative, one that promotes complexity instead of sound-bites, justice instead of vengeance, healing instead of enflamed escalation. Like a song of peace that gently plays through the cacophony of hatred and war, strains of an alternative narrative murmur with a quiet prophetic power—in stories of empowered nonviolence from the Sermon on the Mount, in stories of victims who transformed vengefulness into a sober and poignant forgiveness, and in stories of perpetrators who responded to compassionate accountability over punitive imprisonment.

To this trickling strand of music, the teens added a chorus of their own. The chorus, however, comes with a punch. It tells a story that pleads with us to grapple with painfully difficulty questions. Can we envision a heaven that houses an al-Qaeda terrorist? Can we recognize our own collusion with structures that create violence? Can we hear the whisper of music that longs to play in a perpetrator's soul, and imagine it mingling with the healing song that aches to play in the soul of their victims? If these challenging teenagers are right, the future of our planet depends on us trying.

The teens of "A Third Way" embody the aims and movements of a *critical reflection* approach to narrative pedagogy. Critical reflection narrative pedagogy recognizes that the cultural narratives that shape our consciousness are far from ideologically neutral. Narratives are saturated with assumptions—about gender, race, power, violence, God, the "good," the "bad," the "other"—assumptions that are subliminally absorbed when the stories themselves are assimilated. Many of these assumptions are downright destructive—in, for example, folktales that sexualize children and subjugate women, films that perpetuate racist stereotypes, and storylines that sacralize violence while dehumanizing the people who deserve to suffer it.

Critical reflection narrative educators nurture in young people a critical consciousness about the cultural narratives that shape us. They raise to awareness the stories that are so ingrained that their influence upon us is too close to see—fairy tales, for example, so commonplace a child can recite them; sacred stories sanctified with canonical status; or Hollywood blockbusters with plotlines so familiar we take for granted their mythic pattern. They invite teens to scrutinize the axiomatic assumptions embedded within a narrative, and they empower teens to think for themselves and tell subversive stories. Such pedagogy should come with a warning label. It can be dangerous. Teens become countercultural. And terrorists end up in heaven.

Why are stories so effective for nurturing a critical consciousness?

First, *cultural narratives are means of enculturation.* Religious educators have long realized the unequivocal given of enculturation.[3] Enculturation, sometimes called socialization, is the process by which a person absorbs a community's worldview, beliefs, values, ways of living, even language simply by virtue of participating in that community. Enculturation is so primal, it happens below our awareness. Maria Harris demonstrates this by comparing two headlines when Everest was scaled for the first time. A Western newspaper declared, "Hillary Conquers Everest"; an Eastern paper, on the other hand, rejoiced, "Everest Befriends Humanity."[4] These competing headlines reveal two vastly different cultural worldviews. In one, nature is hostile and to be subdued by dominating lone individuals. In the other, nature is alive and welcoming, eager to receive all of humanity in the interconnection that binds and harmonizes the world. These radically different worldviews are so deeply ingrained that they affect the instinctive and pre-reflective way an event is perceived and interpreted. We are as embedded in our cultural frameworks as fish are immersed in the sea.[5] Our assumptions absorb us so completely, we do not even perceive them. Indeed, they are the lens through which we perceive anything at all.

This process of enculturation happens naturally and prereflectively. It does not require intentional instruction; it occurs informally—through our families and social networks, through the media that surround us, through the casual conversations of everyday life that matter-of-factly reinforce certain mind-sets and behaviors. Our culture is the only social world we know; and we assimilate its assumptions as if it is the only one there is.

A student of mine, Rev. Diane Davis, became the sole pastor at a small church in the desert Southwest. She ministered there for eight or nine years, then was called to another church near Phoenix. It turned out that her parish replacement was a colleague she knew rather well, a man named Robert Marshall. One morning, shortly before she left, she was visiting one of her lay leaders, a young mother raising her four-year-old daughter alone. They were discussing the transition in the mother's kitchen while the four-year-old colored on the table beside them. Diane was describing the new pastor, what a great guy Bob was, and how much he loved to tell stories, when something finally dawned upon the daughter. She stopped her coloring and asked incredulously, "You mean to tell me that the new pastor is going to be a *man*?" Diane nodded. "Well, yes." The daughter shook her head and replied, "I've never heard anything so ridiculous in my entire life."

Before she ever entered a school, without being instructed that such was the case, this young girl believes that only women can be pastors. Why? Because in her world—in its discourse, its practice, its role models—only women *are* pastors. And though she will soon learn that men, also, are capable of ministerial leadership, she will never dislodge the self-evident certainty that women quite exceptionally can lead institutions. Such is the reality of enculturation. Cultural assumptions are so reinforced, a four-year-old gets it.

Narrative educators recognize that cultural assumptions are embedded not just in role models, media images, casual conversation, and communal reinforcement; they are embedded in the narratives a culture tells as well. Stories socialize. In fact, some argue that stories socialize as powerfully as any other cultural influence. Catherine Orenstein, a cultural narrative critic trained at Harvard's Folklore and Mythology Department, observes, "Fairy tales are the first words read to us before we know the meaning of words, and the first models of society we encounter before we ever leave home."[6] We so thoroughly ingest them that they permeate our speech; we talk about "fairy-tale weddings," for example, and bemoan that, after all, "Life is no fairy tale."[7] Some of these stories are so widespread, they saturate us all, like "Little Red Riding Hood," a tale that

Orenstein observes "runs through us all like a current. Each of us carries within an intuitive understanding of what it means to be wolf, Grandma, woodsman, and Little Red Riding Hood."[8]

The cultural phenomena of princess mythology, in no small part fueled by Disney, demonstrates the power that a pervasive narrative can have over young people. As religious educator Katherine Turpin has documented, princess mythology has become a multibillion-dollar industry.[9] Young girls from every social class and racial identity devour princess movies, purchase princess paraphernalia, and spend countless hours dressing up and pretending to be princesses themselves. Princess mythology is so ever-present, Professor Marcia Lieberman has pointed out, that "Cinderella, Sleeping Beauty, and Snow White are mythic figures who have replaced the old Greek and Norse gods, goddesses, and heroes for most children."[10]

This princess fascination has a profound pedagogical impact. Cultural critic Henry Giroux, lamenting what he calls the "Disney-fication of children's culture," argues that Disney films have become a primary "teaching machine" for young people. He writes, "These films possess at least as much cultural authority and legitimacy for teaching specific roles, values, and ideals as more traditional sites of learning such as public schools, religious institutions, and the family."[11] Even mothers with feminist inclinations are at a loss. One such mom's interaction with her daughters could play in homes throughout North America.

> "Girls," I said, "you can do anything when you grow up! You can be scientists or ski instructors or hedge fund managers—I beg you, be hedge fund managers. Why would you want to be passive, anorexic princesses?"
>
> They looked at me as if I had gone mad. "Because princesses wear pretty dresses, Mama," they explained.
>
> I tried again. "Girls," I said gently, "I don't want to shock you, but historically, princesses have not always been popular. Consider the Russian Revolution. Or the French. Does the word guillotine ring a bell?"
>
> "You are a commoner!" my three-year-old shrieked, and adjusting their glittering tiaras, the little darlings ran off to

watch *Disney Princess Enchanted Tales* for the ten billionth time while I glumly cleaned the kitchen.[12]

And it's not just our daughters who are at stake. What princess movies are for girls; action films are for boys. The *Star Wars* franchise goes toe to toe in its duel with Disney over saturating society with its formative mythology (and the marketing lines that reinforce it). Make no mistake about it, narrative cultural critics forewarn, media-driven storylines are shaping values, assumptions, and ways of life. Truly, they are schooling the minds of our young people.

The second reason that narrative critical reflection is so essential for nurturing a critical consciousness is that *cultural and religious narratives often enculturate in oppressive and destructive ways*. While all narratives embody implicit ideologies, many of our dominant cultural narratives—sometimes subtly, sometimes blatantly—promote such problematic agendas as the subjugation of women, the domestication of children, or the glamorization of violence. All stories teach; some teach insidiously.

The imperial pervasiveness of princess mythology, for example, begs for critical analysis. As many feminist educators have observed, the message that these tales teach young women is downright troubling.[13] Princesses are pretty—their beauty defined by cultural standards of body type, hair length, facial features, and skin complexion; they are passive and helpless in the face of hardship, and in need of a male to liberate them—Cinderella, Sleeping Beauty, and Snow White are locked up, in a coma, or poisonously bespelled as they wait for their prince to come; and their longed-for reward is a domestic paradise—marriage to the perfect man and living happily ever after in his castle home. Hardly are these heroines models of female empowerment or achievement. As columnist Rosa Brooks observes, only half-jokingly, Disney princesses "rarely slay dragons, play sports, pilot jets or do open-heart surgery. Instead, they fiddle with their coiffures, linger over invitations to the ball, flee ineffectually from evil, and swoon. You don't have to be Gloria Steinem to realize that these are not, for the most part, useful professional skills in today's world."[14]

Concern is only deepened when we realize the depths to which these mythic stories are internalized. Ethnographer Kay Stone interviewed women of various ages and backgrounds and found that nearly every one of them not only could describe the stories in detail but they, at some point, "openly admired the lovely princesses and hoped to imitate them—especially their ability to obtain a man and a suburban castle without much effort."[15] Unfortunately, disillusionment sets in as Prince Charming never comes, or only in disguise, and cleaning up after him is decidedly unglamorous. "I thought there was something wrong with me," one woman writes of her lack of fulfillment, "not with the fairy stories."[16] The Disneyfication of culture is all too successful. If it not only fails to bring life but blames the death on the one domesticated, then, truly, something is wrong with the story.

Religious narratives also carry assumptions in need of critical reflection. Postcolonial biblical scholars have amply demonstrated how narratives in sacred texts carry cultural biases and serve political purposes.[17] Phyllis Trible has detailed how "texts of terror," such as the slaying of Jephthah's daughter (Judges 11) or the dismembering of the unnamed concubine (Judges 19), reinforce the subjugation of women and legitimate the violence committed against them.[18] The exodus story as well, such a source of liberation for many, is a cause of persecution for others. Scholars who reflect politically on the biblical account of the Israelites conquering the land of Canaan argue that it is clearly written from the perspective of the conquerors—the insinuation that the land was vastly uncivilized and awaiting discovery; the presumption, theologically sanctioned, that the land was "promised" to the chosen ones and "destined" for those who invaded it; and the mandate from God and religious leaders to massacre the indigenous inhabitants, certainly serve the ideological legitimation of the historical conquest. As Native Americans George Tinker and Robert Allen Warrior insist, the insidious way this same storyline was used to legitimate the European "Manifest Destiny" to claim the Americas as their God-sanctioned promised land cries out for a critical reflection that extends not just to the biblical narratives but to how these narratives are interpreted within and applied to new sociopolitical contexts.[19]

In sum, stories are ideological. They serve the political and peda-gogical purposes of the people telling them. Whether they admon-ish children to obey their parents or the big bad wolf will get them, inspire girls to ripen into princesses well-wed and domestically rescued (and adorned in appropriate Disney products), or sanc-tion the latest military invasion that serves the cause of the good and the godly, stories carry assumptions and promote an agenda. For the sake of the people who suffer this agenda—the anorexic young women who once wore tiaras, and the casualties of the neighborhoods bombarded by smart bombs—our cultural narra-tives, even those most hallowed and self-evident, are in need of critical scrutiny.

The third reason that critical reflection narrative pedagogy bears such liberative potential is that *critical reflection itself is a means of personal empowerment and human agency*. For educators like Jack Mezirow and Thomas Groome, critical reflection is funda-mental to what it means to be an adult.[20] Developmentalist James Fowler concurs; he sees critical reflection as central in the transition from the conventional faith of early adolescence to the more reflec-tive and self-chosen faith of young adulthood.[21] After childhood enculturation, in which we unreflectively internalize the assump-tions of our primary communities, fully becoming an adult involves questioning one's beliefs and assumptions, considering alternative perspectives, evaluating them all through reflective criteria, then owning and internalizing those perspectives that are "more inclu-sive, differentiating, permeable (open to other view points), criti-cally reflective of assumptions, emotionally capable of change, and integrative of experience."[22] For cultural activists like Paulo Freire, this critical reflection is the means not just of becoming an adult but of becoming a free and full human being. To be human is to be a subject.[23] No longer the passive consumer of their culture's sto-ryline, a subject is an active agent who sifts out the domesticating plotlines from the liberative ones, and freely chooses the stories by which they will live.

The teens of "A Third Way" demonstrated the liberative power of such critical reflection. For the first time, their eyes were opened to a destructive mythic pattern in films they had viewed since childhood; they were introduced to alternative storylines that promoted a peace they had not thought possible; and they became agents of culture, subjects who told stories that rose out of their inquiry and challenged the conventional wisdom of their community. As they testified from the stage, critical reflection is more than a pedagogical method; it is a tool for transformation. Without it, we are doomed to perpetuate the prejudices of the past; with it, we climb out of the sea of our cultural presuppositions and into a world both reasonable and humane.

Educational movements

Given the power of stories to nurture a critical consciousness, critical reflection approaches to narrative pedagogy seek to do three things:

1. They bring to young people's conscious awareness the cultural and religious narratives that subliminally shape their lives.

2. They invite teens to reflect critically on the ideologies and assumptions embedded within these narratives.

3. They empower young people to construct their own narratives that embody self-consciously liberative assumptions.

A variety of cultural and religious educators promote the use of narrative in nurturing a critical consciousness in young people. Joseph Taylor's "Reel Youth Ministry" raises to teens awareness how the prevalence of violence, the relentless display of sculpted bodies, and the glorification of cigarette, drug, and alcohol use in films marketed to teenagers contribute to aggressive behavior, eating disorders, and substance abuse in the young people who flock to see them. [24] Jina Kim and Hyon-Shim Hong empower Korean young women to critique the patriarchal subjugation of women in popular Korean folktales through the lens of gospel stories reinterpreted to expose the hidden power of the women within them.[25] Herbert Kohl helps young people reflect critically on portrayals of historical legends—for example, how depictions of Rosa Parks as a tired, lone heroine glorifies the hero myth of American individualism, and misrepresents the well-organized and widely networked movement that can inspire contemporary community-based activism.[26]

One representative narrative educator, Jack Zipes, has devoted his professional career to cultivating a new generation of counter-cultural storytellers. He argues that learning to tell stories is intrinsically empowering. It resists the television-stupor passivity of uncritically consuming the stories disseminated by the cultural elite, and it equips us with the techniques needed to narrate our own lives, to form plots that realize the life we imagine for ourselves. "We need to learn strategies of narration," he writes, "in order to grasp that we can become our own narrators, the storytellers of our lives."[27]

Zipes travels to public schools, libraries, and universities to animate a critical consciousness toward the cultural stories that shape us—from Peter Rabbit to Harry Potter; to teach the skills and grammar of storytelling—from folktales to science fiction; and to empower young people to craft narratives that rival those of their culture and more meaningfully inform the navigation of their lives.

To jump-start the process, he often begins with "Little Red Riding Hood," in part because of its reputation as the most popular folktale of all time, and in part out of his indignation that the tale involves a victimized girl who not only is raped and murdered but is blamed and held responsible for both, a storyline all too insidiously pervasive throughout our cultural communities.[28] To help dispel a narrative fossilization—that every story is limited to one "orthodox" version—he shares the tale penned by Charles Perrault, the precursor to that of the Brothers Grimm. It involves a spoiled, gullible, and helpless young girl who is forced to undress, garment by garment, then climb into her grandmother's bed where she is devoured by a creepily lascivious wolf. There is no happy ending—the girl dies—only a moral—that maidens should be more careful around the strangers who stalk them.

Zipes's agenda is to raise a critical consciousness about insidious storylines that domesticate or outright oppress. He selects from several strategies. He might ask provocative questions that stir discussion of the story's troubling themes for example, the sexual exploitation of children, or its blame-the-victim mentality. He might reveal the way this folktale has been used to sexualize women by displaying advertisements he has collected over the years of increasingly seductive femmes fatales dressed in red riding hoods selling to wolves everything from rental cars to Johnnie Walker Red Label.[29]

Another pedagogical strategy would be to share a parallel story where a similar plotline is embodied in an alternative context. For example, a story that often provokes passionate discourse and critical insight is one used to illuminate the legal bias against victims of sexual assault: "The 'Rape' of Mr. Smith."

"Mr. Smith, you were held up at gunpoint on the corner of 16th and Locust?"

"Yes."

"Did you struggle with the robber?"

"No."

"Why not?"

"He was armed."

"Then you made a conscious decision to comply with his demands rather than to resist?"

"Yes."

"Did you scream? Cry out?"

"No. I was afraid."

"Have you ever given money away?"

"Yes, of course—"

"And you did so willingly?"

"What are you getting at?"

"Well, let's put it like this, Mr. Smith. You've given away money in the past—in fact, you have quite a reputation for philanthropy. How can we be sure that you weren't *contriving* to have your money taken from you by force?"

"Listen, if I wanted—"

"Never mind. What time did this holdup take place, Mr. Smith?"

"About 11 p.m."

"You were out on the streets at 11 p.m.? Doing what?"

"Just walking."

"Just walking? You know that it's dangerous being out that late at night. Weren't you aware that you could have been held up?"

"I hadn't thought about it."

"What were you wearing at the time, Mr. Smith?"

"Let's see. A suit. Yes, a suit."

"An *expensive* suit?"

"Well—yes."

"In other words, Mr. Smith, you were walking around the streets late at night in a suit that practically *advertised* the fact that you might be a good target for some easy money, isn't that so? I mean, if we didn't know better, Mr. Smith, we might even think you were *asking* for this to happen, mightn't we?"[30]

After sharing this story, one might ask for similarities seen between it and the folktale, connections to discourse that casts suspicion on the victims of sexual assault and other contexts where women are blamed for their own oppression.

The Grimm's Brothers version of "Little Red Riding Hood" fares no better than that of Charles Perrault. Zipes often shares their version to expose how the same story is modified to serve different cultural agendas. The Grimms tempered the sexuality and altered the tragic ending, but the girl is still gullible, she is still devoured in bed by a wolf, but in this case she is rescued by a man who aids her in her helpless state. The moral is slightly altered as well—children who stray from their parents' direction will suffer the consequences of their disobedience. Young people are often amazed to find out that both the Grimms and Perrault versions are radical distortions of the original coming-of-age story in which a self-reliant and resourceful young maiden outwits a ravenous wolf and triumphantly succeeds her grandmother in a community of needle workers. After inviting reflection that compares the various Red Riding Hood heroines, Zipes frequently shares contemporary feminist versions of the tale that reclaim the empowerment of women, diminish the reliance on male rescuers, and hold devouring wolves accountable and in check.[31]

Throughout this process, young people are reflecting critically on disturbing themes within classic folktales, defusing the orthodox necessity of any one version of the story, and accessing their imaginations to conceive of new, more liberative ways of constructing and telling the story. Zipes completes the process by inviting the youth to write their own version of a "Little Red Riding Hood" story, one that promotes the values and assumptions they want to see embodied in their community.[32]

The five educational movements of critical reflection narrative pedagogy

Whether critiquing folktales so ubiquitous they sell red-label scotch, inspiring princesses to wake up to their personal power, or remythologizing the storylines that inform our response to violence, critical reflection narrative pedagogies have five distinct educational movements. The first movement is *to expose to young people a significant cultural story that shapes them*. The purpose of critical reflection narrative pedagogy is to nurture in young people a critical consciousness toward those narratives that subliminally influence their values and assumptions. Toward that end, we first must bring such narratives to their awareness. The specific narrative chosen as the focus for any given educational event depends on the needs of the young people in attendance, the narratives capturing their current fascination, the pressing concerns within their communities, and the aims and hopes of the educator.

Narratives to focus on could be drawn from:

- *Biblical Stories*—for example, the conquest of Canaan narrative to expose the legitimation of indigenous lands being invaded, or Pamela Cooper-White's use of the rape of Tamar to prompt reflection on violence against women;[33]

- *Classic Folktales*—like Jack Zipes' use of "Little Red Riding Hood," or Hyon-Shim Hong and Jina Kim's use of beloved Korean folktales;

- *Popular Films*—like Disney's portfolio of princess movies; box-office hits that portray teens as insatiable consumers of sex, alcohol, or illegal substances; or action films that embody the myth of redemptive violence;

- *Commercials or Advertisements*—to tease out the hidden narratives of what sex buys you, what body types are celebrated, or the Kobe Bryant glory you will know if only you buy Nike;

- *Stories from Community Leaders*—like the narratives governmental officials recount to justify war, anecdotes by politicians that reflect racial biases, or stories told from pulpits that bear assumptions about gender roles, other religions, or adolescent stereotypes;

- *Water-Cooler Stories*—like tuning into the stories told informally throughout a community to tease out attitudes toward women, gays, or immigrants illegal or otherwise.

Narrative educators develop the antennae necessary to notice the stories alive in a community that subtly or obviously convey destructive assumptions. These are the stories to bring to teens' awareness. Unfortunately, there are often many from which to choose.

The second educational movement is *to surface the ideological assumptions that are embedded in the narrative.* When I was a kid, I joined the Captain Satellite fan club. From the deep recesses of space, the cartoon-host astronaut sent a monthly communiqué printed in unintelligible blue type in case nefarious alien forces ever intercepted them. For $1.99 and two cereal box tops, I purchased the top-secret decoder glasses. They had red lenses. Putting them on, it all became clear. I could instantly read the row of red letters embedded within the blue type.

Narrative educators supply young people with the "red lens glasses" that reveal the subliminal ideological assumptions within a cultural narrative. Several methods are available:

- *Critical questions about the story*—Sometimes ideological assumptions become clear merely by directing attention to them. One can imagine in "A Third Way," or one of Zipes' Red Riding Hood workshops, questions posed such as, "What does this action picture storyline assume about violence, or the possible rehabilitation of 'bad guys?' What stereotypes in this folktale are reinforced about women, witches, or wolves?

How would it feel, in the Exodus narrative, to be a Canaanite hearing this call to genocide?"

- *Critical questions about the storyteller*—Ideological agendas can be revealed by asking such questions as, "Who do you think wrote this story—a man or a woman, an Israelite or a Canaanite, a child or an adult? Whose interests are being secured, and whose are being violated? Who keeps telling this story in our community, and how do they benefit from its implicit agenda?

- *Providing a structural template*—Subliminal ideologies can be discerned by providing a conceptual lens through which to notice them in a story. For the teens in "A Third Way," Wink's myth of redemptive violence offered a grid through which to analyze action movies. Similar templates can be provided about the narrative arc common to all princess storylines, the core message in every teen ad, or the bias to blame the victim in stories involving sexual assault.

- *Contrasting alternative value systems*—Ideological agendas often can be brought into bold relief when set alongside competing values and assumptions. In "A Third Way," the teens were exposed to principles of nonviolence, the practices of forgiveness, and the conditions of an accountable reconciliation. The myth of redemptive violence, as played out in action movies, became all the more apparent when seen in contrast.

- *Exploring a narrative's social function*—Narratives serve ideological purposes, whether justifying a war, selling liquor, selling Disney products, keeping children in their place, keeping women in their place, or keeping the conquered in their place. Ideological agendas can become more evident when teens are asked to reflect on the function this story serves in society, and the assumptions implied therein.

The third educational movement is *to expand the narrative possibilities of the presenting story*. Critical reflection narrative pedagogy seeks to dispel the notions that stories can only be told in their "orthodox" version, that there is such a thing as an orthodox version at all, and that stories can only be created by those with cultural power. One movement of this approach, then, is to expand the imaginative possibilities surrounding a narrative, thus dislodging the "givenness" of the culturally sanctioned version, and nurturing the awareness that ideologically destructive stories can be retold with more liberative values and assumptions. This can be done in several ways:

- *Reimagining the current story*—A favorite method of Zipes, in dislodging the notion that a story is determined, is to ask "What if" questions that provoke different narrative outcomes. What if Little Red Riding Hood was trained in the martial arts? What if the wolf was being hunted down and only wanted safe refuge? What if Jephthah forsook his vow and refused to slay his daughter? What if a terrorist wasn't a monster at all but a grieving father whose daughter was killed by an American bomb?

- *Comparing variations on the same story*—The assumed orthodoxy of a story can be subverted when alternative versions of the same story are presented. The various redactions of "Little Red Riding Hood" that Zipes presents to young people dispel the myth that the story can only be told in one way, and they reveal more obviously the ideological agenda of any given variation. Similar reflection is nurtured when reading the different versions of the same biblical story in the synoptic gospels.

- *Presenting a subversive narrative*—The ideological agenda of cultural narratives can be exposed and subverted when narratives are presented that embody radically different assumptions. Zipes has collected a catalog full of alternative versions of "Little Red Riding Hood."[34] Feminist storytellers have likewise gathered empowering reconstructions of domesticating princess stories.[35] The teens participating in "A Third Way" were exposed to narratives of terrorist biographies, victims who found forgiveness, and perpetrators willing to make amends through processes of restorative justice and accountable reconciliation, all serving as compelling alternatives to the seeming inevitability of redemptive violence.

- ◆ *Exploring a contemporary recasting of the same story*—Attending to how a story is recontextualized in a contemporary setting can expose the story's agenda and expand one's narrative consciousness. Recognizing the blame-the-victim storyline from "Little Red Riding Hood" in contemporary stories of sexual assault, or how the story's sexual themes are exploited in modern advertisements, illuminates the insidiousness of the original version. Similarly, comparing the Israelite version of the conquest of Canaan with the European version of the conquering of the Americas sets both stories' agenda into bold relief.

The fourth educational movement is *to invite teens to articulate the values they want to promote and embody*. The purpose of critical reflection narrative pedagogy is not to indoctrinate young people into an alternative ideology different from the one they have already internalized. Domestication, even with a liberative coating, is still domestication. Critical reflection nurtures independent thinking. This entails becoming conscious of personal and cultural assumptions, holding them to the light of free and rational scrutiny, and choosing for oneself the values and viewpoints that one will espouse and embody. Critical reflection narrative educators, then, create a space for teens to sift through the various perspectives made available and to articulate some synthesis of the values and viewpoints they want to affirm and make their own.

This can be done in a variety of ways. After presenting various characterizations of Little Red Riding Hood—from ditzy to determined—Zipes asks young people which heroine they would most like to be, and why? Often he launches into the telling of a final version, then stops midway through and asks the youth to finish the story for a daughter they can imagine having in the future.

In "A Third Way," after discussing various stories and perspectives on violence and redemptive responses, I asked the teens, as I do with all the drama groups I direct, to free write for three minutes on the message they wanted their play to promote. We recorded them on flip charts, then dialogued and distilled them down to a single-line consensus about their play's central theme. In this case, they wanted to communicate, "We are all terrorists; we are all victims; heaven has room for both." This theme became the spine of the play, an invaluable touchstone against which to test every new idea about dialogue or storyline. More than that, however, it became a communal credo, the encapsulated core of the consecrated truth to which their critical reflection had led them.

The fifth educational movement is *to empower young people to critically reconstruct the story in ways that embody the values they want to promote*. The process of narrative critical consciousness is completed when teens create their own narratives, claiming a self-authorship grounded in the personal truth of their considered viewpoint. Zipes, for example, invites young people to rewrite folktales from critically reflective perspectives—"Little Red Riding Hood" with a feminist consciousness perhaps, or as an animal rights activist raising awareness of the wolf as an endangered species.

Re-creating cultural narratives completes the transformation from passively and uncritically absorbing stories to authoring stories as an active subject. This empowered agency, in turn, contributes to and shapes the culture in which one lives. The stories teens conceive and tell, like those already culturally hallowed, have the power to alter perceptions, influence values, affect discourse, and inspire change. *Terrorists in Heaven*, for example, embodies a radically alternative mythology to cultural narratives currently dominant in North America. It challenges assumptions, stirs controversy, and provokes public dialogue. And it demonstrates not only the teens' critical capacities, but their acceptance of the call to shape the culture they once absorbed so thoroughly. Such is the power of critical reflection narrative pedagogy. Young people rise from the sea of uncritical cultural assimilation and step into society as critical thinkers. It's a radical process; passive consumers become prophets.

In a popular Korean folktale subtitled "The Faithful Daughter," the heroine, Sim-Chung, volunteers as a virgin sacrifice to raise the currency to cure her blind father.[36] She is thrown into the center of a typhoon to appease the tempestuous Sea-King, a gesture that eventually reunites her with her father and restores her father's sight. The story, often told to Korean daughters to reinforce a filial obedience even at the cost of personal sacrifice, was told by a senior pastor within the Korean Presbyterian Church in a sermon denouncing women's ordination. "Women should serve their fathers first, their husbands second; their personal ambitions should be sacrificed. The Bible demands it; the culture confirms it. The church, quite simply, should stop debating it."

Eun Mi was at the sermon. She was also at Jina Kim's Bible study for Korean women.[37] The sermon hit close to home. Once certain of her call, she attended seminary and completed every one of the requirements for ordination, but she was repeatedly turned down because of her gender. Hope was fading. The sermon felt like a final blow.

The women at Jina Kim's Bible study heard her discouragement. They shared similar stories of domination, and together they looked for alternative narrative inspiration. They found it in Jesus' encounter with the Samaritan woman at the well (John 4:1–42). They recognized that Samaritans were an occupied people, and that women were denied both voice and power. Nevertheless, that Samaritan woman questioned Jesus with a resilient audacity and eventually was instrumental in revealing Jesus' identity. Her tenacity gave rise to a surprising priestly role.

With the support of these women, Eun Mi persisted. After *ten* years, she prevailed. She was called by a church and approved by the denominational board. At her ordination service, Eun Mi told Sim-Chung's story, how it had been used for generations to subjugate women, and how it is still used today to deny them the right to claim their gifts and dignity.

"I am Sim-Chung," Eun Mi boldly proclaimed from the pulpit. "I have risen from the sea to serve my people. Not the fathers whose blindness would sacrifice their daughter's personhood, but the daughters themselves, who see all too well and long to hear the truth—Sim-Chung's death was wrong. As is submitting yourself before any patriarch who robs you of life's fullness."

Eun Mi was claiming her vocation. She also names the vocation of critical reflection narrative pedagogy. Stories are diverse. Some bring life; some deal death; some wage war; some birth peace. But stories, to a one, affect us. Too many lives have been sacrificed to the seas of domesticating stories. The time has come to rise from the surf and to claim one's place behind the pulpit and the podium, with eyes that see the storylines of destruction and with words to tell the tales that heal.

Five

How can stories embolden the artist within?

Narrative pedagogy and creative vitality

Tahira was tired of repeating her correct name. Freshly arrived from Pakistan, she had yet to make friends. Hoping to remedy that before school started, she signed up for the summer storytelling workshop. The teens at the program tried, but they just couldn't get it. Teresa? Tamara? Tyra? Finally, when one said, "Terry, right?" Tahira gave up. "Yeah," she said. "Call me Terry."

The ostensible reason the teens were there was to learn to tell stories. For two weeks of half-days, they would hear stories from around the world, explore narrative structure and technique, then write, polish, and practice original folktales to be shared at a family-friendly storytelling festival on the final Friday evening. The program had no other agenda—not that teens learn sacred stories, not that they reflect critically upon their cultural narratives, nor to empower them for social transformation. Its sole aim was to celebrate creativity through the age-old art form of storytelling.

Inspired by Daniel Sklar's brilliant approach to play-making, we started by creating characters.[1] A favorite Sklar exercise is Scribble-Scrabble—where young people fill a blank piece of paper with subconscious doodling, then examine the tangle and tease out objects, feelings, and creatures they can decipher. They choose one, then create a character by fleshing out that character's name, age, habitat, primary relationships, their deepest fear, and their deepest wish. Essentially a self-designed Rorschach blot, the exercise stimulates the imagination while surfacing emotionally laden symbols to explore through story.

Tahira conceived of Bupsala Manresa, an African young girl with two rivals who always teased her. Her deepest wish was to be called by her true name; her deepest fear was that she wouldn't be worthy of it. The teens, then, created storylines where their characters set off to satisfy their wishes and encounter some obstacle where they have to confront their fears. Along the way, I taught techniques in storyboarding and dramatic tension, emotional expression and vocalization.

Tahira, as it turned out, didn't need much help. We discovered she was something of a natural. Then again, she crafted a story that spoke for itself. At the Friday evening festival, she claimed her space behind the mic with such a sense of purpose she forgot to introduce herself. She did not forget, however, to introduce her tale.

She called it, "Boopsie's Breath."

In the heart of the African jungle, a village gathered to celebrate an unusual occurrence. Three babies had been born on the very same day. Tonight was their naming ceremony. In this village, names were special. They described your heart's essence, the essence you would grow into and become if you followed your true path. Only the wisest woman in the village could name a child. And the villagers waited around the fire for the elder to emerge from her hut.

After hours of drumming, the elder appeared. She circled the fire three times for wisdom, then held the first child close to her chest. She peered into the infant's eyes as if reading its very soul. Then she lifted the baby into the air and declared, "You are Ogbanaya—One with the strength to move mountains." The father answered as was their custom, "That's an awfully big name for such a small child." The wise woman responded, "Have no fear. He will grow into his name. Until then, he will be called Oggie."

The wise woman went to the next child and looked deeply into her eyes. Then she lifted the baby into the air and said, "You are Okeechukwu—One who runs with the wind." The mother rejoined as was their custom, "That's an awfully big name for such a small child." "Have no fear," the wise woman assured. "She will grow into her name. Until then, she will be called Okie."

Then the wise woman went to the last child. Now, some who were close say that as the elder looked deeply into the child's eyes, the child burped sour-milk gas into the wise woman's face, and that is why the elder's face curdled and turned away. Others say, no, a sacred spark that burst from the fire caught her eye and caused her to scowl. Either way, the wise woman winced, and as she lifted the child into the air, she intoned, "This is Bupsala Manresa—One with the breath of a lion." The mother rose and started, "That's an awfully big name. . . . Wait a minute," she exclaimed. "That's a horrible name. She'll have bad breath the rest of her . . ." "Have no fear," the wise woman snapped. "Trust me, she will grow into her name. Until then, she will be called Boopsie."

As could be expected, Boopsie grew to hate her name. The villagers cringed and turned away when Boopsie passed them by. And the children plugged their noses, then ran away to play without her. Their favorite game was to pretend to be their real names. Oggie would lift a rock and cry out, "I am Ogbanaya, One with the strength to move mountains," and Okie chased butterflies while squealing, "I am Okeechukwu, One who runs with the wind." But when Boopsie found where they were playing, they stopped and faked like they were sick. "There's Boopsie," they cried. "Her breath could kill a jackal." And they would fall over as if toxic fumes overcame them. Boopsie did not want to grow into her name. She was afraid she already had.

Twelve years passed when a crisis befell the village. A lion as fierce as a dozen dragons terrorized the jungle. The villagers beseeched the wise woman for counsel. She pondered deeply. Then she advised, "We will send out three to stalk the lion." "Only three?" the villagers exclaimed. "Who will they be?" "Oggie, Okie, and Boopsie," the elder replied. "What?" The villagers were outraged. "They are only children. Why not send a team of our bravest hunters?" "Have no fear," the wise woman insisted. "It is time for these three to grow into their names."

For three days, the children followed the lion's tracks until they came to a ridge. At one end of the canyon below, they spied a cave; at the other end, a lion was devouring a jackal's carcass. "I've got a plan," Oggie said, and they made for a tree alongside the cave. Safe on a branch, they scouted the scene. "This is perfect," Oggie said. "Okie, you're a fast runner. You get the lion to chase you toward the cave. But just before you get there, you jump up on this branch. I'm really strong, I'll be waiting just above the cave, and when the lion runs in, I'll get the rocks to avalanche and the lion will be trapped inside."

"What about me?" Boopsie asked. "What can I do?"

"What can you do?" Oggie replied. "Breathe on the lion to make him sick? Here. You gather some sticks and leaves and make a scarecrow in the back of the cave that looks like Okie. Then just get out of the way. Now, Okie, you lead the lion straight this way. The lion will be fooled. Just don't forget; at the last second, jump up onto this branch. You don't want to get trapped in that cave."

A few moments later, the savage beast was snarling for more food when it heard a sing-song voice lilting from the canyon. "Mr. Liiiiii . . . on. Where arrrrrre you?"

"ROARRRR!" The lion growled. "Who dares approach the king of the jungle?"

"It's me," the voice squeaked, "Okie."

"ROARRRR!! And what are you doing here?"

Okie swallowed hard, then let out, "I'm growing into my name."

"ROARRRR! I'LLL give you a name . . . LUNCH!"

The lion sprung and tore after Okie. Okie ran, as fast as she could run. And then something amazing happened. It was as if the wind was lifting her up and carrying her faster than she had ever dreamed possible. She flew down the canyon, around the bend, toward the cave, then just at the last second, she leaped up onto the branch as the lion sped past her and into the cave.

Up above, Oggie was ready. His arms embraced a boulder as big as he was. He strained. His muscles quivered. Then something amazing happened. It was as if all of the strength of the earth erupted right up through him. The rock budged, then shifted, then tumbled over the edge and down in front of the cave. An avalanche of rocks and stones crashed along with it until the mouth of the cave was barricaded completely.

Oggie jumped onto the branch. "Way to go, Okie! It worked!" he screamed. "Way to go, Oggie. It did!" Okie returned. They both turned around. "Way to go Boopsie, we did . . . Boopsie? Where are you?" Okie and Oggie looked at each other. "You don't think . . ." But it was true. Boopsie was still in the cave.

When the rock slide finally settled, the cave was so dark Boopsie could not see her hand in front of her face. The lion was beside himself with rage. "ROARRRR! I will kill whoever's responsible! Then kill them again. ROARRRR!" Then he stopped. He sensed something. "Hmm," he toyed, "somebody's in here. I smell your breath. It's a human's breath. A very scared human's breath."

Boopsie couldn't believe it. Her breath would kill her yet. She covered her mouth with her hands and retreated to the back of the cave. The lion slowly stepped toward her. Boopsie cowered, more and more afraid. The lion was feet away, inches away, so close she could feel its breath. And then something amazing happened. It was as if a warrior's ferocity ruptured right up through her. She screamed as if a lion herself and leaped. Before the lion could raise its claws, Boopsie had it by the throat. They wrestled and rolled—face to face, eye to eye, nose to nose—Boopsie squeezing that lion's neck while roaring into its face until she squeezed the breath right out of that beast and pinned it on its back. "Enough! Enough!" the lion gasped. "You win, I say. Enough!"

Boopsie loosened her grip, just a bit. The lion gulped for air. Then he looked at her and conceded, "You are a fierce fighter," the lion acknowledged. "You have done what no one has ever done before you. You have breathed the breath of a lion and survived. So now, I give you the lion's secret. His power is in his breath—it is what makes him roar, what makes him stand tall, what makes him the king of the jungle. Today, I pass that breath to you. From this day forward, I will live with your people in peace; and you, young warrior, will walk in the power of the lion's breath."

Oggie and Okie were crestfallen as they dug through the rock slide to retrieve Boopsie's bones. When they broke through, though, they could not believe their eyes. Boopsie was standing tall in wait for them; she was, quite clearly, breathing; and at her side, the lion meekly knelt.

Three nights later, the villagers held a ceremony in honor of the conquering heroes. They sat around the fire as the wise woman stood before Oggie and invited him to claim his true name. "I am no longer Oggie," the young man announced. "I am Ogbanaya, for I have the strength to move mountains." The elder then stood before Okie and invited her to claim her true name. "I am no longer Okie," the young woman declared. "I am Okeechukwu, for I can run with the wind." Then the wise woman stood before Boopsie and invited her to claim her true name. Boopsie stood tall, as radiant as royalty. "I am no longer Boopsie," the young warrior proclaimed. "I am Bupsala Manresa, for I have the breath of a lion." She paused a beat, then added with a smile, "And I love my name."

The clapping came from adult and child alike. You would have thought the audience itself had just evaded a monster. When the acclaim subsided, one of the teens remembered the oversight. "Hey," he yelled from the wings, "you forgot to tell them your name."

"Oh, yeah," the storyteller recalled. She started, then caught herself. "They call me Terry," she announced, "but my real name is Tahira."

Bupsala Manresa would be proud.

Theoretical underpinnings

Like most teens, Tahira signed up for the storytelling workshop with motives little related to a love for narratives. She wanted to make friends; she wanted to get out of the house; perhaps she sought any excuse to escape the task of unpacking boxes. While she was at the workshop, however, something happened. She developed a fondness for folktales to be sure—hearing a few told by the facilitator, playing around with different genres, screening videos of trained professionals for tips and skills in performing them. But more, something came alive within her. Once a character materialized out of the gossamer regions of her imagination, and an enticing storyline took hold, Tahira was captured—held captive by the ecstatic delights of timeless artistic creativity. She spent hours consumed with fleshing out her characters, mapping out a plot, measuring out the beats of the pace, and polishing the ending precisely. Then she walked around as if in a trance—mouthing the story under her breath, absorbing the arc of its flow, and memorizing turns of phrase as she rehearsed how to tell it in the way that she felt it. Storytellers create a spell when they tell. Tahira was entranced with the craft itself. And as she hit her final note in front of a crowd transfixed by her words, she glowed. She sparkled as one at the height of her powers—claiming her voice, speaking her truth, and perceiving her beauty. She was Tahira—perhaps for the first time, a young woman who knew her name, and who felt the life spirit restoring her to herself.

Tahira embodies the aims and movements of a *creative vitality* approach to narrative pedagogy. Creative vitality narrative educators have a love for narratives in and of themselves. They are storytellers who treasure legends and folktales, playwrights who marvel at the magic of the theater, writers who know the healing power of fiction, and filmmakers enthralled at the stories a camera can convey. Creative vitality narrative educators recognize that these are time-honored activities—crafts unto themselves with traditions and techniques, precepts and protocols. And they seek to pass on these narrative crafts to young people—that teens might learn the trade, so to speak, take a stab at it themselves, and come to celebrate the beauty and joys intrinsic to the act of merely telling stories.

The aim, however, is not solely to transmit the traditions of storytelling. These traditions are alive for a reason. They are art forms. Like music, painting, dance, and the like, storytelling, in all of its variety, is first and foremost an artistic enterprise. It is a way of connecting with one's deepest emotions, discovering one's voice and truth, and communicating, through acts of beauty and self-expression, the unique way one experiences the world. Further, creativity is intrinsically self-renewing. It connects us with a spirit of vitality that courses through every art form like a crackling current of electricity. Art regenerates. It is so revitalizing that some see creativity as a spiritual path—an intentional way of connecting with a life force that not only brings untold delight, it restores us to the splendor of being more fully human, of being more fully ourselves.[2]

Teens already know this energy. Adolescence is a time of seemingly boundless creativity. Forming bands inside the garage, honing dance moves at the park, making movies with hand-held cameras, sketching landscapes on one's homework, drawing graphic novels, writing verse and rhyming rap: teens give themselves to their artistic impulses. Tahira sure did. She did not call it a spiritual path, but it was one all the same. Through following her creativity, she experienced what it was like to be an artist. More important, however, through the art of telling stories, she experienced what it was like to be herself. Not just Tahira, but Tahira radiant with the sparkle of the spirit.

Why are narrative art forms so effective for nurturing creative vitality?

First, *artistic activity connects us with the sacred spirit of life*. St. Irenaeus classically proclaimed, "The glory of God is humanity fully alive."[3] Contrary to misconceptions in toxic images of the divine, God does not denigrate humanity. God's deepest desire is that all of creation, humanity included, flourish with the fullness of life. Indeed, if Irenaeus is right, when humanity swells in radiant glory, God's own glory swells as well. Like all of us, I have been graced with glimpses of human abundance that could serve as icons of divine glory.

At a wedding reception I once attended, I noticed a teenaged young lady sitting at one of the dozens of round tables stationed throughout the social hall. She was in a wheelchair, paralyzed, as I was to discover later, from the waist down after a car accident the year before. She was not talking with anyone, her head was cocked listening to the music from the small wedding ensemble playing love songs from the dais. Seemingly on an impulse, she wheeled herself to the modest dance floor, nestled herself within several couples, then tilted her head back, and rocked herself in rhythm with the music.

A woman at my table turned out to be a dance therapist. She saw the young lady as well. Watching the teen sway by herself, the woman felt moved to wander toward the dance floor. Once there, she bent down and asked the young lady, "May I share this dance with you?" The young lady met her gaze and beamed. "I would love to," she said. And for the next several minutes, the two of them glided, whirled, and twirled with such grace the couples stopped dancing and edged to the side, the people at the tables interrupted their chatter, and the musicians, nodding one to another, sustained the serenade with "Over the Rainbow" then segued into "It's a Wonderful World." The onlookers, while dabbing at tears, broke into applause as the teenage dancer nodded at her partner while glowing like the noonday sun.

A few moments later, when left to themselves, the girl shared her gratitude with the stranger. "Thank you," she said. "I haven't danced since the accident. I used to be a dancer, and oh, how I have missed it. You have reminded me—when I dance, I feel loved. When I dance, I feel the very power of God lifting me up into life."

There is a dance that moves through our world, a flow of sacred vitality that invites all of creation to rest in its music, move to its

rhythms, and through its restoring melody, be lifted up into the fullness of life. Some call this dance the spirit of God; some call it the
cosmic life force; others call it the flow of creativity. Julia Cameron,
whose vocation is coaching artistic recovery for anyone artistically
wounded, defines it as the "underlying, in-dwelling creative force
infusing all of life—including ourselves."[4] This spiritual energy is the
life-blood of the universe, a river of creativity that flows within all
things, inspiring and sustaining fullness and vitality. It is the force
that makes the flower bloom, the eagle soar, and the dancer swell with
radiant delight. It is life. Indeed, it is the livingness that keeps life alive.

For Christians, this creative spirit is foundational to the nature of
God.[5] The Scriptures begin with the story of an artist God mixing
colors, arranging shapes, and fashioning clay into the masterpiece
of Creation, then insists that it is God's very breath that sustains
Creation in an ever-renewing infusion. Likewise, fashioned in the
image of God as we are, creativity is foundational to being human.
Beverly Shamana, a bishop, musician, and painter, writes, "We are
the offspring of a creative God whose hand print is stamped indel-
ibly on our soul, marking us for continuing creativity in the world."[6]
Creativity is our essence, our birthright, our sacred endowment.
We are most fully human, most fully *alive*, when we are at one with
this fountain of fecundity flowing from the divine.

While this sacred renewing energy is ever flowing, humanity
must cultivate a living connection to it. "Think of the universe as
a vast electrical sea," Cameron writes, "in which you are immersed
and from which you are formed; opening to your creativity changes
you from something bobbing in that sea to a more fully functioning,
more conscious, more cooperative part of that ecosystem."[7] Art is
one way of connecting to and participating with the currents in this
sea of sacred vitality. Artists know this. Whether musicians in the
flow, writers in the zone, dancers carried away in the moment, even
storytellers caught up in the mysterious spell woven through their
words—artists soak in and soar within this mystical union where
human discipline, talent, and drive are graced by a divine energy
that flows through them with ecstatic intensity.

The arts, in essence, are dance steps that mediate this connection
with the sacred; art does not manipulate the spirit, as any writer can

attest when their words feel like trudging through mud. Art does, however, place you on the dance floor where a sacred presence can steal up out of nowhere, grab your hand, and partner with you in bringing beauty into the wedding hall of our world. A "mighty symphony" fills the universe, Evelyn Underhill observes, "the very self-expression of the Eternal God."[8] The sacred invitation extended to each of us is to be an instrument in this symphony of life, to follow the lead of our artistic impulses, and to play the music to which a paralyzed teen can dance.

The second reason narrative art forms are effective for nurturing creative vitality is that *artistic activity is intrinsically restorative.* Art not only connects us with the sacred; art restores us to ourselves. Daniel Judah Sklar, in teaching playwriting at public schools in inner-city New York, suggests that the value of teaching an art form to young people goes beyond the delights of the craft itself; art nurtures a way of being in life, a way of looking "at the world with the eyes of an artist."[9] In several ways, artists, when in the flow, remind us all of what it looks like to be vital human beings.

First, artists are *alive to their experience.* Like Shakespeare's Gloucester, artists "see the world feelingly."[10] Whether Itzhak Perlman playing the violin or Vincent van Gogh painting a starry night, artists are in touch with the deep yearnings of the soul, and they allow the events of life to ripple through them with an unbridled delight, a raw fierceness, or a brokenhearted anguish. Artists are not numb to their feelings; life guts through them with piercing clarity.

In teaching a drama workshop to young adults at a city college in Los Angeles, I once walked in and asked the students, "How was the drive over?" The responses were various riffs off of, "Fine." "Okay." "A little traffic but no big deal." I gave them an exercise—imagine experiencing your drive over this evening with the openness of an onscreen Meryl Streep. They had no trouble with it. One saw a dog dead on the road and wept; another saw a father scolding his daughter and kindled with the instinct to kill; still another imagined a gorgeous blonde driving by with a smile prompting from him an impromptu aria. Actors do not sleepwalk through the tedium of the day. They are alive to their experience. And if they can access it honestly, we pay good money to go see it. It's real; it's energy; it's alive. As Kafka ascertained, it is "the axe for the frozen sea inside us."

Second, artists *tell their personal truth.* When asked why he loved being an actor, Jeff Goldblum once described, "If I'm in a subway and someone steps on my toe and says, 'Sorry,' I say, 'It's okay, no problem.' If I'm on the stage, however, I can jump up and down in pain, throw a tantrum, call the person names, or sob like a child." As James Dean put it, actors "portray publicly what we all feel privately." Artists are not prisoners to social niceties or cultural conventions. They access their experience, they find their voice, and, with it, they tell their personal truth.

Feminist scholars have underscored how empowering this can be.[11] Denying one's experience—whether from shame, insecurity, or having it silenced from the outside—is a diminishment of our humanity. Our experience is the source of our personal truth. It is what we know, deep in the soul where all the things that we know are known. Contexts that value our experience, help us claim it, and empower us to voice it honestly are as liberating as they are in short supply. Dori Grinenko Baker's inspiring work with young women is testimony to this. She invites young women to tell stories from their experience and look for the presence of the divine within them; in so doing, they discover that their lives are "fifth gospels . . . sacred texts where God continues to reveal God's self."[12] In the words of Nelle Morton, Baker is "hearing young women into speech."[13]

Art is a uniquely powerful avenue for nurturing such inner authority and self-emergence.[14] In the movie *Magnolia* a sexual abuse survivor displays above her wardrobe the collage she created at an art therapy session. Images of violation flood the canvas while pasted, in tiny letters at the bottom, are the words that quietly proclaim, "It's true." Some theologians recognize that the impulse to resist the despair of silence and to speak one's painful truth through art is the pulse beat of the spirit of God birthing life out of suffering and death.[15] As Dee Dee Risher writes, inspired by political prisoners composing poetry and Chilean women remembering the slain through folk art, "These courageous compulsions to create in the midst of death bear testimony to the irrepressible presence of God's creative power within us and its urgent need to speak."[16] Whether abuse survivors revealing their secrets, orphaned boys putting God on trial, or a teenage immigrant giving expression to the pain of having one's name belittled, telling one's personal truth is empowering, and an empowered voice bears the echo of the spirit that resists the silence of oppression.

Finally, artists, each in their own way, *give beautiful shape to their experience.* While open to their emotions and aware of their truth, artists do not simply vent their feelings or scream their point of view. Rather, they take the raw material of their experience and, using the gifts particular to them, transform their experience into an artistic piece that provokes the mind and pierces the heart. As Thomas Wolfe says about writing, "Fiction is not fact, but fact selected and understood. Fiction is fact arranged and charged with purpose."[17] In arranging the facts of our experience and charging it with purpose, we become creators. We search for the medium—painting or music, folk tale or film—that combines our personal gifts with our aesthetic vision, and we fashion an artistic piece that bears our unique perspective and pulsates with the heartbeat of our creative spirit. The miracle is that making art remakes us. We not only create objects of beauty, we become the objects of beauty we were created to be.

Doug Lipman narrates his version of the well-known Talmudic tale:

Once, the great Hasidic leader, Zusia, came to his followers. His eyes were red with tears, and his face was pale with fear.

"Zusia, what's the matter? You look frightened!"

"The other day, I had a vision. In it, I learned the question that the angels will one day ask me about my life."

The followers were puzzled. "Zusia, you are pious. You are scholarly and humble. You have helped so many of us. What question about your life could be so terrifying that you would be frightened to answer it?"

Zusia turned his gaze to heaven. "I have learned that the angels will not ask me, 'Why weren't you a Moses, leading your people out of slavery?'"

His followers persisted. "So, what will they ask you?"

"And I have learned," Zusia sighed, "that the angels will not ask me, "Why weren't you a Joshua, leading your people into the promised land?'"

One of his followers approached Zusia and faced him squarely. Looking him in the eyes, the follower demanded, "But what will they ask you?"

"They will say to me, 'Zusia, there was only one thing that no power of heaven or earth could have prevented you from becoming.' They will say, 'Zusia, why weren't you Zusia?'"[18]

An artistic way of engaging life entails being alive to one's utterly unique experience of the world, beholding and claiming the truth within it, and engaging one's creative gifts to bring a beauty into the world that sparkles with one's personal essence. Through living one's life artistically, Zusia becomes Zusia for real; Tahira becomes Tahira; we each become freely and authentically ourselves.

The third reason narrative arts are effective in nurturing creative vitality is that *artistic activity heals the soul.*

When my son, Justin, was about four years old, we found ourselves stumbling through life within the rather snug confines of a one-bedroom apartment. We were doing pretty well—we shared a bedroom, and the coffee table doubled as a writing desk and Lego station—but we were fine. Until our close friends, a family of four, moved to Southern California. Their new house was just a couple of days from closing, and they needed a place to stay in the meantime. No problem. Except that a couple of days turned into a week, one week turned into two, and two turned into three. For a solid month, six of us crowded a space that felt cramped when there were only two. Justin, I feared, had the worst of it. He gave up his bedroom to sleep on the floor; he had to share his toys; he had to share his father, for that matter, but he was hanging in there the best he could.

Until one day, he had just had it.

Our sliding-glass door opened onto a mound of dirt where kids from around the complex came to dig and play. Justin had a shovel and was digging up a boulder that really was the jawbone of a Tyrannosaurus Rex. A kid from the neighborhood needed the shovel, so he walked over to Justin, and grabbed it right out of his hands. Justin grabbed it right back, but it turned into a tug of war, each pulling it back and forth, until the neighbor kid gave a final yank that knocked Justin to his knees. Justin stood up and gave the kid a look that could kill. When it didn't, he kicked the dirt, stomped down the mound, fumed into the apartment, slammed the sliding-glass door behind him, then threw himself into his chair in the corner and folded his arms to pout.

"What's the matter?" I asked him.

"I'm mad," he said. "I'm never playing with my friends ever again in my entire life." I understood. And I let him sit it out.

My godson, Jackson, was oblivious to the entire scene. Also four years old, he sat on the floor playing Legos in the living room. Apparently, he was listening to the radio as well, because, after a commercial break, a song floated out of the speakers that caught his attention. It was one of those songs—a Kenny G saxophone solo—that wraps itself around you, seeps into your bones, then induces you to tap your toes before you are aware you are doing it. The song was working its magic on Jackson. He bobbed his head and rocked his shoulders until, unable to constrain himself any longer, he leaped up from the Legos and commenced to dance right in the middle of the living room. Bopping to the music, he looked into the corner and said, "Hey Justin, you want to dance with me?" Justin just stared at him a moment, then said, "Sure, why not?" And he got up and started dancing with Jackson.

For the next several minutes, the two of them were giddy. They do-si-doed, twirled and shuffled, twisted and skipped like some slapstick combination of Fred and Ginger, John Travolta, and the Three Stooges taking on an Argentinean tango. They were lit up—giggling and squealing as if drunk on life, so drunk that when the song ended, the magical melody still lingering in our midst, Jackson turned to Justin and said, "Hey, you want to go out and dig for dinosaur bones?" and Justin answered, "Sure, let's go." They were already rushing out the sliding-glass door before I could get their attention.

"Justin," I said, "where are you going?"

"I'm going out to play with my friends," he answered.

I said, "I thought you were never going to play with your friends ever again in your entire life."

He looked at me like he didn't know what I was talking about. Then it came back to him, as if it was a lifetime ago. "Oh yeah," he said, then thought, "You know, I think the dancing took my mad away."

The world wounds us. Sometimes the wounds are severe—through child abuse, assault, or the loss of a loved one; sometimes the wounds are less severe but no less absorbed by the soul—through the everyday violations that make us mad if not numb or defeated. Art is an activity with a musical spirit—be it blues or jazz or the edginess of rap. And the music, regardless of the art form itself, works on the soul and heals our wounds. Art takes the mad away. Or if not away, it transforms it into an instrument of life.

The healing power of art lies in the way it processes difficult experiences and the emotions that such experiences produce within us. Trauma generates painful emotions—rage, terror, shame, and despair. Normally, we respond to such emotional pain in one of two ways—either the emotions consume us and we are pawns in their passionate grip, or we swallow them and bleed unawares behind dissociated numbness and the suppression of memory. Art offers a third way—that of integration.[19] It surfaces painful events—perhaps consciously, perhaps symbolically; it provides an imaginative space where we can engage difficult emotions without being consumed by them; and it makes new meaning of the traumatic experiences by representing them in all of their brutal horror, or transforming them in ways that uncover the heartbeat that pulsates new life from the crucible of pain. Shaun McNiff, a recognized leader in art therapy, puts it succinctly, "Art heals by accepting the pain and doing something with it."[20]

Daniel Judah Sklar recognizes that the narrative arts, as well, activate this integrative function. In his work with inner-city young people, he observes that the youth have difficulty controlling their impulses. Writing plays and performing them offers a way of objectifying their impulses into symbolic characters, then asserting them as choices. Acting is not acting out. It involves a self-conscious decision about a character's responses that bestows a distance from and a power over the available emotional options. Tahira demonstrated this through storytelling. When feeling belittled, she could have acted out and vented her pain, or she could have suppressed it and simply moved on. She chose neither. She created characters that symbolically carried her wounds, then accessed a current of narrative creativity that healed these characters and, through them, herself. Louise DeSalvo recognizes a similar dynamic in the art of creative writing. She describes how survivors of trauma—from concentration camps to rape, sexual abuse to parental abandonment—have used memoir and fiction to tell their stories as a form of "symbolic repair" of the soul. One such survivor, novelist Dorothy Allison, sums up the healing hope of narrative, "Two or three things I know for sure, and one of them is that to go on living I have to tell stories."[21]

Storytelling pulsates with a healing rhythm. Like the mournful sway at a communal wake or the lighthearted tango of two tow-headed toddlers, giving in to its movements accesses a current of restorative music. That music is the song of life. It is a song that takes something of the soul's madness away.

Educational movements

Given the intrinsically life-giving power of the narrative arts, creative vitality approaches to narrative pedagogies seek to do three things:

1. They introduce young people to the tradition and craft of various narrative art forms.

2. They nurture and affirm teens' uncensored creative self-expression.

3. They celebrate teenage creativity through public performances and festive receptions.

A variety of educators introduce young people to narrative art forms and celebrate the teens' artistic creations. Kevin Cordi, the first full-time high school storytelling teacher in the country, is founder of

Voices of America, a resource and advocacy project dedicated to creating teenage storytelling troupes around the country.[22] Mark Yaconelli, creator of "The Hearth," organizes intergenerational events in Ashland, Oregon, where regular folks tell real stories on such monthly themes as "From the Heart: Love Stories," "Into the Wild: Wilderness Tales," and "Holiday Disasters and Other Tales of Family Dysfunction."[23] Chris Hendrickson, founder of Street Poets, Inc. and Dreamyard/LA, empowers incarcerated teens and ex-cons to develop their voices as artists and as human beings through a creative writing curriculum and a monthly open mic for them to share their poetry and stories.[24] The Virginia Avenue Project equips young people with the tools to write original theater pieces, then recruits professional actors to stage their plays in regional theaters.[25] A host of other narrative advocates provide resources for teachers to incorporate storytelling or playwriting within their regular curriculum.[26]

One representative educator, the aforementioned Sklar, teaches young people how to write and produce their own plays, partly out of his love for the dramatic craft, and partly out of his conviction that the theater can transform young people into artists of the stage and artists of life.[27] A trained actor and published playwright himself, Sklar walks young people through every dimension of the theatrical creative experience. He teaches them how to write a script with attention to dialogue, narrative structure, and the beats that constitute a scene; he trains them to see acting not as pretending to be something they really are not but as "living truthfully under imaginary circumstances,"[28] and he mentors them in directing a production that includes casting their own play, blocking their scenes, fashioning costumes, and designing sets with background, props, and lights. His goal is twofold—to celebrate the theater as a time-honored art form, and to help teens discover that the stuff of their lives is a valid source for art; indeed it is the inspiration for the art of living their own lives.

Common to each of these narrative educators is an investment in teaching a narrative craft, a commitment to the free and honest self-expression of young people, and an insistence on some form of communal performance that celebrates the young people as artists.

The five educational movements of narrative pedagogy

So how do we foster creative vitality through the narrative arts? Walking through storytelling and the staging of original plays as our two primary examples, creative vitality narrative pedagogy has five distinctive movements. The first movement is *to engage the group of participants*. In creative vitality narrative pedagogy, young people are invited to explore, in a communal setting, a narrative art form as a means of expressing their emotional truth. For this work to be real and alive, a hospitable context needs to be created, and the teens' animated engagement within it needs to be cultivated. This process of engaging the teens includes the following dimensions:

Teens need to be hooked: A facilitator cannot assume that the young people who show up for a particular workshop necessarily have a passion for telling stories or staging plays. The teens' interest needs to be recruited, their hearts inspired by the possibilities. Sklar often starts a new drama program by showing a video of plays that inner-city kids have written and produced. I start most storytelling sessions by telling a story myself that models the craft and piques the interest for what a story can do.

Teens need to feel safe: Artistic self-expression is vulnerable. Many of us carry wounds from people who have ridiculed, dismissed, or ripped apart our personal artistic creations, or from people who have critiqued or minimized our experience. Teens need to feel safe, and facilitators need to be vigilant in sustaining that safety throughout the program. Ground rules should be established about confidentiality, attentive listening, affirmation and support, and taking each other seriously as artists.[29]

Teens need their bodies warmed up: For actors and storytellers, our bodies are our instrument. As Sklar observes, they also store our emotions, senses, and impulses. If our bodies are tense, numb, or simply disconnected from our awareness, we cannot access or express, indeed we cannot *know*, who we really are. Warm-up exercises, therefore, are indispensible—from stretching our muscles to exercising our vocal cords.[30]

Teens need their imaginations activated: Narrative creativity depends upon supple imaginations. Warm-up exercises should invite imaginative play. Examples include: Group Storytelling—where the facilitator tells a story that invites the teens, along the way, to supply all the sensory details; or Imaginative Milling Around—where teens walk around the stage as if on the moon, in concrete shoes, walking on coals, going down the aisle, and other scenarios called out by the group.

Teens need to energize the space: Creativity is fuelled by spirit and energy. Lethargic space creates sluggish art. Animated space creates dynamic art. Circle games are an excellent way of energizing a space. Examples include:

- Sound and Motion—where a scenario is called out like, "You got an 'A' on your final exam," and one teen spontaneously reacts with a sound and a bodily motion that they repeat while approaching another teen who mirrors the sound and motion until a new scenario is called out and the second teen responds with a different sound and motion;[31]

- Circle Dash—where one teen in the circle's middle tries to fill another teen's space while the teens around the circle are dashing to trade places before getting caught;[32]

- Defender—where teens mill around the space while secretly targeting one person who is out to get them and another person who will be their defender; then at the whistle, everyone scrambles to keep their defender between them and their enemy.[33]

Teens need to develop a group connection: As Kevin Cordi observes, storytelling is a communal art.[34] Warm-up exercises should nurture teamwork and a sense of collective connection. Two excellent examples are:

- Walk-Stop-Fall—where the teens mill around the space when someone calls "Walk," stay frozen in one place when someone calls "Stop," and crouch to a knee when someone calls, "Fall," and continuing the game until commands can be changed without anyone using any words;

- Follow the Leader—where one teen is designated the leader after another teen has left the room. The leader flows through a sequence of improvised actions such as snapping their fingers, patting their belly, and drumming on the floor. The rest of the circle mirrors the leader with such precision that the teen who returns is unable to guess who the real leader is.

Through such exercises, teens are engaged in the artistic process, their creative capacities are activated, and a sense of communal connection is cultivated.

Crafting stories for an oral storytelling event

The second educational movement is *to craft the narrative piece.* Whether the art form is storytelling or staging an original play, the bulk of the program—certainly throughout the beginning—entails helping the young people write the narratives they will perform for their community. Though the process for writing stories and crafting plays is similar, the differences are nuanced enough to warrant describing them separately. Crafting a story for an oral storytelling event involves five distinct steps:[35]

1. **Find the seed of a story:** The first step is identifying the story the teen wants to tell. I describe this as finding the story's "seed" because we are simply looking for the basic idea, not the final word-for-word draft. Even if the story is found in a compilation, the teen will thoroughly reconstruct it to make it her own. Seeds for stories can be found in many places:

- *Cultural Stories*: Myths, legends, allegories, fables, fairy tales, folktales, and tall tales proliferate every culture. They are a treasure trove to sift through.

- *Biblical Stories*: Parables, myths, wisdom tales, biographical anecdotes, and historical pericopes fill the sacred texts of all religious traditions. The jewels within them are inexhaustible.

- *Creative Reconstruction:* Akin to Jewish Midrash, cultural tales and biblical stories can be recrafted backward, sideways, inside out, and upside down. This can include: changing the point of view—the three little pigs from the perspective of the wolf, or Noah's ark from an animal's point of view; changing the context: the three little pigs go to churches, or the prodigal son goes to seminary; changing the characters: Little Red Riding Hood becomes the Big Green Top Hat, or the Good Samaritan becomes a teenage gang member; or changing the central theme: Cinderella becomes self-reliant, or Jepthah's daughter refuses her father.

- *Religious Heroes and Heroines:* Religious traditions contain a wealth of stories that engage and inspire, like Francis of Assisi taming the wolf at Gubbio, St. Valentine inventing the very first valentine, Hagar and Ishmael founding the well at Mecca, or Harriet Tubman forming the Underground Railroad.

- *Personal Stories:* The experiences from one's real life provide endless fodder for crafting terrific stories. Generative prompts include: your most embarrassing moment, your most terrifying moment, how you got a scar, the best teacher you've ever had, the best present you've ever received, the best holiday of your life, the worst holiday of your life, if you've ever seen a ghost, if you've ever seen God, a time you got lost, a time you were found, a time you lost someone else you feared would never be found. Truly the possibilities are endless. These are not only potential stories for performing, they are excellent practice exercises at the beginning of sessions that can connect a group of teens to each other while revealing that our lives are reservoirs of stories.

- *Family Stories:* A lovely exercise is to invite teens to ask family or community members for stories, then sharing them at a family reunion, or a Founder's Day, or even a potluck dinner. Such stories could include: when our family came to America, how you became a Christian, how you got your name, heroes who inspire you, or seminal moments that made us who we are today. A fun get-acquainted exercise for a group is to invite teens to tell two family stories, only one of which is true, with the rest of the group guessing between the two.

- *Original Stories:* Tahira made up her own story in the tradition of an African folktale. Teens can make up similar stories modeled after various narrative genres—like myths about the gods of love and hate, tall tales about beloved community members, fairy tales about princesses tired of the same old story, or legends about heroes enduring a spiritual crisis.[36]

Basic Guidelines (The bottom line: Stories that teach and touch): When choosing a story to tell, two guidelines are helpful. First, all stories teach; in other words, all stories embody values and assumptions. Only tell stories that have your name on it, stories that embody the values you cherish. Second, if a story has not touched you, it is unlikely to touch another. Consider only those stories that leap out and stir something within you. Or as some storytellers put it, only tell stories that have first told you.[37]

2. Identify the story's narrative elements: Whether retelling a story written down elsewhere or crafting their own original tale, teens should develop the story's various narrative elements. This teaches them the essential components common to all stories while helping them refine these elements within the particular story they are crafting. The essential elements of any story can be summarized as: Somebody, Somewhere, Has Some Problem, and Does Something about it.[38] These narrative elements are:

- *Character:* Stories revolve around "somebody." The protagonist, antagonist, and secondary characters should be as three-dimensional as possible. Teens should fill out characters by considering at least each character's name, age, gender, species, personality, appearance, vocation, and the soulful elements of their deepest fear, and their deepest wish. Rich discussions can emerge by filling out characters even further, such as asking how these characters feel about God, what crises they have endured, or what gift they are aching to develop.

- *Setting:* Stories take place "somewhere." These contexts should be developed with imaginative detail and can be enriched by asking teens to use all of their senses in describing each setting within their story.

- *Conflict:* Stories revolve around "some problem," or the narrative tension that emerges when something threatens the protagonist's core needs or desires. Teens' stories are sharpened when they are able to articulate the conflict in a single sentence. For example, Bupsala Manresa's wish for a name to be proud of is threatened by a naming that provokes ridicule and shame.

- *Plot:* Stories are the unfolding of the "something that happens" in response to the character's conflict—for example, the story of Boopsie growing into a name of which she will be proud, or her failure in trying to do so.

- *Theme:* Stories embody a theme, sometimes several. Teens' stories are sharpened when they can identify, again in a single sentence, the central message of their story, or the one thing from it they want an audience to take away with them. Tahira's theme, for example, can be described as the personal power that emerges when we claim and embody the name we truly are. The theme serves as the spine of the narrative. Identifying it helps teens set up the story, keep the story on track, and bring the story to a clear climax and resolution.

3. Storyboard a sequence of scenes around a narrative structure. As the elements for the story come into shape, teens should sketch the story's sequence. This can be a literal sketch, like screenplay writers often do, with a piece of paper for each scene taped to a wall in order, or a written outline of the scenes and how they link to one another. Every story should embody the following narrative structure:

- *An Introduction:* where the characters are established and the core conflict is exposed (Boopsie is born and named in a seemingly demeaning manner);

- *The Body:* where dramatic tension builds to a climax as the character responds to the conflict (a belittled Boopsie is thrown into a crisis where her name may or may not be the cause of her ruin);

- *Resolution:* where, like a good blues riff, the conflict dissolves into some resolution that feels narratively satisfying even if only tragically so (Boopsie discovers her name's hidden meaning and accesses it to save the day);

- *A Conclusion:* the denouement where the audience savors the resolution and the story's theme is underscored (Boopsie becomes Bupsala Manresa and claims her pride in her name).

4. Enhance the story's vitality: Once the story has been sketched, details can be added that make the story sparkle and pop. These might include:

- *Sensory Concreteness:* Like all art, the story is in the details. Scenes and characters can be brought to life by evoking sounds, smells, tastes, sights, and physical sensations—like a gassy burp of sour milk, or a lion eating a jackal's carcass. Teens can be invited to close their eyes and imagine each scene as if they were filming it from beginning to end.

- *Memorable Lines:* Certain lines can pop for an audience and linger in their awareness—like chants or repetitive phrases. Tahira, for example, had a ritualized pattern for the naming ceremony that was echoed in the conclusion. Special attention should be given to the opening and closing lines, the only two lines that categorically should be crafted word for word.

- *Audience Participation:* Some storytellers enhance audience participation with chants, refrains, echoes, songs, and improvised suggestions called out along the way. Teens can be invited to experiment, but only as they feel comfortable, for it demands them to be flexible in front of a live group.

5. Draft the story in detail, but not necessarily verbatim: Teens, finally, should draft the story in a detailed outline that captures the story's arc and all of its essential components. I do not necessarily encourage teens to write the full story verbatim, as it is easy to get lost in the minutiae and lose the gestalt of the whole.

Crafting original plays

Daniel Judah Sklar's process for crafting an original play flows through four distinct steps.[39]

1. Conjuring characters: Like Aristotle, Sklar's approach to playwriting begins with compelling characters. The storyline comes second; if the characters are complex, the plot comes organically from the characters' needs. Evading temptations in young people to cull characters as carbon copies from their favorite television shows, Sklar has created a variety of exercises to conjure symbolically laden characters from the soul's imagination. Bupsala Manresa emerged from Sklar's favorite exercise, the Scribble-Scrabble described at the beginning of this chapter. Other exercises include:

- *The Baffling Moment:* where teens free-write about an encounter they had where something baffling happened to them. They circle emotions and narrative details, then create characters that represent them.

- *Props:* where teens pick from random objects (or pictures), then create a character of someone in crisis symbolized by the prop.

- *Animals:* where teens imagine a favorite animal, perhaps an animal totem, then convert the animal into a character.

◆ *Contexts:* where teens exploring, for example, the war in Iraq, immigration, discrimination at school, or even a biblical story, brainstorm together imaginary persons who might inhabit the context, then choose an intriguing character from among them.

2. Bringing the characters into three-dimensional life: Once the cardboard outline of a character has been identified, that character needs to be deepened until it takes on a pulsating life of its own. Playwrights can deepen their characters through the following exercises:

◆ *Character Profiles*: As was done with Bupsala Manresa, each character should have a name, species, age, hangout, and important relationships. Three further details brilliantly illuminate the character's soul—their deepest wish, their deepest fear, and a secret gift they cherish. To these characteristics, other qualities can be added along the way—the character's hobbies, religion, relationship with God, a crisis they have endured, an achievement of which they are proud.

◆ *The Interview Game:* Teens can discover interesting details of their character by becoming the character and submitting to an interview. The interviewer, either a partner or the entire group, asks any intriguing question that comes to mind, for example, the character's favorite movie, the clothes they like to wear, or the things that haunt them in the dark of night.

◆ *A Day in the Life:* Teens can describe a typical day in the life of their character from waking to sleeping.

◆ *Monologues:* Teens can write a dramatic monologue to the audience in which their character reveals a secret that no one else in the character's world is aware of, and the consequences that would occur if that secret ever leaked out.

◆ *Letter to the Playwright:* Teens can write a letter from the character to themselves as the playwright about some conflict in the character that the character thinks would make a great story.

3. Crafting scenes: Once characters are enfleshed, their souls revealed, and their contexts understood, dramatic scenes can be created. The most straightforward way to do this is to invite the teens to craft a scene where their character sets out to meet their deepest desire and, along the way, encounters some obstacle; in the ensuing conflict, the character either succeeds or fails. Improvisation is another technique to tease out a scene—here teens write scenarios where their characters encounter a conflict, then ask teen actors to spontaneously dramatize it for the rest of the group. The group can then offer suggestions for further improvisation until the playwright has a sense of where to take the scene. In crafting such scenes, Sklar teaches teens proper script formatting, how to convey action through dialogue, and the beats that constitute the arc of a scene.

4. Weaving the scenes into a play: Creative vitality narrative pedagogy moves from teens writing scenes to crafting an entire play to be performed. The simplest play to evolve from a group of teens' individual scenes is a final performance that merely strings them together in a series of vignettes. Often—for example, in the groups that produced *Finding God in the Graffiti* and *The Night That God Got Nailed*, teens prefer to weave characters and scenes into a single piece collectively created. This involves a creative alchemy difficult to prescribe. As a director, I look for the following possibilities in weaving scenes into a single organic whole: Is there a common theme or issue—for example, taking one's grievances about suffering before God—common to all of the scenes? Is there a generative context, such as a courtroom where God is put on trial, that can contain the various characters the teens have created? Is there a metanarrative, like the Passion from the Gospel of Mark, that can ground the scenes and transvalue their meaning?

If the teens have the energy to produce an integrated piece, I involve them in the process. We brainstorm together and improvise possibilities to see what takes hold. They conceive of multiple endings to scenes and dialogue until they reach consensus about which ones ring true. And they free-write the fundamental message of the play, share the free-writings with one another, then synthesize and streamline until the message can be summarized in a single line—for example, that hope can be found in even the darkest of crises. This message forms a baseline around which to weave the entire play.

Rehearsing for a storytelling event

The third educational movement, once stories and plays have been crafted, is *to rehearse for the actual performance.* Once again, though similar, the rehearsal process for storytelling and the staging of original plays have distinctive nuances.

In preparing storytellers for a performance, I coach them through the following guidelines:

Internalize the story, don't memorize it: After an evening of captivating stories, one child asks another, "Do you think the storyteller memorized all those stories?" "Don't be silly," the second child answers. "She knows them all by heart." Storytelling is a live event. The teller weaves a spell that descends upon an audience. This spell is diluted when tellers read from a text, or when they are lost in trying to remember words they had attempted to memorize earlier. Stories should be internalized, but not memorized. They should be known by heart. To aid in this process, I suggest that teens learn the outline of their story, its overall arc, the key phrases, and most important, the opening and closing lines. Then the teens should practice it at least ten times, even if only to themselves.

Use your body to keep the story alive: Stories can fizzle by being too flat or by being overly dramatic. Telling a tale from a frozen monotone would be too flat; forced emotion and exaggerated expressions would constitute being overly dramatic. Between these two extremes, natural body gestures, facial expressions, and emotional vocalization can keep the story's heartbeat pumping.

Maintain a connection with the audience: As hard as it is for many, an oral event creates a relationship between the teller and the audience. A teller is inviting the audience into the teller's world.

The teller should be intentional about keeping them there. First and foremost, maintain eye contact; it sustains a connection like nothing else. In addition, use silence to heighten suspense and keep the audience from drifting. Finally, take a deep breath and talk at the pace the story invites. Talking too fast is anxiety's default.

Speak from the heart: Finally, an ounce of heart, when telling one's story, outweighs pounds of polished technique. Before you take your place on the stage, remember how the story touched you in the first place. Then allow the lifeblood of this connection to pulsate through the telling by being simple, and by being real.

Rehearsing for an original stage production

In preparing teen actors for staging an original production, I coach them through the following guidelines:

Know the arc of the scene more than the words on the page: Usually, when directing young people, I invite teens to sketch each scene's beats rather than draft word-for-word dialogue. (The beats are the incremental steps in the tension of a scene. For example, when Boopsie is in the cave, Beat 1: the lion rages at being trapped; Beat 2: the lion recognizes a human presence; Beat 3: Boopsie cowers while the lion approaches; Beat 4: Boopsie pounces on the lion and the two wrestle; Beat 5: Boopsie vanquishes the lion.) When memorizing scripts by rote, teens tend to become so concerned with the words that it takes them out of the scene. Improvisation should rehearse the actors' understanding of their characters' motivation, a living connection to the other actors, and a sense of the key moments in the scene. The words will follow naturally.

Bring the same creativity that inspired the story to the design of the entire set: Plays need costumes, lighting, props, and scenery. They need not be elaborate. Very simple set design—like a cinderblock wall littered with graffiti—can set the mood and enhance the play. Invite the teens to bring their gifts and creativity to inform the design. Often, some teens will find designing the set more life-giving than acting in their own scene. Put them in charge and showcase their talents.

Resist over-rehearsing: Original stage productions, unlike scripted theater productions, are chimera phenomena. They are usually meant for a single performance, and are performed by teens with little dramatic experience. That they wrote the play themselves suggests that it is living within them and internalized. Overworked, it becomes stilted. Once the entire play has been conceived, I usually direct one dress rehearsal. Kinks and miscues abound to be sure, but the intensity of the actual performance has a way of ironing them out. Too much polishing beforehand results in flattened performances.

Settle anxiety with silliness: Marie-Claire Picher of the Theater of the Oppressed Laboratory has a brilliant technique that I use immediately before the final performance of any group I work with: have the teens rehearse the entire play one final time as if the remote was stuck on super-fast-forward.[40] The technique does two things: First, it breaks the teens free of the compulsion to try and remember every word of a scene, thus forcing them to focus on only the absolutely central beats through which each scene flows. Second, the silliness settles some of the nervousness while sustaining teen animation. Settled, but poised with tensive anticipation, the teens are ready to perform.

The fourth educational movement is *the actual performance itself.* It is counterintuitive, but from a pedagogical perspective, the performance is the least important part of the process. A connection with the creative spirit, the liberating thrill of claiming your truth, healing engagement with symbolically laden images from the soul—these all occur through the crafting and refining of stories as they are prepared in the sessions leading up to the performance. The performance itself is usually preoccupied by spastic butterflies and peeks through the curtain to see who's sitting in the audience. That being said, the performance is absolutely indispensible. A community that takes the time to attend a teen exhibition, and which receives their work with engaged acclamation, gifts the teens with public legitimation and honors them as artists. The radiant smiles of the teens after the performance say it all, as does having a stranger approach you, perhaps with tears in his eyes, to thank you because, "That was my story, too."

The fifth and final movement of creative vitality narrative pedagogy is *to party*. As peculiar as it sounds, for this approach to narrative education, partying is part of the pedagogical process. Creativity begs to be celebrated. Teens have opened their souls, discovered their truth, and claimed their voices. Communal acknowledgment empowers, but pizza and Coke consecrate.

The elements of the festivities are secondary. Viewing a video of the actual performance, passing out certificates and tongue-in-cheek awards, or taking a field trip to a professional production with a late-night dinner like the real actors do it—these are wonderful ways to celebrate. But it does not really matter. Whatever the menu, the final feast is Eucharistic.

Rola was getting seconds of M&M'S and sheet cake. The rest of the sixth-graders were scattered across the floor. The videotape of the play they performed at the end-of-the-year school assembly was playing on a monitor up front. *The Wizard of Zo* was quite the sensation. A twisted remake of the one from Oz, it featured a band of misfit schoolkids petitioning the wizard to take on the evil Lord Rage, who had overthrown their school with his nefarious sidekick, the dark warlock Dr. Togwaddle. Rola was the lead character's Toto. Or to be more precise, Tutu—the caterpillar who dreamed of being a ballerina but slithered on the floor behind Dorothy like a tail that had fallen off and was straining to get back.

The play climaxed with a surprise cameo by the beloved principal retiring after thirty-two years of service to the school. While the audience expected a sixth-grade actor, the real Ms. Perkins followed a spotlight the length of the auditorium like a resplendent good witch Glenda. Though brief, her appearance was poignant. Summing up her professional career, she told the ragtag band of kids that they already had all the power they needed—it was lodged within their souls. To demonstrate, she invited Tutu to shed her caterpillar disguise. Underneath, Tutu was dressed like a ballerina—

with sequin tights and butterfly wings. "She's right," Tutu exclaimed with delight. "I can not only dance. . . . I can fly!"

Sensing her moment was seconds away, Rola dashed with her treats to her place on the floor. Before she could make it, however, she was caught short. There on the screen, it was already happening. Tutu was dancing her flight.

"Ahhh," Rola sighed, as if watching her idol on television. "Look at me. Aren't I beautiful?"

Creative vitality narrative pedagogy is in the business of transforming caterpillars into butterflies. It leaves to others the agenda of religious literacy or cultural critical reflection. Artistic self-emergence is its own satisfaction. Young people glimpsing their beauty is its own intrinsic reward.

The documentary *Man on Wire* chronicles what some have dubbed as the artistic crime of the century—Philippe Petit's 1974 daring high-wire walk between the Twin Towers of the World Trade Center. With a team of assistants disguised as janitors, Petit scaled a cable between the two skyscrapers and, for nearly an hour, stunned onlookers in the streets below by walking on a wire with the grace of a dancer over a thousand feet in the sky. When asked why he did it, Petit looked quizzically at the man asking the question. Then he said, "Why do so many ask me 'why?' I did something singularly beautiful. There is no 'why.'"

Why do narrative educators teach for creative vitality? Watching Rola transfixed before her image on the screen, and before her, Tahira, claiming her name with boldness, I can only agree with Petit. There is no why. Teens alive in their glory—beauty speaks for itself.

Six

How can stories inspire social transformation?

Narrative pedagogy and societal empowerment

The social justice group at St. Timothy's, a local parochial high school, gathered for a late-summer planning retreat. They sought an issue on which to focus during the upcoming school year, a global concern with enough substance to sustain months of mobilization and enough significance to satisfy their drive to make a difference. It never occurred to them to look in their own backyard.

When they introduced themselves to each other and expressed their hopes for the year, the teens named a number of issues that weighed on them—the crisis in Darfur, global warming, sex trafficking, the enduring war in Iraq. Each concern prompted nods of assent, but none of them kindled widespread fervor. We needed to keep looking. Assent was not enough. We were after passion.

In empowerment approaches to narrative pedagogy, the facilitator helps a community discover and name the social issues that smolder within them, rooted as they are in their own wounds and worries. Paulo Freire calls such issues "generative themes" because, when surfaced and channeled, they generate a spontaneous passion that burns with the strength necessary to sustain long-term justice work. Finding these themes is like drilling for oil within a seemingly barren landscape. Underneath the perfunctory politeness of social routine, indignations and broken dreams are buried. The facilitator designs exercises as exploratory soundings through a community's functional façade to surface the energy lying within. Occasionally, a trickle's worth of curiosity will be accessed around a concern that arouses a degree of intrigue, but intrigue and curiosity dry up swiftly in the heat of protracted labor. So the facilitator keeps taking soundings in search of that geyser of a strike when everyone in the room is passionately engaged. For this, the facilitator must be vigilant. A strike can blow at any time.

After several group-building activities and warm-up games with the St. Timothy's social justice group, I laid several dozen pictures on the floor—a random collection of nameless wounds within our world including a starving child, a sewage dump, mass grave sites, a clear-cut forest, nuclear silos next to a preschool. I invited each teen to find one picture that particularly moved them, and to create a fictitious character that knows that wound directly. Then they each wrote and read aloud a monologue of that character expressing his or her experience. Such an exercise often accesses emotional identifications that symbolize deeper passions. In this case, the monologues were tender and empathetic. The group received each one with care and polite support. Even the cut-up athlete giving voice to the flag-waving chicken sacrificing himself for the cause of fast-food prompted an appreciative amusement from the others. It was energy, to be sure, yet it was still tepid—the energy of camaraderie, but not the raw passion that strikes when something vital is at stake. We took a break before trying another tack.

The energy broke through before we got back.

"Did you hear what happened to Troy?" one boy asked another at the soda machine.

"Yeah," the other gushed. "That was severe, man."

"A whole year of expulsion!" the first returned. "Who does Mr. O'Brien think he is anyway?"

"Totally! He's like the prison warden from hell."

Several others joined in, and I eavesdropped long enough to cull the bare details. Troy, a rising senior, star athlete, student body president, debate captain, and All-American finalist for a prestigious collegiate scholarship, got drunk at a party, staggered to his car, drove with a blood alcohol level twice the legal limit, and barreled through a random front yard so fast he took out a picket fence, a bed of roses, an oleander bush, and a three-year-old aspen tree before totaling the sedan parked in the driveway. Tragically, the man whose car and yard Troy destroyed had had a daughter who was killed several years earlier by a driver under the influence. The man petitioned the court to prosecute Troy to the full extent of the law, then lobbied the school for Troy's expulsion. Mr. O'Brien, the school's vice principal, bypassed the disciplinary review board and complied. Before the first class of his senior year, Troy was expelled and his collegiate future was as damaged as the property he had destroyed.

When the group regathered, I narrowed the focus to the context that was most immediate to them. I invited the teens to create human sculptures that depicted some form of pain or oppression currently happening within their high school. As we surveyed them, several sculptures prompted trickles of reaction—groaning recognition at a strict teacher giving unfair grades, and indignation at the capricious new curfew decreed for all campus events. However, as I suspected, it was the sculpture of a shamed teen being castigated by a vindictive despot that set off the explosion. Everybody knew the situation. And everybody had an opinion.

"That's *exactly* what Mr. O'Brien did. He ruined Troy's life and he doesn't even care."

"He didn't even go through the proper channels. Where was the review board? Where was the students' *voice*?"

"What difference would it have made?" one teen rejoined, representing an opposing perspective. "Troy screwed up big time. He totally thrashed a man's property. What about *that guy*?"

"Yeah, he screwed up, but the punishment doesn't fit the crime. He smashed a car and got his life ruined—a car for a life? Where's the justice in that?"

"Plus, he's totally sorry for what he did. Aren't we supposed to be about forgiveness?"

"Sorry doesn't cut it, man. So he's sorry. He still caused thousands of dollars of damage. I say it again, where's the justice in *that*?"

"Yeah, anybody can say they're sorry. That doesn't mean they've really changed. What if he killed somebody?"

"What *if* he killed somebody? Can't that be forgiven, too?"

"Not without justice."

"So what is justice?"

What is justice indeed. Clearly, we had stumbled upon a generative theme. I suggested we explore the issue dramatically. We brainstormed fictitious characters living within this scenario and developed their perspectives. Then we designed scenes where these characters would have to wrestle with the issues. In one scene, a drunk-driving teenager met the adult he violated while under the influence. It ended in a stalemate. The adult could not get past the rage at his loss. The teen cried he was sorry so long he screamed it and stomped away. Though the scene failed to resolve the dramatic tension, it succeeded in raising the complex questions that preceded any resolution in the first place. What would it take for a violated person to authentically embrace forgiveness? What would it take for a perpetrator of violence to really understand the pain he had caused? What is the role of accountability? What is appropriate restitution? Is there a way that punishment for wrongdoing can be healing for all of the parties involved?

The questions drove the teens into research. They studied the difference between retributive and restorative justice and found that the two are quite distinct. *Retributive justice* metes out punishment for acts of wrongdoing—a person steals a car, they receive ten years in prison. The problem with such a system is that the convicted is offered little chance for rehabilitation, punishments more often intensifying the wrongdoing propensities. In addition, the victims, while assuaging a sense of justice, are denied an opportunity at healing or restitution. *Restorative justice*, on the other hand, offers a tough-love process through which both parties can heal. It recognizes that, when someone commits a violent act, that person should suffer consequences. Yet these consequences need not be capricious nor vindictive. Root causes of the problem can be addressed—a drinking problem, perhaps, or a lack of healthy mentoring. In addition, the guilty party can commit to reparations, repaying stolen property or working off damages. Even in the event of a killing, restorative actions can be performed—practices of grief and remembrance, or a commitment to causes and projects that honor the victim and care for others who are disadvantaged. Responsibility and choice are placed in the hands of the perpetrator. That person can follow a path that promises healing and some measure of redemption, or the person can simply suffer the retributive consequences of one's actions.[1]

Impassioned by the promise of restorative justice, the teens returned to the stage. They role-played the scenes once more, improvising their way into discovering how such justice could be embodied in the scenario with which they were wrestling. As the principles took hold, a play emerged. The teens were so emboldened by their discovery, they lobbied to perform it for the entire school. In fact, they were impassioned to do far more. Their play was simply the introduction for a schoolwide assembly on the promise of restorative justice. Their goal was not to entertain. It was to inspire change. They argued that the school's disciplinary process be transformed to embody restorative principles. To make their case, they invited two special guests. This is the play they saw.

Scene one takes place at a high school party. Trent, a football star and world-class partier, is drunkenly bragging about how well he can hold his liquor. Binge drinking while throwing a football at a butcher paper target, he is egged on by his inebriated buddies. The more he drinks, the louder his bravado, and the wilder his throws. When it is time to leave, his girlfriend begs him not to drive. The guys tease him, mocking both his apparent inability to hold liquor after all and the emasculating belittling by his lady. Trent erupts, grabs his keys, and storms off stage. "Watch this," he calls over his shoulder. The sound of squealing tires rips from offstage.

Scene two takes place in the living room of two grief-stricken parents. The mother mourns how her daughter was only thirteen years old, her whole life ahead of her. She can't believe her daughter was run over as she walked home from a friend's, the driver so drunk he left no skid marks when he hit her full speed. The father is beside himself with rage, wishing the driver had died in the crash as well, hoping that the monster will be sent to prison, enduring untold punishments, until he's a very old man. The mother cannot get over that the driver was just a teenager. The father is disgusted that the teen was no more than a self-centered jock who thinks he could do whatever he wants without consequence. Typical of a prima-donna football star.

Scene three takes place in a courtroom. A judge finds the defendant, Trent, guilty of vehicular manslaughter. She listens to the parties as they appeal for the type of punishment Trent should suffer. The attorney for the parents argues that, given the egregious nature of the accident, the habitual pattern of the defendant's drinking, and the tragic loss that ensued, Trent should be sent to prison for the highest number of years allowed. The father makes a statement. His daughter is dead. For the rest of their lives, he and her mother will mark time by the proms the daughter will miss, the wedding that will not happen, and the thriving career and tow-headed grandkids that never will materialize. A life has been lost. Nothing can bring it back. It is only just that Trent loses his as well, locked away and forced to live with the horror he brought into the world.

Trent's attorney argues that given the youth of the defendant, the tragic nature of his fatherless childhood, and the depth of his remorse, Trent should be placed on probation, his driver's license suspended, with the conditions that he attend an alcohol recovery program, refrain from drinking, and perform community service by volunteering for a junior high girls' sports program. Trent reads a statement. Every night he closes his eyes with the image of that girl in front of his car. He knows he can never bring her back. But he wants the parents to know that he will forever be sorry for what he did to all three of their lives. The judge takes the matter under advisement.

Scene four takes place at Trent's home. The victim's parents knock on the door. With great effort, the father tells Trent how difficult it is to lose your only child. Trent listens with some understanding. The father rehearses the probation plan that Trent suggested to the court, then asks if Trent has found a sponsor for such a program. Trent says that he has yet to find one, but is diligently searching. The father tells Trent that part of him is consumed with hate toward Trent and wishes that Trent would be thrown into jail. He is grateful for a judge who takes so seriously the victim's needs for justice. But part of him wants to let go of such hatred. He tells Trent that he would be willing to recommend to the judge that she accept Trent's plan, and that he would volunteer to be Trent's sponsor. He will take Trent once a week to his recovery meetings and monitor his community service. He will keep Trent out of jail. On one condition. Every week that they drive to the meeting, they make one stop. At the grave of the daughter that Trent killed.

He gives Trent twenty-four hours to decide. If Trent agrees, he is to meet the father at the girl's grave the following afternoon.

Scene five takes place on a sidewalk the next day. Trent walks toward the side of the stage. From that direction, his partying friends walk toward him, drinking beer and carousing loudly. When they see Trent, they bemoan, with stifled giggling, the tough break that befell Trent. Trent shrugs. They ask Trent where he is going. He tells them he is supposed to meet someone in a few minutes. The friends say that there is a great party getting started, Trent should come with them. Trent evasively demurs. They urge Trent to put the past behind him, and to make a comeback with his legendary drinking endurance. If nothing else, the party can help him forget about it all for a while. Trent hesitates. The friends coax. Trent says he'll think about it. The friends start walking off the stage telling him not to wimp out. Before they exit, they call a last time. "Here," one yells, pulling a beer out of brown paper bag. "It'll help you make your decision." He tosses the beer to Trent. The friends head off to the party.

Trent pauses center stage. He looks in the direction of his absent friends. He turns around and looks toward the unseen graveyard. Then, he studies the beer.

The lights go out.

The poignant ending of the play belies the invitation of restorative justice. Parties damaged by violence—the perpetrators and the victims—are confronted with a choice: a cycle of destructiveness or an accountable reconciliation. The teens who wrote the play wanted the school to wrestle with this choice as well. Disciplinary procedures could remain mired in punitive consequences that kill the soul, or they could nurture restitution, healing, and eventual restoration. To prove that such a process could work within the grittiness of real-life situations, they invited their two guests on-stage to respond to their play.

During the months before the play, the teens researched how restorative justice might be embodied in concrete realities. Wondering if this process is truly realistic and effective, they approached Troy and inquired into his willingness to claim responsibility, to reach out to the man whose property he violated, and to make restorative amends. He was willing. The teens then approached the violated older man. Troy came with them. After a series of painful conversations—often laced with three grief-filled years' worth of tears and frustration—the older man was won over. Troy worked off his debt and volunteered at a local girls' athletic center. The older man joined him and softened into forgiveness. The two of them partnered to share their story. They became passionate advocates of the process. They even spoke at school assemblies. When they took the stage, their testimony was simple.

"That play you saw. It is our story. And we are here to tell you. This process works."

Their words had prophetic power. By year's end, Troy graduated with his senior class and the school incorporated restorative justice principles into its official disciplinary policy. The teens' play found its ending. What bubbled up in a drama workshop ended in social transformation. The teens were transformed as well. Through play-acting their way through their generative concerns, they became agents of change for real. And through them, like cascading waters from the mountaintops, justice rolled down off the stage and into a community's life.

Theoretical underpinnings

The teens of today live within a wounded world. Ethnic cleansing, children trafficked for sex, the AIDS pandemic in Africa—unimaginable horrors fill the news and weigh on the hearts of the adolescents inheriting the future of the planet. These wounds extend into their own communities as well. In their schools and homes, churches and neighborhoods, teens experience firsthand violence and abuse, poverty and prejudice, pressures to perform, and powerlessness before the petty tyrannies of those who dominate their lives. Some people suggest that youth are a besieged minority, as lacking in voice and influence in the institutions that rule over them as others belittled by virtue of race, gender, social class, or sexual orientation.[2] The depth of pain youth are exposed to, and the sophistication of the systems that sustain it, are so overwhelming it is often difficult to resist giving in to their inevitability or numbing out and ignoring them altogether.

All the more impressive, then, is what the teens at St. Timothy's were able to accomplish. In the face of a tragedy whose complexity ranged from the legal to the interpersonal, and constrained by an administration whose mind was made up and whose authority was unimpeachable, these teens beat back the drag of hopeless passivity and channeled their frustration into a determination to find a better way.

They found it through narrative. Through stories, they surfaced the conditions they were most impassioned to change and the energy necessary to see that change through; through improvisational role-play, informed by their research, they rehearsed their way into liberative alternatives; and through a dramatic presentation, and the testimonials that followed it, they awakened their community to a new form of justice and successfully advocated for its adoption. Quite simply, narrative leveraged transformation. Through it, a teenager's life was restored to him, a grieving father found healing, and a group of high school students discovered the power to induce institutional change.

The teens of St. Timothy's embodied a *social empowerment* approach to narrative pedagogy. Social empowerment narrative pedagogy focuses, not on the sacred stories that constitute a faith tradition nor on the artistic creations from teens' narrative imaginations, but on the stories of social pain or oppression alive within one's community. It problematizes these stories—frames them as problems to be resolved as opposed to social inevitabilities to be endured—then it uses situational role-plays to explore interventions, try out alternatives, and "rehearse" ways of responding that truly alter the social conditions that inhibit the flourishing of life. This process strives for genuine social transformation, but it transforms the teens as well. Powerless pawns before impenetrable political realities become empowered social players affecting public policy; political spectators, as it were, become cultural actors, taking the stage and shaping the storyline of the social worlds in which they live.

If the past is any indication, the powers-that-be should be on alert. In movements throughout history—for women's suffrage, civil rights, and the end of the Vietnam War—empowered young people have made a difference, so much so that scholars of youth culture suggest that a central vocation of adolescents is that of social prophet.[3] Mobilized teens are compelling, even to a high school's vice principal's office.

Why are stories so effective for fostering social transformation?

First, *Christian faith involves participation in the story of God's social project.*

An associate pastor had the rather daunting task of preaching the children's sermon on Trinity Sunday. She began by asking the youngsters huddled on the altar steps, "How many of you are you?" A couple of kids started counting the group. "No," the minister interrupted, "I mean, just you—how many of 'you' are there?" One child mused, "Well, there's me, and my sister, and my little brother." "No," the pastor tried again, "I mean, you, all by yourself. How many of *you* are there?" One child ventured a guess, "One?" "That's right," the minister affirmed, "there's only one of you. Now, how many of God are there?" "Oh, there's only one God," the children assured. "That's right, there's only one God. Now is God the Creator God?" "Oh, yeah," the kids confirmed. "Is Jesus God?" "Oh, yeah." "Is the Holy Spirit God?" "Oh, yeah." "So how many is that?" "Three." "That's right. Do you know the cool thing about God? God can be three and one at the same time." The kids looked confused. The minister pulled out a banana. "How many bananas do I have?" Still befuddled, the kids were quiet. "One," she says. "Now look at this." She loosens the banana up a bit and peels the skin. Then, from the tip, she separates the white fruit into three equal sections lengthwise. "God," she declares, "is just like this banana—three and one at the same time."

A couple of days later, a four-year-old present at the sermon bounces into her kitchen before preschool and stops short. Her dad is slicing a banana into a bowl of cereal. She studies him awhile, then asks, "Daddy, does God cry when you do that?"

Does God cry when we do that? Does God cry when we slice our seas with sewage or slice the air with toxic waste? Does God cry when we slice one another with weapons of war or cut with the blades of violence and abuse? Liberation theologians in recent decades have argued that God not only cries when humanity is violated. God's personal project, Trinitarian or otherwise, is freedom—freedom from injustice, and freedom for human restoration.[4] For such theologians, this project has several dimensions. First, it is *historical*—God's desires for humanity are not limited to admission into an otherworldly realm, but include the very this-worldly realm where suffering cries out for healing. Second, it is *social*—salvation and spirituality are not confined to the state and destination of one's soul, but include liberation from every form of human diminishment, be it rooted in race, gender, class, ability, or sexual orientation. Third, it is *participatory*—God's liberation does not entail a unilateral rescue of helpless human puppets, but empowers humanity as free and determining subjects to participate with God in the healing of creation.

God's project, significantly, is also a *narrative* project. It has a specific goal toward which it moves: the kin-dom of God. Liberation theologians have revealed with a burning clarity the "Utopian Vision" of the gospel.[5] At the core of Jesus' ministry was his commitment to a radical vision of a world where totalitarian powers are toppled, practices of cultic exclusion are dismantled, and economic disparity is reproportioned in a Jubilee of extravagant debt relief.[6] It is good news for the disenfranchised—a social gospel—where the oppressed are set free, the poor know abundance, and outcasts of all kinds are welcomed at the feast of universal inclusion. This is the vision Jesus proclaimed. And this is the vision for which he gave his life. To be his disciple is to take up his cause. As Leonardo Boff attests, "Following Jesus means translating that utopia into action. We must try to change the world on the personal, social, and cosmic level."[7] Christian faith involves weeping with God at the wounds of the world, being captured by the dream of a kin-dom whose structures embody justice and whose spirit breathes compassion, then setting off on the communal quest of making that dream a reality. In short, it is partnering with God in the story of the world's restoration. Social empowerment pedagogy invites young people to claim their Christian vocation—grounded in the call of Jesus—to join forces with the sacred in the narrative project of God's social agenda.

The second reason narratives are so central in fostering social transformation is that *educational settings are narratively constructed.* Within social contexts saturated with structures and mind-sets that sustain racism and sexism, poverty and homophobia, there is no such thing as neutral education. As popular educator Paulo Freire has classically made clear, all education is political; it either subverts the status quo or supports it.[8] Abstention is not an option. Silence, too, is complicity. Freire argues that a careful analysis of "the teacher-student relationship reveals its fundamentally *narrative* character."[9] Educational encounters incarnate either the story of a student's rise to empowered agency or the tragedy of their domestication. As he surveys traditional schooling, he comes to the unfortunate conclusion, "Education is suffering from narration sickness."[10]

For Freire, most educational contexts are based on a "banking" philosophy in which teachers with the currency of cultural knowledge deposit their wisdom into the minds of passive student receptacles. Such education is intrinsically dehumanizing—it treats students as objectified depositories; it domesticates them into docile listeners; and it denies them the agency inherent to being human. This is especially insidious for students who are already victims of injustice within their social context as it only integrates them into the structures of oppression rather than empowering them to question those structures and transform them altogether.

Freire calls for education to embody an alternative, more liberative narrative. Recognizing that educational method is "structural content"—that the *way* one teaches is as instructive as the content that one teaches—Freire advocates that education be dialogical rather than monological; connected to the context's social concerns, not abstracted from nor oblivious to them; and carried out in a spirit of collaborative co-investigation as opposed to the hierarchical transmission of social capital by an expert to the culturally illiterate. "Banking" teaching methods should be replaced with "problem-posing" education, where the generative concerns of a community are explored by students and teachers engaged in mutual inquiry to analyze causes, explore resources, create interventions, and mobilize for concrete acts of transformation. Such praxis-based education structurally embodies an alternative narrative to the transmissive tragedy of student domestication. In Freire's pedagogy, teaching embodies the story of marginalized students emerging as empowered protagonists bringing justice to their communities.

The teens of St. Timothy's exemplified such liberative education. We could have taught them Bible studies to increase their narrative literacy, or coached them in storytelling techniques to access their creative vitality. While potentially engaging and perhaps entertaining, such pedagogies in Freire's estimation would be socially subjugating, nurturing an implicit acquiescence to the power structures of their society. Instead, the teens problematized a generative concern, discovered liberative possibilities, and mobilized to leverage change. The story of a teen whose dreams were crushed became the story of a teenage coalition rising to claim its power.

The third reason that stories are so effective for fostering social empowerment is that *involvement in narrative activity is intrinsically transforming.* For liberation theologians, "Orthopraxis precedes orthodoxy," or more literally, "right action" comes before "right belief."[11] This means more than the popular notion that walking our talk is more important than talking our walk. It recognizes that our "walk," in fact, transforms our "talk." This is counterintuitive. The commonsense assumption behind traditional education is that, if we enlighten people's minds—say about the plight of the poor or the violation of human rights in Gaza—it will result in altered behavior that pledges solidarity in eradicating injustice. Liberative educators observe that it more often happens the other way. In works of solidarity and justice—regardless of how enlightened the motives or the substance of the belief system behind it—the actions themselves expand attitudes, melt prejudices, raise consciousness, and secure more radical commitments to the cause of liberation. In short, personal transformation is a result of social action, not a precondition for it.

When I was in high school, my church youth group embarked on a mission trip to Mexico. For seven sun-scorched days, we renovated a parsonage, installed a septic system, and volunteered at a Vacation Bible School. Stephanie was a high school senior in our group. And of one thing we were all certain. Stephanie had *no* desire to be there.

Stephanie came from the wealthier side of the tracks than us working-class folk. She wore designer clothes, had her hair styled after fashion magazines, and drove the brand-new bright yellow Mustang convertible her parents bought her for her sixteenth birthday. She was used to sunbathing in Mexican resorts, not serving the Mexican poor. And yet, her parents, vacationing in Europe, thought this trip would be "good for her." So she showed up at the church parking lot, her Armani luggage bulging with chocolates and make-up accessories, beach novels and gourmet popcorn, and boarded the school bus for the barrios of Cancun.

We soon discovered that Cancun is a two-tiered city. On the sea side of town, it sports the posh hotels, five-star restaurants, and glittering white sand beaches that entice people from all over the world to soak in their luxurious beauty. Yet, not a quarter's throw away, a vast barrio stretches with corrugated tin shacks, cardboard latrines, and fly-infested dumping grounds where children vie for edible scraps. The wealth does not trickle down. Understandably, therefore, some of the poor venture into the opulent neighborhoods and beg, panhandle, perhaps even pickpocket from the vast swarms of tourists. This threatens business because, if harassed, tourists will not return. So a turf war has developed with packs of well-off teens patrolling the streets to keep the poor on their side of town and occasionally raiding into the barrio to avenge a violation with a savage beating. One such raid occurred while we were in Cancun.

Throughout the week, Stephanie kept somewhat to herself. She dutifully painted plywood siding during her shifts and cut out biblical characters with kids at the church school, but once relieved she would steal away to read in the shade or stroll alone along the beaches. She was walking back early one evening when a young boy clad in nothing but cutoffs darted from behind a shack and across the dirt road in front of her as fast as a hunted jackrabbit. Pursuing like frenzied hounds, a gang of seven or eight older boys, all bearing the social badges of shoes and button-shirts, chased the child into an empty field, pounced upon him, then commenced to beat the child senseless.

As she later described it, something in Stephanie just broke. Without fully realizing it, she found herself screaming, "Enough! Enough!" then raced into the field and pulled at the boys consumed with beating the child. Pushed to the side, she got to her knees and threaded her way through their legs until she could wrap the child in her embrace, shielding the gang's punches with her body. Only then did the boys stop. They looked at her incredulously, then peeled away and scampered back to the skyscrapers, leaving her to tend the whimpering child.

On the night we left Cancun, our entire youth group was seated on the school bus eager to return home to fast-food hamburgers and reruns on TV. All except Stephanie. She stood in front of the bus beside our youth minister, and with tears of compassion streaming down her cheeks, she pleaded with him, "Please, can't we stay just a few days more? There's just too much pain here."

Today, Stephanie works as an immigration rights attorney just south of San Diego. She traces her current vocation to that day in Cancun when her heart, quite simply, broke open of its own accord.

Stephanie, at first, engaged in acts of care for all of the wrong reasons. Her motives for taking the trip were hardly informed by altruism; her privileged consciousness was far from transformed. Yet, in spite of her resistance, the acts of care worked on her. Going through the motions of social compassion allowed the motions to take hold and a genuine compassion to wash over her. Solidarity with the poor has the power of enlightening the mind and melting the heart. Action shapes consciousness. Working for justice gives rise to personal transformation.

In the same way, narrative activity that role-plays social empowerment is liberative for the people who give themselves to it. When young people, like the teens at St. Timothy's, dramatize social conflicts, then improvise interventions that claim dignity and promote justice, something shifts within them. The make-believe of the stage grabs hold and makes them true believers. They act out a new form of justice and discover that it really works. They try on the part of having a voice and access a personal power they did not know they had. They perform a play that imagines redemption, then mobilize to make the imagined come true. In essence, they are acting their way into a new self-consciousness, role-playing their way into becoming social agents. As these teens at St. Timothy's attest, and as Stephanie did before them, the power of liberative narrative pedagogy is this: role-play becomes real-life; quite literally, rehearsal becomes the part of a lifetime.

Educational movements

Given the power of stories and the stage to foster liberative involvement with the world, social empowerment approaches to narrative pedagogy seek to do three things:

1. They expose and name the social conditions within a community that inhibit the life of that community's participants.

2. They create narrative scenarios that problematize these issues so young people can reflect critically and practice liberative interventions.

3. They empower the participants to mobilize for social change in their communities beyond the stage and the classroom.

A number of educators recognize the power of narrative to explore oppression and empower teens as agents of liberation. Many of these use scripted material—plays, stories, or films—that dramatize social issues teens commonly face. These narratives—dealing with such topics as drug use and child abuse, eating disorders and sexual assault—are performed *for* the teens in classrooms, youth groups, and assemblies, and then used to spark discussion about life-giving forms of intervention.[12] Such events are often invaluable for raising awareness and providing safe space to discuss difficult issues. They run the risk, however, of perpetuating a spectator mentality in which an audience of teens observes social empowerment, perhaps even imagines it for themselves, but are not mobilized to concretely enact it.

Other narrative educators use the stage to invite teens to tell their own stories of social oppression, actively explore them through role-play and improvisation, then organize collectively to implement promising forms of liberative response. Norma Bowles of Fringe Benefits explores issues of tolerance and diversity with high-school students through her "Theater for Social Justice Workshops."[13] David White employs "Theater of the Oppressed" techniques to help Christian teens discern acts of hope and resistance within their communities.[14] *Acting Out*, a traveling theater troupe of actors and educators, creates issue-oriented, audience interactive, improvisational scenes for young people to explore such critical issues as HIV/AIDS and STDs, suicide and substance abuse.[15]

These latter programs of participatory theater take their inspiration from Augusto Boal, the representative educator who perhaps most radically embodies a liberative approach to narrative pedagogy.[16] Boal, political comrade and Brazilian compatriot of Paulo Freire, is the grandfather of theater activism. In the same way that Freire recognizes that all education is political, Boal observes that all *storytelling* is political. Every narrative venue—whether films in movie theaters, plays on Broadway, stories told at festivals, or skits performed at summer camps—either reinforces social passivity or empowers people for social transformation. Boal laments that almost all socially sanctioned narrative presentations are performed by professionals and produced by the cultural elite. The general public is reduced to the role of spectator, the audience who watches the narrative productions written and directed by those with cultural power. Spectating, for Boal, is intrinsically domesticating. An audience either unreflectively internalizes these narratives or instinctively dismisses them, but their personal and collective power to critically engage the culture's stories and contribute as active narrative agents is not intentionally nurtured. This passive cultural consumption both mirrors and perpetuates a political passivity before the other institutions that dictate a community's life. In short, Boal argues, the theater has become a weapon of the ruling classes.[17]

Boal advocates for narrative contexts to be reclaimed as weapons of liberation, as arenas for mobilizing social change. This does not mean more plays and films *about* social issues that keep people in the seats as spectators.[18] Rather, it means revolutionizing narrative space entirely, separating the distance between the audience and actor, in fact, blurring it altogether. In Boal's participatory use of narrative space, the audience becomes the actors, the voiceless tell the stories, and the stage becomes a "Theater of the Oppressed."

First with peasants throughout Brazil and Peru, then with marginalized persons throughout the world, Boal creates dramatic venues where members of a community are empowered to perform scenes depicting the oppressive conditions in which they live; to dialogue about these conditions—the causes of the oppression, the structures that sustain it, and resources from which to inform interventions; and finally, to role-play any and every idea that emerges from the people about ways of resisting dehumanization and promoting their own liberation. The genius of the process is that abstract issues of injustice become concretized in real-life settings; impenetrable forms of oppression become open-ended problems with which to be creative; subjugated people discover the power to think for themselves; and liberative interventions are generated with enough dramatic force to be practiced in their real lives.

Boal's method not only transforms our understanding of narrative venues; it transforms the people who participate in it. Poor Peruvian peasant women discover how to stop their husbands from siphoning money to their mistresses in the city;[19] Latino mothers emerge from their seclusion to curb the gangland violence that plagues their neighborhood;[20] a teenage social justice group campaigns to transform its school's disciplinary procedures. Passive bystanders before political realities impossible to surmount become active subjects capable of transforming the drama of their real lives. In essence, spectators become inspired actors—agents of change on both the stage and the street.

The Five Movements of Social Empowerment Narrative Pedagogy

So how can we use narratives to socially empower a group of young people? Whether working with teens from a parochial high school, or with burdened women in the barrios of Peru, social empowerment narrative pedagogy has five distinct educational movements. The first movement is *to warm up the group of participants.* In social empowerment narrative pedagogy, a space is created in which a group of young people share charged stories, name hard realities, discuss difficult topics, claim their truth, dream new directions, discover their power, and role-play together until liberative directions for their lives emerge and solidify. The work is, at once, inviting and demanding. It requires communal solidarity, bodily involvement, emotional expressiveness, creative fluidity, broad participation, team work, trust, playfulness, and energy. Warming up a group, a necessary task at every session no matter how long the group has worked together, is more than recollecting names and stretching muscles. It is a sequence of exercises designed to activate body, soul, and imagination; engage the teens' participation; build collective trust and connection; and dynamize the space with energy and emotional vitality.

A facilitator's repertoire of warm-up exercises can draw from the abundance of exercises developed in theater companies, improv groups, summer camps, and youth organizations.[21] In choreographing a sequence for a particular session, the following considerations are helpful:

- ◆ *Circling-Up:* Beginning and ending each session in a circle focuses the group, connects them to each other, and establishes a sense of solidarity that builds throughout the program.

The closing circle after the final performance is often the most moving moment the young people share.

- *Warm-Up Rituals:* While introducing new games and activities keeps the warm-up time fresh, starting each session with the same initial sequence creates a ritual that, as the program evolves, instantly captures the group's attention and connects them to one another. Our young people became so attached to our opening three activities—a shakedown, the name game, and a round of Zip-Zap-Zop—we could corral the occasional squirreliness at any time by circling up and commencing our ritual.[22]

- *Deepening the Circle Connection:* Warm-up activities within the circle—such as Follow the Leader, Circle Dash, and the Sound and Motion Game—are uniquely valuable in nurturing communal connection and cooperation.[23] Ample time should be given to such exercises, especially early in the program when the group identity is still forming and scene work has yet to solidify.

- *Dynamizing the Space:* As invaluable as circle games are, they should be followed by exercises—like Imaginary Milling Around, Walk-Stop-Fall, Cover the Space, and Defender—that invite the group to move throughout the working area.[24] This creates an energy that reverberates throughout the space and lingers through the later activity.

While warming up may feel like fun and games, it is indispensable for activating dramatic muscles, stoking contagious energy, and building group connection. Indeed, it is time well spent.

The second educational movement is *to surface the generative themes of a community*. The purpose of liberative narrative pedagogy is to explore, through storied scenarios, the social concerns that are most personally relevant to a particular group of people. To discern which concerns are most alive in a community, the educator looks for energy—those issues that trigger anger or sorrow, outrage or animation. This energy is essential. It reveals the depth

of investment the participants have in that issue, and its discharge—
breaking through the numbing façade of resignation, apathy, and
dejection—releases the vitality of the human spirit necessary to sustain the long, belaboring haul toward liberation. Like an oil driller in
search of a strike, the facilitator takes soundings until such energy is
surfaced. These soundings can take a variety of forms.

- *Narrative Excavation:* A straightforward approach is to
  invite teens to share stories in which young people experience oppression. David White organizes listening groups and
  town-hall meetings to surface pressing concerns; he also creates survey teams in which young people interview the teens
  of their community and return with stories of social wound-
  ing.[25] Norma Bowles will ask a group to list all of the ways
  people are discriminated against; then she invites each person
  to pick one from the list and tell a story of a teen who suffers
  from that form of intolerance.

- *Narrative Presentations:* The facilitator can present external
  stories or case studies of teen oppression with the hope of
  activating latent passion. The Acting Out drama troupe per-
  forms a variety of issue-based scenarios to see which ones
  spark energy within a particular group. Paulo Freire spends
  time within a community beforehand, listening for the issues
  that people bemoan in the coffee houses and the marketplace.
  He then shows pictures or shares vignettes that portray people
  suffering these issues with the hope of activating an impassioned recognition.

- *Body Exercises:* Augusto Boal observes that we carry oppression in our bodies, and often our deepest concerns, sometimes below our awareness, need bodily expression to be
  exposed. After warming up a group's connection to their
  bodies through yoga stretches, say, or untying human knots,
  he might lead a group of teens through a series of physical
  activities to surface generative concerns. One example would
  be rhythm machines, where a group creates a syncopated collage of motion and sound depicting the teens' sense of love,

perhaps, or hate, or their honest experience of high school. Another example, used with the teens of St. Timothy's, is to invite groups of four to create human sculptures that capture different teens in various forms of crisis.[26]

- *Props Exercises:* Another way to access generative themes is through creative indirection. Random objects collected from the home and garage—a baseball bat and spatula, crucifix and soccer trophy—can be strewn across the stage floor, enticingly awaiting the teens' arrival. Warm-up games—like a group juggle, minefield, and trust walks through them—can play off the props and heighten anticipation.[27] Then the teens can each pick a prop and, in groups of six, create a commercial selling the items to a new kid in town as surefire necessities in surviving the worst conditions at school or in the neighborhood. A final exercise, uniquely powerful, is to invite each young person to use the prop to tell the story of a teen in crisis.

- *Party Games:* Teens often love to play party games—improv exercises from *What's My Line*, theater games from Comedy Sports, or icebreakers from summer camps. These can be easily adapted to surface their concerns. One group we worked with adored "Family Feud" so we played with such topics as "top ten crises teens endure" and "top five questions they would pose to God."

- *Group Improvisation:* Improv exercises are excellent ways of surfacing generative issues while teaching teens how to sustain dramatic connection between actors in a scene. Warm-up activities to ease into the process could include Mirrors—where one teen mimics another as if the first were staring into their reflection; Columbian Hypnosis—where one teen leads another throughout the theatrical space while staring at the leader's palm;[28] and Cock-Fight, a teen favorite, where two actors improvise a scene while repeating throughout the same two lines of dialogue, one saying, "I want it," the other responding, "You can't have it."[29] Once warmed up, teens can improvise typical scenes of adolescent conflict. The scenes that occur to them will reveal their own concerns percolating below the surface.[30]

Each of these exercises is a sounding into the well of teen experience. Some will fall flat; others may flicker with amusement. Still others, however, will tap a spring that spews with passionate force. This is what we look for. The stories that quiet the crowd, the scenes that incite recognition, the characters that move with pathos and delight—these are the torrents that point to the themes bubbling in the depths of their souls.

The third educational movement is *to problematize the generative themes in activating scenes that capture the core of the social conflict.* Michael Rohd, a liberative theater educator in the tradition of Boal, describes an "activating scene" as a vignette that poses a social conflict without presenting a resolution.[31] An example would be a teenage girl told to meet her coach after hours if she wants to make the tennis team, or Trent faced with the decision between drinking with his friends or entering rehabilitation. The scenes are open-ended. They do not present answers to a passive audience; they force reflection about forms of intervention that either liberate or dehumanize.

A generative concern, once identified, can be transposed into an activating scene in various ways. The facilitator, after sensing the energy around teenage sexual harassment, for example, can craft a scene for the teens to enact where such harassment would typically be encountered. Or the teens can take an issue as a prompt, brainstorm various contexts where it is experienced, then craft their own scenes that depict the essential conflict. Another option is for the teens to start with a controversial topic, say "Should young people consume alcohol?" There the teens can list collectively various perspectives on both sides of the issue, create characters for each of these perspectives, and craft scenes where the characters meet in some context in which the stakes are high.

Regardless of how the scenes are created, they are most effective when embodying the following criteria: a core conflict is clearly depicted, the context is believable and realistic, a moment of decision is reached with the outcome still undetermined, and the characters—a sympathetic protagonist and an antagonist who is not a cardboard cartoon—are credible, recognizable, and complex.[32] Activating scenes provoke genuine questions; they do not, subtly or obviously, promote a predetermined agenda.

The fourth educational movement is *to invite the participants to discuss and role-play liberative interventions within the social conflict in question.* Once an activating scene is presented, the tiger is out of the cage. If the scene realistically depicts an issue of generative passion within the community, the lack of resolution will activate a flurry of responses. A facilitator can channel these reactions into a dialogical and liberative exploration. This exploration should have the following components:[33]

- *Initial Debriefing:* First, the facilitator invites the group to debrief the initial activating scene with such questions as, "Is it realistic? Did the character get what she wanted? What prevented her from meeting her needs? And what else could she have done?"

- *Replaying the Scene:* Second, the role-play is performed multiple times with audience members acting out various interventions brainstormed by the group. After each one, the group debriefs—"What was done differently? Is it any more satisfying? Is it a realistic option in our community? What would it take to do it for real?"

- *Researching the Issue:* Third, along the way, the group identifies dimensions of the conflict that need further research—"What more do we need to know to fully understand the issue? What are the systemic causes of the problem? What resources offer us new perspectives? What skills or tools do we need to develop?" For example, the teens at St. Timothy's talked to the various parties involved, boned up on their school's disciplinary procedures, and discovered alternative visions of justice that turned them on with their liberative promise.

- *Resolution:* Finally, consensus is reached about the most satisfying intervention the participants have discovered thus far. At some point, dialogue and research come to an end. The scene is role-played, and a realistic resolution clicks into place. Often the sense is palpable. The group has stumbled upon its power, and a path to liberation is glimpsed.

The fifth educational movement, following from the last, is *to embody the liberative agency rehearsed on the stage in the real-life contexts of the participants' lives.* In response to the question of when a session of participatory theater should come to an end, Augusto Boal replied, "Never . . . In truth, a session of Theater of the Oppressed has no end, because everything which happens in it must extend into life. . . . Theater of the Oppressed is located precisely on the frontier between fiction and reality—and this border must be crossed. If the show starts in fiction, its objective is to become integrated into reality."[34] The purpose of liberative narrative pedagogy is not to provoke impassioned conversation, nor to fill an evening with inspiring social role-play. It is to discover within social oppression empowering interventions and mobilize for their implementation. If the process does not leave the stage and stream out onto the streets, its fundamental driving force is violated and subverted. To paraphrase Boal once more, perhaps the theater is not itself the revolution, but have no doubt: it is a rehearsal for the revolution to come.[35]

Maria did not care to share the character she created from her coffee-mug props. I told her that was fine. She was rather timid already. Her best friend, though, Lupita—as boisterous as Maria was meek—had other designs. When I asked the group to pair off, Lupita all but dragged Maria to a corner where they huddled and crafted a scene. Then she took center stage like a linebacker poised to blitz, and read their play for the rest of us.

Minnie, a senior coed named after the mouse, has a full ride to Harvard—on the one condition that she ace her English class. Mr. C., short for Mr. Cool, is all too accommodating. He offers to help her in his classroom after school. The first day Minnie arrives, Mr. C. is changing his shirt; she catches him bare-chested. The second time, he is tucking his shirt in, his pants partly unbuttoned. The third time he suggests they meet at the Starbucks across the street from his pad. When Minnie demurs, Mr. C. is indignant—there are plenty of students with promise to tutor. She has one week to decide. Their next session is at the coffee shop, or she should start considering her backup colleges.

The group got it at once. "Why doesn't she turn the creep in?" one teen shouted.

"Cuz no one would believe her," Lupita shot back. "He's Mr. Cool on campus. She's a nobody."

"Why doesn't she tell her father?" another threw out.

"Her father wouldn't believe her," Lupita threw back.

"Why doesn't she . . . "

"Why doesn't she what?" Lupita interrupted. "There's *nothing* she can do."

For several days of the spring break program, the teens agonized over options. Beating him up with a baseball bat was satisfying emotionally but hardly realistic. Dropping out for a junior college felt like a kick in the gut of Minnie's collegiate dreams. Giving in, of course, was out of the question. The teens were stumped. Maria was beat. Until a teen had an idea. What if Minnie carried a recorder and taped his innuendoes, and then, when she gave the signal, twenty of her friends hiding in the corners jumped out and denounced the man? "I have a better idea," Maria volunteered. "What if Minnie writes that scene as a play and invites Mr. C. to watch it?"

The scene was but one of a series of vignettes the teens performed for their high school. Even so, it hardly went unnoticed. When Minnie revealed her recorder and a dozen teens leaped out from all sides with the cry, "You'll never teach again, Perv," the audience erupted. Catcalls and wild applause were the universal acclamation from the entire high school assembly. Or nearly universal, so it seems. Lupita assured me afterward. There was one teacher who just sat there, and took it all in.

I met up with Maria at graduation a couple of months later. She was breezing by in her cap and gown. "How's Minnie?" I volleyed her way. Her beaming smile belied a story that I would never know.

"She's going to Disneyland," Maria shared. "And then she's going to Harvard."

Teens live in a tragic world. Barrio poverty, sexual harassment, death at the hands of drunk drivers—indeed, it's enough to make God weep.

If God does weep, the tears form pools. They flow within the wounds of the world and well up in pockets of healing waters. Those pools are disguised as stories. They look like social action groups role-playing new forms of justice, like gangland mothers improvising antidotes to violence, and like spring-break drama groups using the stage to expose exploitation.

Though in disguise, they are pools all the same. And they bear renewing properties. Teens find power soaking in those waters; wounds are healed, hope revived, a belief in justice is rekindled.

As teens splash in the waters that birth liberation, the pools become replenished. God's eyes remain moist. Not with sorrow. But with the sparkling gaze of one who delights in a daughter's restoration.

Conclusion

It is hard to admit, but I had it in for Miguel right from the start. He thought the circle games were childish—and the role-plays too serious. He mimicked the others behind their backs but wanted no part of performing up front. He insisted his guitar was a necessary prop, then plucked it through other people's scenes. Interventions and group covenants were but temporary deterrents. He would spit out he was sorry like it was all our fault and then retreat into his writing tablet.

When I finally pushed him to create an original character, he scribbled one out and dared me to reject it—a tagger so determined to join a local gang, the Brick City Boys, that he graffitied **"BCB"** on every space he could find. "Oh," Miguel added when he shared it with a sneer, "he also plays guitar." I told him the character had promise. He shrugged it off, slouched in his chair, and doodled—**BCB** in bold black letters—on every square inch of his pad. As the other teens' scenes coalesced into a play, Miguel saw no place for his character within it. So we invited him to play his guitar at the party set in the play's climactic conclusion. Miguel was noncommittal.

The play was being performed at a posh private school some twenty miles from the barrio where the workshop was held. The complex sparkled with the glint of fresh money; the equipment was state-of-the-art. After four weeks in the dilapidated auditorium at the local Catholic church, the teens gawked like yokels at the World's Fair. On the mammoth stage, complete with an orchestra pit, they were afraid to unpocket their hands. Which was just as well. The place was donated for just one day on the single condition that, when we were through with it, it looked untouched "right down to the knobs on the computerized tech board."

As it turned out, Miguel did show; he was an hour early. He brought a mic and an amp, and set them up himself in the back corner of the stage. Then he killed time jamming on the guitar until he tired and explored the theater. I didn't pay too much attention. We had yet to have a dress rehearsal, the show but a couple of hours away, and we were still figuring out how to work the lights and where to set the food for the postshow reception.

Twenty minutes before the performance, Joe, one of my assistants, found me frantically folding programs in the theater's foyer. I thought he was anxious to open the doors for the crowd starting to arrive. He wasn't. "Frank," he said, "we have a problem. Follow me." He took me to the choir room located behind the stage. We used it as our home base where we stored all of our gear. On the freshly painted surface, beside the mounted technicolor television console, someone had graffitied the wall. In bold black blocks, "**BCB**" blared in our face.

My heart pounding, I hunted down Miguel. I found him in the parking lot back behind the theater. "I'm not accusing you," I said, my voice trembling with accusation. "I just want to know if you know anything about this."

His indignation exploded like a grenade. "Of course you would think I did it. That's messed up, man. I had nothing to do with it. And you shouldn't accuse people if you don't know for sure."

"I'm not accusing," I said. "I just needed to ask. If you didn't do it, who do you think did?"

"How do I know? Everyone of them's got it in for me. It could be anybody."

"Well, let's deal with this as a group," I told him. "We'll meet in the choir room."

The others were already there. Word had gotten out. I circled us up. "We've got a problem," I started. "And we need to find a way to resolve it."

"But the play starts in like five minutes," one teen said.

"I know," I said, "but this is more important. The show doesn't mean a thing if we pretend everything's okay." The teens shuffled in the awkwardness. "Does anybody have anything they want to say about it?"

One teen did. "I think the person who did it should confess and apologize, so he doesn't ruin it for the rest of us."

I could feel Miguel's ire from across the circle. I tended to agree with the teen, but I responded by saying, "How do we know it's a 'he'?"

"Well, *whoever* then," the teen continued, "but I bet it's a 'he.'"

I sensed murmurs of assent. For the first time, I took it seriously, "What if it wasn't Miguel?" I thought. I'd be ticked too. "We don't know who it is," I said. "We just know that someone in this circle graffitied a wall. And we need to figure out what we're going to do about it."

"Why would anybody do such a thing?" one of the younger teens questioned.

"I don't know," I said. "What do you think?"

"All kinds of reasons," another teen offered. "Maybe they don't like the school."

"Maybe they don't like the play."

"Maybe they don't like the rest of us."

"Or maybe," one teen volunteered, "they don't like just one of us."

"What do you mean?" another one asked.

"Maybe somebody did it to make it look like somebody else did it."

"Yeah," Miguel said, his fury leaking. "Everybody just keeps assuming it's me."

"So, let's not assume," I said. "We really don't know who did it. What if it was somebody else, any one of us, what must that person be feeling right now to do something like this?"

"Well," one said, "they don't really care about what's going on. I mean they're ruining the whole thing."

"So what would they be feeling instead?" I pushed.

"I don't know," one mused. "Maybe they're just hanging out and watching it all."

"How would that feel?" I continued.

"I don't know, it would suck, man. Maybe they're jealous, at all the fun we're having."

"Maybe they feel left out," another offered.

"I bet they feel lonely," Teresa offered, my senior stalwart. "I mean, here we've been doing this for a month and, if they're still feeling like they're not part of the group—that's lonely."

I followed her lead. "So, if that's what this person is feeling, what would you want to say to them?"

"God," one said, "we just didn't know. We didn't mean to leave anybody out."

"I guess we could have tried harder," another said.

"I don't know, I just feel bad," still another said.

"You know," Teresa suddenly realized, "I don't want to know who did it. If somebody is feeling this left out, and like none of the rest of us really care, then we all did it. And we all should take responsibility for it."

"What would that look like?" I asked.

"It starts," she continued, "by not trying to find out who did it anymore. Whoever you are, I'm sorry. We all helped you feel this way. We all did it."

I scanned the rest of the circle. "Is that how the rest of us feel? We all did it?" In various degrees, they got it; or at least they got the possibility of it. Somehow, we were all in it together. "So, how do we take care of it?" I asked.

"My dad got this stuff from Home Depot," one teen remembered, "and it took off permanent marker on my sister's wall. Maybe we can get some of that, and we can all take turns scrubbing it off—each one of us around the circle."

"I'm happy to run to Home Depot," Joe volunteered. "I can have it here by the end of the show."

I surveyed the group. They were in. "Okay," I summed up, "we'll meet right here after the show."

After the teens took their bows and received the applause, they did not rush out to greet the guests who had come to see them. We met back in the choir room. A single line formed in front of the graffiti. Each teen took their turn. Even Miguel. He still simmered as if suspicious of being falsely accused, but he swiped at the marker on the wall all the same. As the last teen scrubbed, the graffiti was wiped clean—by the group that had put it there in the first place.

In the reception area, a few moments later, the teenage actors were soaking up adoring praise for their play in huddles of family and friends. Miguel was by himself. No family or friends had taken the time. I walked toward him sipping his soda in the corner. He shook his head as I approached.

"You still think I did, it, don't you?" he asked.

"No," I said. "I really think Teresa's right. We all did it. Me too. And I'm sorry."

He eyed me to see if I meant it. I did. "Yeah, well," he allowed, "maybe I did it too." He paused but a second before adding, "But that doesn't mean I did it."

To this day, I do not know who graffitied that classroom wall. Perhaps Miguel. Perhaps a teen angry at Miguel. Perhaps a teen unconcerned about Miguel, just furious at the opulence that taunted with callous indifference. Such is how it is with narrative pedagogy. We tell stories, we coax stories, we stage the stories that teens create, but we never know the end of the story, how these stories live on in the teens as their lives continue to unfold.

It is not that we know nothing, however. We know the power of narrative. By now it should be clear—I am a story advocate. I have set out in this book to detail the various ways that stories enliven and liberate; and in so doing, I have passionately argued for each approach in hopes of enticing others to explore them with young people. It is not empty enthusiasm. I have seen them in action. And through them, I have seen the sacred restoring life on the stage of teenage souls.

But I have seen something else as well. As thrilling as being an artist can be, as emboldening as it is to claim your storied identity, as profound as it can be to touch the holy in a sacred text, as empowering as it is to see your play inspire social change, narrative pedagogies are merely techniques. As liberative as they promise to be, they can just as easily distract us from the humanity in our midst.

The story is not always the one on the stage. Sometimes, the wall graffitied in the classroom is where the real story is taking place. While the company is claiming its voice through circle games and public performances, a faceless teen is screaming in the shadows. The scream looks like sabotage and it sounds like self-destruction, but it is equally self-expressive. "I want to be known," the graffiti cries out. "I want my story to be heard as well."

Where is the God who hears the cry in whatever tangled form it wails? God is not center-stage. God is in the graffiti. In the vandalized back room of every teenage soul, a sacred presence whispers, "I hear the cry of your story. Your story is mine. The graffitied anguish on the wall. . . . I did it, too."

Notes

Introduction

1. Excellent character profiling techniques can be found in Daniel Judah Sklar, *Playmaking: Children Writing and Performing Their Own Plays* (New York: Teachers' and Writers' Collaborative, 1991).

2. Irving Greenberg, "Cloud of Smoke, Pillar of Fire: Judaism, Christianity and Modernity after the Holocaust," in *Auschwitz: Beginning of a New Era?* ed. E. Fleischner (New York: KTAV, 1977), 23.

3. For a helpful introduction to such techniques see Peter Pitzele, *Scripture Windows: Toward a Practice of Bibliodrama* (Los Angeles: Alef Design Group, 1998).

Chapter 1

1. Stephen Prothero defines religious literacy as "the ability to understand and use in one's day-to-day life the basic building blocks of religious traditions—their key terms, symbols, doctrines, practices, sayings, characters, metaphors, and narratives." Stephen Prothero, *Religious Literacy: What Every American Needs to Know—and Doesn't* (San Francisco: HarperSanFrancisco, 2007), 11–12.

2. Lest we scapegoat adolescents, it should be pointed out that some researchers have found Americans as a whole, though deeply religious, "profoundly ignorant about religion," indeed "a nation of religious illiterates" (ibid., 1).

3. Chris Smith with Melinda Lundquist Denton, *Soul Searching: The Religious and Spiritual Lives of American Teenagers* (New York: Oxford University Press, 2005), 131 (emphasis in original).

4, James McClendon, *Biography as Theology* (Nashville: Abingdon Press, 1974).

189

5. See Michael Root, "The Narrative Structure of Soteriology," in *Why Narrative?* ed. Stanley Hauerwas and L. Gregory Jones (Grand Rapids: Wm. Eerdmans, 1989), 263–78.

6. See particularly Stanley Hauerwas, *Truth and Truthfulness, The Peaceable Kingdom* (Notre Dame, Ind.: University of Notre Dame Press, 1983), and McClendon, *Biography as Theology*.

7. Gabriel Fackre summarizes various articulations of this grand narrative arc; see Gabriel Fackre, "Narrative Theology: An Overview," *Interpretation* 37, no. 4 (October 1983): 350–51. For a discussion of the Bible as a single cosmic story, see George W. Stroup, *The Promise of Narrative Theology: Recovering the Gospel in the Church* (Eugene, Ore.: Wipf and Stock Publishers, 1981), 136–69.

8. (The church's) "most important social task is nothing less than to be a community capable of hearing the story of God we find in Scripture and living in a manner that is faithful to that story." Stanley Hauerwas, *A Community of Character* (Notre Dame, Ind.: University of Notre Dame Press, 1981), 1.

9. Patricia Griggs, *Using Storytelling in Christian Education* (Abingdon: Parthenon Press, 1981), and Susan Shaw, *Storytelling in Religious Education* (Birmingham: Religious Education Press, 1999). See also William White, *Speaking in Stories: Resources for Christian Storytellers* (Minneapolis: Augsburg, 1982); Marlene Lefever, *Creative Teaching Methods* (Colorado Springs, Colo.: Cool Ministry Resources, 1996); and Mark Miller, *Experiential Storytelling: (Re)Discovering Narrative to Communicate God's Message* (Grand Rapids: Zondervan Press, 2003).

10. Sarah Arthur, *The God-Hungry Imagination: The Art of Storytelling for Post-Modern Youth* (Nashville: Upper Room Books, 2007).

11. Ibid., 15.

12. Ibid., 31.

13. Ibid., 111.

14. Ibid., 96.

15. For tips on retelling biblical narratives as stories, see the Network for Biblical Storytellers and the School for Sacred Storytelling. For cultivating storytelling skills, see chapter 6.

16. Walt Wangerin, *The Book of God: The Bible as a Novel* (Grand Rapids: Zondervan, 1996); Anita Diamant, *The Red Tent* (New York: St. Martin's Press, 2005); Malcolm X with Alex Haley, *The Autobiography of Malcolm X* (New York: Random House, 1973).

17. Miller, *Experiential Storytelling*.

18. For helpful discussion suggestions, see Lefever, *Creative Teaching Methods*, 202–16.

19. For creative ideas, see ibid., 58–201.

20. For suggestions in helping others craft stories, see chapter 6.

21. For suggestions on helping youth craft dramatic productions, see chapter 6.

22. See Miller, *Experiential Storytelling*, 91–148.

Chapter 2

1. Erik Erikson, *Youth: Identity and Crisis* (New York: W. W. Norton and Co., 1968).

2. The narrative character of personal identity is developed more fully in Paul Brockelman, *Time and Self* (New York: Crossroad Publishing Company, 1985); Stephen Crites, "The Narrative Quality of Experience," in *Why Narrative? Readings in Narrative Theology*, ed. Stanley Hauerwas and L. Gregory Jones (Grand Rapids: Wm. Eerdmans, 1989), 65–88; Stanley Hauerwas, *A Community of Character* (Notre Dame, Ind.: University of Notre Dame Press, 1981), 129–52; Stanley Hauerwas, *Vision and Virtue: Essays in Christian Ethical Reflection* (Notre Dame, Ind.: University of Notre Dame Press, 1974); 68–89; Donald E. Polkinghorne, *Narrative Knowing and the Human Sciences* (Albany: State University of New York Press, 1988), 101–23; George W. Stroup, *The Promise of Narrative Theology: Recovering the Gospel in the Church* (Eugene, Ore.: Wipf and Stock Publishers, 1981), 100–131.

3. George Stroup makes this observation in *Promise of Narrative Theology*, 111.

4. On what constitutes personal identity, see Stroup, *Promise of Narrative Theology*, chap. 4; and Dan McAdams, *The Stories We Live By: Personal Myths and the Making of the Self* (New York: Guilford Press, 1993), chap. 7.

5. For the narrative structure of meaning, see Polkinghorne, *Narrative Knowing*, chaps. 1, 6; and Herbert Anderson and Edward Foley, *Mighty Stories, Dangerous Rituals: Weaving Together the Human and the Divine* (San Francisco: Jossey-Bass, 1998), chap. 1.

6. For Hauerwas, narrative is defined as a description of events linked in a temporal sequence that unfolds according to a plot. See Hauerwas, *Truthfulness and Tragedy* (Notre Dame, Ind.: University of Notre

Dame Press, 1977), 28. Paul Brockelman defines narrative similarly; see Brockelman, *Time and Self*, 65.

7. Richard Gardner, *Therapeutic Communication with Children: The Mutual Storytelling Technique* (Northvale, N.J.: Jason Aronson Inc., 1986). Other narrative therapists include Michael White and David Epston, *Narrative Means to Therapeutic Ends* (New York: W. W. Norton and Co., 1990); Christie Neuger, *Counseling Women: A Narrative, Pastoral Approach* (Minneapolis: Fortress Press, 2001); Alan Parry and Robert Doan, *Story Re-visions: Narrative Therapy in the Post-Modern World* (New York: Guilford Press, 1994); and Jill Freedman and Gene Combs, *Narrative Therapy: The Social Construction of Preferred Realities* (New York: W.W. Norton and Co., 1996).

8. Dan P. McAdams, *The Redemptive Self: Stories Americans Live By* (Oxford: Oxford University Press, 2006).

9. Robert Stone, "Narrative Theology and Religious Education," in Randolph Crump Miller ed., *Theologies of Religious Education* (Birmingham: Religious Education Press, 1995), 271.

10. See Stroup, *Promise of Narrative Theology*, 109–10.

11. For the narrative character of Christian faith, see Paul T. Brockelman, *The Inside Story: A Narrative Approach to Religious Understanding and Truth* (Albany: State University of New York Press, 1992), chap. 5; Stroup, *Promise of Narrative Theology*, chap. 6; and Hauerwas, *Vision and Virtue*, chap. 4.

12. Two helpful examples are: McAdams, *Stories We Live By*, and David Feinstein and Stanley Krippner, *The Mythic Path: Discovering the Guiding Stories of Your Past—Creating a Vision for Your Future* (New York: Jeremy P. Tarcher/Putnam Books, 1997).

13. Helpful examples include: Richard Morgan, *Remembering Your Story: Creating Your Own Spiritual Autobiography* (Nashville: Upper Room Books, 2002); Richard Patterson, *Writing Your Spiritual Autobiography* (Allen, Tex.: Thomas More Publishing, 2002); Richard Peace, *Spiritual Autobiography: Discovering and Sharing Your Spiritual Story* (Colorado Springs, Colo.: NavPress, 1998); and Dan Wakefield, *The Story of Your Life: Writing a Spiritual Autobiography* (Boston: Beacon Press, 1990).

14. Peter Morgan, *Story Weaving: Using Stories to Transform Your Congregation* (St. Louis : CBH Press, 1986).

15. Dori Grinenko Baker, *Doing Girlfriend Theology: God-Talk with Young Women* (Cleveland: Pilgrim Press, 2005).

16. Anne E. Streaty Wimberly, *Soul Stories: African American Christian Education,* rev. ed. (Nashville: Abingdon Press, 2005).

17. McAdams, *Stories We Live By,* 102–9.

18. Other narrative arcs advocated include framing one's life through the trajectory of "creation–fall–redemption–kingdom of God" or that of "paradise–paradise lost–paradise quest–paradise regained."

19. See, for example, The Wheel Council, *Storytelling Power Book: Substance Abuse Prevention* (Prescott, Ariz.: Wheel Council, 1997); Liz Greene and Juliet Sharman-Burke, *The Mythic Journey: The Meaning of Myth as a Guide for Life* (New York: Fireside, 2000); Sam Keen and Anne Valley-Fox, *Your Mythic Journey: Finding Meaning in Your Life through Writing and Storytelling* (Los Angeles: Jeremy Tarcher, Inc., 1989).

20. Morgan, *Story Weaving,* 53.

21. Stanley Hauerwas, *The Peaceable Kingdom: A Primer in Christian Ethics.* (Notre Dame, Ind.: University of Notre Dame Press, 1983), 22; Wimberly, *Soul Stories,* 33.

Chapter 3

1. For helpful discussions on myth, see Susan Shaw, *Storytelling in Religious Education* (Birmingham: Religious Education Press, 1999), 148–61, and Belden C. Lane, "Myth," in *The New Dictionary of Catholic Spirituality,* ed. Michael Downey (Collegeville, Minn.: Order of St. Benedict, 1993), 692–95.

2. Joseph Campbell, *The Hero with a Thousand Faces* (Princeton, N.J.: Princeton University Press, 1949), 3.

3. Karl Barth, *The Word of God and the Word of Man* (Gloucester, Mass.: Peter Smith Publisher, 1978), 29.

4. Ibid., 62–63.

5. Ibid., 34.

6. Carl Jung, et al., *Man and His Symbols* (Garden City, N.Y.: Doubleday, 1964), 98.

7. See for example, Samuel Laeuchli, Evelyn Rothchild-Laeuchli, and Bjorn Krondorfer in *Body and the Bible: Interpreting and Experiencing Biblical Narratives,* ed. Bjorn Krondorfer (Philadelphia: Trinity Press International, 1992).

8. Some theologians argue that honoring such reactions threatens the authority of the text. Depth encounter scholars suggest that the authority of the text is not in its historical accuracy, but in its sense of being "true to

life" and its ability to deepen authentic human experience. See, for example, John Bowden, "Narrative Theology," in *The Westminster Dictionary of Christian Theology*, ed. Alan Richardson and John Bowden (Philadelphia: Westminster Press, 1983), 391–92.

9. Samuel Laeuchli and Evelyn Rothchild-Laeuchli, "Mimesis: The Healing Power of Myth," *Quadrant* 22, no. 2 (1989): 56; and Krondorfer, *Body and Bible*.

10. Walter Wink, *Transforming Bible Study: A Leader's Guide* (Nashville: Abingdon Press, 1980), 19–20.

11. Aristotle, *On the Soul*, part VII.

12. See Jung, *Man and His Symbols*, and Robert A. Johnson, *Inner Work: Using Dreams and Active Imagination for Personal Growth* (San Francisco: HarperSanFrancisco, 1986).

13. See, for example, Marlene Lefever, *Creative Teaching Methods* (Colorado Springs, Colo.: Cook Ministry Resources, 1996); Gloria Durka and Joanmarie Smith, *The Aesthetic Dimensions of Religious Education* (New York: Paulist Press, 1979); and Maria Harris, *Teaching and the Religious Imagination* (San Francisco: Harper and Row, 1987).

14. Wink, *Transforming Bible Study*, 13.

15. Peter Pitzele, *Scripture Windows: Towards a Practice of Bibliodrama* (Los Angeles: Alef Design, 1998).

16. Ibid., 13.

17. See William A. Barry, S.J., *Finding God in All Things: A Companion to the Spiritual Exercises of St. Ignatius* (Notre Dame, Ind.: Ave Maria Press, 2006), and David Lonsdale, *Eyes to See, Ears to Hear: An Introduction to Ignatian Spirituality* (Maryknoll, N.Y.: Orbis Books, 2005).

18. For warm-up exercises particularly helpful for narrative pedagogy, see chapters 5 and 6.

19. Tim F. Schramm, "Bibliodrama in Action: Reenacting a New Testament Healing Story," in Krondorfer, *Body and Bible*, 63.

20. See Pitzele, *Scripture Windows*, 53–75.

21. See Wink, *Transforming Bible Study*, 39–43.

22. Ibid., 40.

23. Pitzele, *Scripture Windows*, 199.

24. For the significance of such material integration, see Robert Johnson, *Inner Work*, 97–134.

Chapter 4

1. For a variation on this tale, see Ed Brody et al., *Spinning Tales, Weaving Hope* (Philadelphia: New Society Publishers, 1992), 137–39.

2. Walter Wink, *Engaging the Powers* (Minneapolis: Fortress Press, 1992), 13.

3. See for example, John H. Westerhoff III, *Will Our Children Have Faith?* (New York: Seabury Press, 1976); C. Ellis Nelson, *Where Faith Begins* (Atlanta: John Knox Press, 1976); Maria Harris, *Fashion Me a People* (Louisville: Westminster/John Knox, 1989); and Thomas Groome, *Christian Religious Education* (San Francisco: Harper and Row, 1980), chap. 6.

4. Maria Harris, "Completion and Faith Development," in *Faith Development and Fowler*, ed. Craig Dykstra and Sharon Parks (Birmingham: Religious Education Press, 1986), 119.

5. H. Richard Niebuhr, *The Meaning of Revelation* (New York: Macmillan Co., 1955).

6. Catherine Orenstein, *Little Red Riding Hood Uncloaked: Sex, Morality, and the Evolution of a Fairy Tale* (New York: Basic Books, 2002), 10.

7. Ibid., 11.

8. Ibid., 245.

9. Katherine Turpin, "Princess Dreams: Children's Spiritual Formation in Consumer Culture," in *Children, Youth, and Spirituality in a Troubling World*, ed. Mary Elizabeth Moore and Almeda M. Wright (St. Louis: Chalice Press, 2008), 45–61.

10. Marcia R. Lieberman, "'Some Day My Prince Will Come': Female Acculturation through the Fairy Tale," *College English* 34, no. 3 (December 1972): 384.

11. Henry Giroux, "Animating Youth: The Disneyfication of Children's Culture," in Henry Giroux, *Fugitive Cultures* (New York: Routledge, 1996), 90–91.

12. Rosa Brooks, "Resist the Princesses," *Los Angeles Times*, March 27, 2008.

13. Along with Marcia Lieberman and Katherine Turpin, see Carol P. Christ, *Diving Deep and Surfacing: Women Writers on Spiritual Quest* (Boston: Beacon Press, 1980).

14. Brooks, "Resist the Princesses."

15. Kay Stone, "Things Walt Disney Never Told Us," in *Women and Folklore*, ed. Claire R. Farrer (Austin: University of Texas Press, 1975), 42–50 (48).

16. Ibid., 49.

17. For a representative sample, see Richard Bauckman, *The Bible in Politics: How to Read the Bible Politically* (London: SPCK, 1989); Cain Felder, *Stony the Road We Trod: African-American Biblical Interpretation* (Minneapolis: Fortress Press, 1991); Elisabeth Schüssler Fiorenza, *Bread Not Stone: The Challenge of Feminist Biblical Interpretation* (Boston: Beacon Press, 1984); Kwok Pui-Lan, *Discovering the Bible in the Non-Biblical World* (Maryknoll, N.Y.: Orbis Books, 1995); Fernando F. Segovia, *Decolonizing Biblical Studies: A View from the Margins* (Maryknoll, N.Y.: Orbis Books, 2000); R. S. Sugirtharajah, ed., *Voices from the Margin: Interpreting the Bible in the Third World* (Oxford: Oxford University Press, 2002). For religious educators detailing the implications for biblical pedagogy, see Fernando F. Segovia and Mary A. Tolbert, *Teaching the Bible: The Discourse and Politics of Biblical Pedagogy* (Maryknoll, N.Y.: Orbis Books, 1998), and Boyung Lee, "A Postcolonial Approach to Biblical Pedagogy," *Religious Education* 102, no. 11 (2007): 44–66.

18. Phyllis Trible, *Texts of Terror: Literary-Feminist Readings of Biblical Narratives* (Philadelphia: Fortress Press, 1984).

19. George Tinker, "Native Americans and the Land," *Word and World* 6 (1986): 66–74; and Robert Allen Warrior, "A Native American Perspective: Canaanites, Cowboys, and Indians," in Sugirtharajah, *Voices from the Margin*, 277–87.

20. Jack Mezirow, "How Critical Reflection Triggers Transformative Learning," in *Fostering Critical Reflection in Adulthood: A Guide to Transformative and Emancipatory Learning*, ed., Mezirow and Associates (San Francisco: Jossey-Bass Publishers, 1990), 1–20; Jack Mezirow, "Learning to Think Like an Adult: Core Concepts of Transformation Theory," *Learning as Transformation: Critical Perspectives on a Theory in Progress*, ed., Jack Mezirow and Associates (San Francisco: Jossey-Bass, 2000), 3–33; Groome, *Christian Religious Education*, chaps. 8–9.

21. James Fowler, *Stages of Faith* (San Francisco: Harper and Row, 1981).

22. Mezirow, "Learning to Think Like an Adult," 19.

23. Paulo Freire, *Pedagogy of the Oppressed* (New York: Continuum, 1984).

24. Joseph Taylor, *Reel Youth Ministry: Empowering Young People to Become Agents of Change through Critical Consciousness and Narrative Pedagogies* (Claremont School of Theology, Calif.: unpublished Ph.D. dissertation, 2010).

25. Hyon-Shim Hong, my student at the Claremont School of Theology, critiques classic folktales compiled in Tae Hung Ha, *Folk Tales of Old Korea* (Seoul: Yonsei University Press, 1958); Jina Kim, another CST student, documents her work in Jina Kim, *Transformative Education through Narrative Pedagogy in the Korean Women's Context* (Claremont School of Theology, Calif.: unpublished D.Min. project, 2007).

26. Herbert Kohl, *Should We Burn Barbar? Essays on Children's Literature and the Power of Stories* (New York: New Press, 1995), 30–56.

27. Jack Zipes, *Creative Storytelling* (New York: Routledge, 1995), 4.

28. Jack Zipes, ed., *The Trial and Tribulations of Little Red Riding Hood* (New York: Routledge, 1993), and Zipes, *Creative Storytelling*, 23–35.

29. Ibid., 8–12.

30. Connie K. Borkenhagen, "The Legal Bias against Rape Victims (The Rape of Mr. Smith)," *American Bar Association Journal* (April 1975); reprinted in Sheila Ruth, *Issues in Feminism: An Introduction to Women's Studies* (Mountain View, Calif.: Mayfield Publishing Co., 1990).

31. See for example, Zipes, *Trials and Tribulations*; Zipes, *Don't Bet on the Prince: Contemporary Feminist Fairy Tales in North America and England* (New York: Methuen, 1986); Alessandra Levorato, *Language and Gender in the Fairy Tale Tradition: A Linguistic Analysis of Old and New Storytelling* (New York: Palgrave Macmillan, 2003).

32. Zipes has an abundance of creative methods to explore all types of stories—from myths and wish tales to fables and science fiction. See Zipes, *Creative Storytelling.*

33. Pamela Cooper-White, *The Cry of Tamar: Violence against Women and the Church's Response* (Minneapolis: Fortress Press, 1995).

34. Zipes, *Trials and Tribulations.*

35. Zipes, *Don't Bet on the Prince*, and Robert Munsch, *The Paper Bag Princess* (Buffalo, N.Y.: Annick Press, 1980).

36. For a version of this tale, see Suzanne Crowder Han, *Korean Folk and Fairy Tales* (Elizabeth, N.J.: Hollym Corporation, 1991).

37. Kim, *Transformative Education*, 74–85.

Chapter 5

1. Daniel Judah Sklar, *Play-Making: Children Writing and Performing Their Own Plays* (New York: Teachers and Writers Collaborative, 1991).

2. See, for example, Nancy Azara, *Spirit Taking Form: Making a Spiritual Practice of Making Art* (York Beach, Maine: Red Wheel, 2002); Ellen

Langer, *On Becoming an Artist: Reinventing Yourself through Mindful Creativity* (New York: Ballantine Books, 2005); Cathy Malchiodi, *The Soul's Palette: Drawing on Art's Transformative Powers for Health and Well-Being* (Boston: Shambhala Publications, 2002); Thomas Ryan, *Soul Fire: Accessing Your Creativity* (Woodstock, Vt.: Sky Light Paths, 2008); Beverly Shamana, *Seeing in the Dark: A Vision of Creativity and Spirituality* (Nashville: Abingdon Press, 2001); Robert Wuthnow, *Creative Spirituality: The Way of the Artist* (Berkeley: University of California Press, 2001).

3. Irenaeus, *Adversus Haereses (Against Heresies)* 4.34.5–7.

4. Julia Cameron, *The Artist's Way: A Spiritual Path to Higher Creativity* (New York: Tarcher/Putnam Books, 1992), 3.

5. See, for example, Ryan, *Soul Fire.* and Shamana, *Seeing in the Dark.*

6. Shamana, *Seeing in the Dark*, 12.

7. Cameron, *Artist's Way*, 1.

8. Evelyn Underhill, *The Spiritual Life* (London: Hodder and Stoughton, Ltd., 1937), 19, 84.

9. Sklar, *Play-Making*, 135–36.

10. William Shakespeare, *King Lear*, 4.6.

11. Mary Field Belenky et al., *Women's Ways of Knowing: The Development of Self, Voice, and Mind* (New York: Basic Books, 1986); Carol Lakey Hess, *Caretakers of Our Common House: Women's Development in Communities of Faith* (Nashville: Abingdon, 1997); Rosemary Radford Ruether, *Sexism and God-Talk: Toward a Feminist Theology* (Boston: Beacon Press, 1983).

12. Dori Grinenko Baker, *Doing Girlfriend Theology: God-Talk with Young Women* (Cleveland: Pilgrim Press, 2005).

13. Nelle Morton, *The Journey Is Home* (Boston: Beacon Press, 1985).

14. See, for example, Patrice Vecchione, *Writing and the Spiritual Life: Finding Your Voice by Looking Within* (New York: Contemporary Books, 2001).

15. See Elizabeth Johnson, *She Who Is: The Mystery of God in Feminist Theological Discourse* (New York: Crossroad, 1992).

16. Dee Dee Risher, "Roots and Branches: More Than Just Bread," *The Other Side* (September–October 2000): 54.

17. Thomas Wolfe, *Look Homeward Angel* (New York: Scribner, 1957), i.

18. Doug Lipman, *The Storytelling Coach* (Little Rock, Ark.: August House Publishers, 1995), 31–32.

19. For excellent sources on art therapy, see Margaret Frings Keyes, *Inward Journey: Art as Therapy* (Chicago: Open Court Publishing, 1983);

Shaun McNiff, *Art Heals: How Creativity Cures the Soul* (Boston: Shambhala Publications, 2004); David Rosen, *Transforming Depression: Healing the Soul through Creativity* (New York: Penguin Books, 1993).

20. McNiff, *Art Heals*, v.

21. Louise DeSalvo, *Writing as a Way of Healing: How Telling Our Stories Transforms Our Lives* (Boston: Beacon Press, 1999), 29.

22. Kevin Cordi and Judy Sima, *Raising Voices: Youth Storytelling Groups and Troupes* (Littleton, Colo.: Libraries Unlimited, 2003); and *www.youthstorytelling.com*.

23. See *www.thehearthstorytelling.wordpress.com*.

24. See *www.streetpoetsinc.com*.

25. See *www.virginiaavenueproject.org*.

26. See, for example, Bob Barton and David Booth, *Stories in the Classroom: Storytelling, Reading Aloud and Role-Playing with Children* (Portsmouth, N.H.: Heinemann Educational Books, 1990); Rives Collins and Pamela Cooper, eds., *The Power of Story: Teaching through Storytelling* (Needham Heights, Mass.: Allyn and Bacon, 1997); Patsy Cooper, *When Stories Come to School: Telling, Writing, and Performing Stories in the Early Childhood Classroom* (New York: Teachers and Writers Collaborative, 1993); Kieran Egan, *Teaching as Storytelling: An Alternative Approach to Teaching and Curriculum in the Elementary School* (Chicago: University of Chicago Press, 1986); Harriet Mason and Larry Watson, *Everyone a Storyteller: Integrating Storytelling into the Curriculum* (Portland, Ore.: Lariat Publications, 1991); Betty Rosen, *And None of It Was Nonsense: The Power of Storytelling in School* (Portsmouth, N.H.: Heinemann Educational Books, 1988).

27. Sklar, *Play-Making*.

28. This is Sanford Meisner's famous definition of acting. See Sanford Meisner and Dennis Longwell, *Sanford Meisner on Acting* (New York: Vintage Books, 1987).

29. For excellent suggestions from an empowering coach, see Lipman, *Storytelling Coach*.

30. Sklar, *Play-Making*, 12.

31. Ibid., 29.

32. Michael Rohd, *Theater for Community, Conflict and Dialogue* (Portsmouth, N.H.: Heinemann, 1998), 10.

33. Ibid., 17.

34. Kevin Cordi, "How Do Storytellers Help Novice Storytellers Learn the Craft?" Youth Storytellers, *www.youthstorytellingcom/articles/html* (accessed August 13, 2009).

35. Excellent sources for teaching young people how to craft stories include: Augusta Baker and Ellin Greene, *Storytelling: Art and Technique* (New York: R. R. Bowker, 1987); Martha Hamilton and Mitch Weiss, *Children Tell Stories: A Teaching Guide* (Katonah, N.Y.: Richard C. Owen Publishers, 1990); Kendall Haven, *Super Simple Storytelling* (Englewood, Colo.: Teacher Ideas Press, 2000); Norma Livo and Sandra Rietz, *Storytelling Activities* (Littleton, Colo.: Libraries Unlimited, Inc., 1987); Margaret Read MacDonald, *The Storyteller's Start-Up Book: Finding, Learning, Performing, and Using Folktales* (Little Rock, Ark.: August House, Inc., 1993).

36. For excellent exercises exploring various narrative genres, see Jack Zipes, *Creative Storytelling: Building Community, Changing Lives* (New York: Routledge, 1995).

37. Syd Lieberman, "Going to the Well: Choosing Stories for Telling," in *The Power of Story*, ed. Rives Collins and Pamela J. Cooper, 40.

38. Michael Parent, "Story-Activities to Do with Children," Youth Storytellers, *www.youthstorytelling.com/articles/html* (accessed August 13, 2009).

39. For excellent resources in teaching young people how to write original plays, see Sklar, *Play-Making;* and Herbert Kohl, *Making Theater: Developing Plays with Young People* (New York: Teachers and Writers Collaborative, 1988).

40. *See www.toplab.org.*

Chapter 6

1. For a primer on restorative justice, see Howard Zehr, *The Little Book of Restorative Justice* (Intercourse, Pa.: Good Books, 2002).

2. Brian Dominick and Sara Ebrahimi, "Young and Oppressed," National Youth Rights Association, *www.youthrights.org*, 2010; Marian Wright Edelman, *Families in Peril: An Agenda for Social Change* (Cambridge, Mass.: Harvard University Press, 1989).

3. David White, *Practicing Discernment with Youth: A Transformative Youth Ministry Approach* (Cleveland: Pilgrim Press, 2005); Brian Mahan, Michael Warren, and David White, *Awakening Youth Discipleship: Christian Resistance in a Consumer Culture* (Eugene, Ore.: Wipf and Stock, 2007).

4. For helpful introductions to liberation theology, see Deane Ferm, *Third World Liberation Theologies: An Introductory Survey* (Maryknoll, N.Y.: Orbis Books, 1986), and Susan Thistlethwaite and Mary Potter Engel, *Lift Every Voice: Constructing Theologies from the Underside* (San

Francisco: HarperSanFrancisco, 1990). For religious educators who have advocated liberative approaches to religious education, see George Albert Coe, *A Social Theory of Religious Education* (Garden City, N.Y.: Doubleday, Doran and Co., 1929); Allen Moore, ed., *Religious Education as Social Transformation* (Birmingham: Religious Education Press, 1989); Daniel Schipani, *Religious Education Encounters Liberation Theology* (Birmingham: Religious Education Press, 1988); Carol Lakey Hess, *Caretakers of Our Common House* (Nashville: Abingdon Press, 1997); Letty Russell, *Christian Education in Mission* (Philadelphia: Westminster Press, 1967); White, *Practicing Discernment*; Elizabeth Conde-Frazier, *A Many Colored Kingdom: Multicultural Dynamics for Spiritual Formation* (Grand Rapids: Baker Academic, 2004).

5. Schipani, *Religious Education,* and Leonardo Boff, *Jesus Christ Liberator: A Critical Christology for Our Time* (Maryknoll, N.Y.: Orbis Books, 1978).

6. Marcus Borg, *Jesus, A New Vision* (San Francisco: Harper and Row, 1987); Walter Wink, *Engaging the Powers* (Minneapolis: Fortress, 1992); Ched Myers, *The Biblical Vision of Sabbath Economics* (Washington, D.C.: Tell the World Press, 2001).

7. See Boff, *Jesus Christ Liberator,* 280, 291–92.

8. Paulo Freire, *Pedagogy of the Oppressed* (New York: Continuum, 1970).

9. Ibid., 57 (italics in original).

10. Ibid.

11. See Juan Luis Segundo, *The Liberation of Theology* (Maryknoll, N.Y.: Orbis Books, 1976).

12. For excellent examples, see Jim Hancock, *Dramatic Pauses: 20 Ready-to-Use Sketches for Youth Ministry* (Grand Rapids: Youth Specialties, 1995); Nancy Duffy Hery, *Drama That Delivers: Real-Life Problems, Students' Solutions* (Englewood, Colo.: Teacher Ideas Press, 1996); R. William Pike, *Stop, Look, Listen Up!: and Other Dramas for Confronting Social Issues in Elementary Schools* (San Jose, Calif: Resource Publications Inc., 1993); R. William Pike, *Act for Health: Using Theater to Teach Tough Teen Topics* (Santa Cruz, Calif.: ETR Associates, 1991); Joan Sturkie and Marsh Cassady, *Acting It Out: 74 Short Plays for Starting Discussions with Teenagers* (San Jose, Calif.: Resource Publications, Inc., 1990–2000).

13. Norma Bowles, ed., *Friendly Fire: An Anthology of 3 Plays by Queer Street Youth* (Los Angeles: A.S.K. Theater Projects, 1997); Norma Bowles,

Cootie Shots: Theatrical Inoculations Against Bigotry for Kids, Parents, and Teachers (Los Angeles: Theater Communications Group, 2001).

14. White, *Practicing Discernment.*

15. Mario Cossa et al., *Acting Out: The Workbook* (Washington D.C.: Accelerated Development, 1996).

16. Augusto Boal, *Theatre of the Oppressed* (New York: Theatre Communications Group, 1985); Boal, *Games for Actors and Non-Actors*, trans. Adrian Jackson (London: Routledge, 1992); Mady Schutzman and Jan Cohen-Cruz, *Playing Boal: Theater, Therapy, Activism* (New York: Routledge, 1994). An excellent organization that trains facilitators of Boal's method is the Theater of the Oppressed Laboratory in New York. Other helpful resources include Michael Rohd, *Theatre for Community, Conflict, and Dialogue* (Portsmouth, N.H.: Heinemann, 1998), and Patricia Sternberg and Antonina Garcia, *Sociodrama: Who's in Your Shoes*, 2nd ed. (Westport, Conn.: Praeger, 2000).

17. Boal, *Theater of the Oppressed*, ix.

18. Freire compares performing liberatory actions *for* the oppressed to saving objects from a burning building. Without being empowered themselves, they melt away and become one of the nameless masses that can be manipulated (*Pedagogy of the Oppressed*, 52).

19. Boal, *Theatre of the Oppressed*, 132–33.

20. This example is from Proyecto Pastoral, Delores Mission in Los Angeles.

21. Excellent sources include Viola Spolin, *Improvisation for the Theater* (Chicago: Northwestern University Press, 1999); Keith Johnston, *Impro: Improvisation and the Theater* (New York: Routledge, 1987); Charna Halpern and Del Close, *Truth in Comedy: The Manual of Improvisation* (New York: Meriwether Publishing, 1994); Stanley Pollack, *Moving beyond Icebreakers* (Boston: Center for Teen Empowerment, 2005); Rohd, *Theater for Community.*

22. A "shakedown" involves counting to ten as a group while shaking the left hand, then the right, the left leg, then the right, then repeating while counting to nine, then eight, then seven, and so on; the "name game" involves each person saying their name with an emotion and a gesture that is echoed and mirrored by the rest of the circle; "Zip-Zap-Zop" involves one person saying "Zip" while clapping their hands toward another, that person saying "Zap" while clapping their hands toward yet another, and

that person saying "Zop" while clapping their hands to still another who cycles to someone else with "Zip" and a clap.

23. See Rohd, *Theater for Community*, 10; and Daniel Judah Sklar, *Play-Making: Children Writing and Performing Their Own Plays* (New York: Teachers and Writers Collaborative, 1991), 29.

24. Rohd, *Theater for Community*, 12, 17.

25. White, *Practicing Discernment*, 99, 104.

26. For these exercises, see Boal, *Games for Actors*, 67, 90; and Rohd, *Theater for Community*, 26, 62, 66.

27. Rohd, *Theater for Community*, 20, 34.

28. Boal, *Games for Actors*, 63.

29. Ibid., 160.

30. For excellent improv exercises, see Rohd, *Theater for Community*, 72–96.

31. Ibid., 97–111.

32. These are adapted from ibid., 102–3.

33. See ibid., 112–27.

34. Boal, *Games for Actors*, 245–47.

35. Boal, *Theatre of the Oppressed*, 155; see also 141–42.

Bibliography

Anderson, Herbert, and Edward Foley. *Mighty Stories, Dangerous Rituals: Weaving Together the Human and the Divine.* San Francisco: Jossey-Bass, 1998.

Arthur, Sarah. *The God-Hungry Imagination: The Art of Storytelling for Post-Modern Youth.* Nashville: Upper Room Books, 2007.

Azara, Nancy. *Spirit Taking Form: Making a Spiritual Practice of Making Art.* York Beach, Maine: Red Wheel, 2002.

Baker, Augusta, and Ellin Greene. *Storytelling: Art and Technique.* New York: R. R. Bowker, 1987.

Baker, Dori Grinenko. *Doing Girlfriend Theology: God-Talk with Young Women.* Cleveland: Pilgrim Press, 2005.

Barry, William A., S.J. *Finding God in All Things: A Companion to the Spiritual Exercises of St. Ignatius.* Notre Dame, Ind.: Ave Maria Press, 2006.

Barth, Karl. *The Word of God and the Word of Man.* Trans. Douglas Horton. Gloucester, Mass.: Peter Smith Publisher, 1978.

Barton, Bob, and David Booth. *Stories in the Classroom: Storytelling, Reading Aloud and Role-Playing with Children.* Portsmouth, N.H.: Heinemann Educational Books, 1990.

Bauckman, Richard. *The Bible in Politics: How to Read the Bible Politically.* London: SPCK, 1989.

Belenky, Mary Field, et al. *Women's Ways of Knowing: The Development of Self, Voice, and Mind.* New York: Basic Books, 1986.

Boal, Augusto. *Games For Actors and Non-Actors.* Trans. Adrian Jackson. London: Routledge, 1992.

———. *Theatre of the Oppressed.* Trans. Charles A. and Maria-Odilia Leal McBride. New York: Theatre Communications Group, 1985.

Boff, Leonardo. *Jesus Christ Liberator: A Critical Christology for Our Time.* Maryknoll, N.Y.: Orbis Books, 1978.

Borg, Marcus. *Jesus, A New Vision.* San Francisco: Harper and Row, 1987.

Borkenhagen, Connie K. "The Legal Bias against Rape Victims (The Rape of Mr. Smith)." *American Bar Association Journal* (April 1975); reprinted in Sheila Ruth. *Issues in Feminism: An Introduction to Women's Studies.* Mountain View, Calif.: Mayfield Publishing Co., 1990.

Bowden, John. "Narrative Theology." In *The Westminster Dictionary of Christian Theology*, eds. Alan Richardson and John Bowden, 391–92. Philadelphia: Westminster Press, 1983.

Bowles, Norma. *Cootie Shots: Theatrical Inoculations Against Bigotry for Kids, Parents, and Teachers*. Los Angeles: Theater Communications Group, 2001.

———, ed. *Friendly Fire: An Anthology of 3 Plays by Queer Street Youth*. Los Angeles: A.S.K. Theater Projects, 1997.

Brockelman, Paul T. *The Inside Story: A Narrative Approach to Religious Understanding and Truth*. Albany: State University of New York Press, 1992.

———. *Time and Self*. New York: Crossroad, 1985.

Brody, Ed, et al. *Spinning Tales, Weaving Hope*. Philadelphia: New Society Publishers, 1992.

Brooks, Rosa. "Resist the Princesses." *Los Angeles Times* (March 27, 2008).

Cameron, Julia. *The Artist's Way: A Spiritual Path to Higher Creativity*. New York: Tarcher/Putnam Books, 1992.

Campbell, Joseph. *The Hero with a Thousand Faces*. Princeton, N.J.: Princeton University Press, 1949.

Christ, Carol P. *Diving Deep and Surfacing: Women Writers on Spiritual Quest*. Boston: Beacon Press, 1980.

Coe, George Albert. *A Social Theory of Religious Education*. Garden City, N.Y.: Doubleday, Doran and Co., 1929.

Collins, Rives, and Pamela Cooper, eds. *The Power of Story: Teaching through Storytelling*. Needham Heights, Mass.: Allyn and Bacon, 1997.

Conde-Frazier, Elizabeth. *A Many Colored Kingdom: Multicultural Dynamics for Spiritual Formation*. Grand Rapids: Baker Academic, 2004.

Cooper, Patsy. *When Stories Come to School: Telling, Writing, and Performing Stories in the Early Childhood Classroom*. New York: Teachers and Writers Collaborative, 1993.

Cooper-White, Pamela. *The Cry of Tamar: Violence against Women and the Church's Response*. Minneapolis: Fortress Press, 1995.

Cordi, Kevin, and Judy Sima. *Raising Voices: Youth Storytelling Groups and Troupes*. Littleton, Colo.: Libraries Unlimited, 2003.

Cossa, Mario, et al. *Acting Out: The Workbook*. Washington D.C.: Accelerated Development, 1996.

Crites, Stephen. "The Narrative Quality of Experience." In *Why Narrative? Readings in Narrative Theology*, ed. Stanley Hauerwas and L. Gregory Jones, 65–88. Grand Rapids: Wm. Eerdmans, 1989.

Denton, Melinda Lundquist. *Soul Searching: The Religious and Spiritual Lives of American Teenagers*. New York: Oxford University Press, 2005.

DeSalvo, Louise. *Writing as a Way of Healing: How Telling Our Stories Transforms Our Lives.* Boston: Beacon Press, 1999.

Diamant, Anita. *The Red Tent.* New York: St. Martin's Press, 2005.

Durka, Gloria, and Joanmarie Smith. *The Aesthetic Dimensions of Religious Education.* New York: Paulist Press, 1979.

Edelman, Marian Wright. *Families in Peril: An Agenda for Social Change.* Cambridge, Mass.: Harvard University Press, 1989.

Egan, Kieran. *Teaching as Storytelling: An Alternative Approach to Teaching and Curriculum in the Elementary School.* Chicago: University of Chicago Press, 1986.

Erikson, Erik. *Youth: Identity and Crisis.* New York: W. W. Norton and Co., 1968.

Fackre, Gabriel. "Narrative Theology: An Overview." *Interpretation* 37, no. 4 (October 1983): 340–52.

Feinstein, David, and Stanley Krippner. *The Mythic Path: Discovering the Guiding Stories of Your Past—Creating a Vision for Your Future.* New York: Jeremy P. Tarcher/Putnam Books, 1997.

Felder, Cain. *Stony the Road We Trod: African-American Biblical Interpretation.* Minneapolis: Fortress Press, 1991.

Ferm, Deane. *Third World Liberation Theologies: An Introductory Survey.* Maryknoll, N.Y.: Orbis Books, 1986.

Fiorenza, Elisabeth Schüssler. *Bread Not Stone: The Challenge of Feminist Biblical Interpretation.* Boston: Beacon Press, 1984.

Fowler, James. *Stages of Faith.* San Francisco: Harper and Row, 1981.

Freedman, Jill, and Gene Combs. *Narrative Therapy: The Social Construction of Preferred Realities.* New York: W. W. Norton and Co., 1996.

Freire, Paulo. *Pedagogy of the Oppressed.* Trans. Myra Bergman Ramos. New York: Continuum, 1984.

Gardner, Richard. *Therapeutic Communication with Children: The Mutual Storytelling Technique.* Northvale, N.J.: Jason Aronson, 1986.

Giroux, Henry. "Animating Youth: The Disneyfication of Children's Culture." In Henry Giroux, *Fugitive Cultures,* 89–114. New York: Routledge, 1996.

Greene, Liz, and Juliet Sharman-Burke. *The Mythic Journey: The Meaning of Myth as a Guide for Life.* New York: Fireside, 2000.

Griggs, Patricia. *Using Storytelling in Christian Education.* Abingdon: Parthenon Press, 1981.

Groome, Thomas. *Christian Religious Education.* San Francisco: Harper and Row, 1980.

Ha Tae Hung. *Folk Tales of Old Korea.* Seoul: Yonsei University Press, 1958.

Halpern, Charna, and Del Close. *Truth in Comedy: The Manual of Improvisation.* New York: Meriwether Publishing, 1994.

Hamilton, Martha, and Mitch Weiss. *Children Tell Stories: A Teaching Guide.* Katonah, N.Y.: Richard C. Owen Publishers, 1990.

Han, Suzanne Crowder. *Korean Folk and Fairy Tales.* Elizabeth, N.J.: Hollym Corporation, 1991.

Hancock, Jim. *Dramatic Pauses: 20 Ready-to-Use Sketches for Youth Ministry.* Grand Rapids: Youth Specialties, 1995.

Harris, Maria. "Completion and Faith Development." In *Faith Development and Fowler,* ed. Craig Dykstra and Sharon Parks, 115–33. Birmingham: Religious Education Press, 1986.

————. *Fashion Me a People.* Louisville: Westminster/John Knox, 1989.

————. *Teaching and the Religious Imagination.* San Francisco: Harper and Row, 1987.

Hauerwas, Stanley. *A Community of Character.* Notre Dame, Ind.: University of Notre Dame Press, 1981.

————. *The Peaceable Kingdom: A Primer in Christian Ethics.* Notre Dame, Ind.: University of Notre Dame Press, 1983.

————. *Vision and Virtue: Essays in Christian Ethical Reflection.* Notre Dame, Ind.: University of Notre Dame Press, 1974.

————, with Richard Bondi and David Burrell. *Truthfulness and Tragedy.* Notre Dame, Ind.: University of Notre Dame Press, 1977.

Haven, Kendall. *Super Simple Storytelling.* Englewood, Colo.: Teacher Ideas Press, 2000.

Hery, Nancy Duffy. *Drama That Delivers: Real-Life Problems, Students' Solutions.* Englewood, Colo.: Teacher Ideas Press, 1996.

Hess, Carol Lakey. *Caretakers of Our Common House: Women's Development in Communities of Faith.* Nashville: Abingdon, 1997.

Johnson, Elizabeth. *She Who Is: The Mystery of God in Feminist Theological Discourse.* New York: Crossroad, 1992.

Johnson, Robert A. *Inner Work: Using Dreams and Active Imagination for Personal Growth.* San Francisco: HarperSanFrancisco, 1986.

Johnston, Keith. *Impro: Improvisation and the Theater.* New York: Routledge, 1987.

Jung, Carl, et al. *Man and His Symbols.* Garden City, N.Y.: Doubleday, 1964.

Keen, Sam, and Anne Valley-Fox. *Your Mythic Journey: Finding Meaning in Your Life through Writing and Storytelling.* Los Angeles: Jeremy Tarcher, Inc., 1989.

Keyes, Margaret Frings. *Inward Journey: Art as Therapy.* Chicago: Open Court Publishing, 1983.

Kim, Jina. *Transformative Education through Narrative Pedagogy in the Korean Women's Context.* Claremont School of Theology, Calif. Unpublished D.Min. project, 2007.

Kohl, Herbert. *Making Theater: Developing Plays with Young People.* New York: Teachers and Writers Collaborative, 1988.

————. *Should We Burn Barbar? Essays on Children's Literature and the Power of Stories.* New York: New Press, 1995.

Krondorfer, Bjorn, ed. *Body and the Bible: Interpreting and Experiencing Biblical Narratives*. Philadelphia: Trinity Press International, 1992.

Kwok Pui-Lan. *Discovering the Bible in the Non-Biblical World*. Maryknoll, N.Y.: Orbis Books, 1995.

Laeuchli, Samuel, and Evelyn Rothchild-Laeuchli. "Mimesis: The Healing Power of Myth." *Quadrant* 22, no. 2 (1989): 53–62.

Lane, Belden C. "Myth." In *The New Dictionary of Catholic Spirituality*, ed. Michael Downey, 692–95. Collegeville, Minn.: Order of St. Benedict, 1993.

Langer, Ellen. *On Becoming an Artist: Reinventing Yourself through Mindful Creativity*. New York: Ballantine Books, 2005.

Lee, Boyung. "A Postcolonial Approach to Biblical Pedagogy." *Religious Education* 102, no. 11 (2007): 44–66.

Lefever, Marlene. *Creative Teaching Methods*. Colorado Springs, Colo.: Cool Ministry Resources, 1996.

Levorato, Alessandra. *Language and Gender in the Fairy Tale Tradition: A Linguistic Analysis of Old and New Storytelling*. New York: Palgrave Macmillan, 2003.

Lieberman, Marcia R. "'Some Day My Prince Will Come': Female Acculturation through the Fairy Tale." *College English* 34, no. 3 (December 1972): 384.

Lieberman, Syd. "Going to the Well: Choosing Stories for Telling." In *The Power of Story*, ed. Rives Collins and Pamela J. Cooper, 39–45. Needham Heights, Mass.: Allyn and Bacon, 1957.

Lipman, Doug. *The Storytelling Coach*. Little Rock, Ark.: August House Publishers, 1995.

Livo, Norma, and Sandra Rietz. *Storytelling Activities*. Littleton, Colo.: Libraries Unlimited, Inc., 1987.

Lonsdale, David. *Eyes to See, Ears to Hear: An Introduction to Ignatian Spirituality*. Maryknoll, N.Y.: Orbis Books, 2005.

MacDonald, Margaret Read. *The Storyteller's Start-Up Book: Finding, Learning, Performing, and Using Folktales*. Little Rock, Ark.: August House, Inc., 1993.

Mahan, Brian, Michael Warren, and David White. *Awakening Youth Discipleship: Christian Resistance in a Consumer Culture*. Eugene, Ore.: Wipf and Stock, 2007.

Malchiodi, Cathy. *The Soul's Palette: Drawing on Art's Transformative Powers for Health and Well-Being*. Boston: Shambhala Publications, 2002.

Malcolm X with Alex Haley. *The Autobiography of Malcolm X*. New York: Random House, 1973.

Mason, Harriet, and Larry Watson. *Everyone a Storyteller: Integrating Storytelling into the Curriculum*. Portland, Ore.: Lariat Publications, 1991.

McAdams, Dan P. *The Redemptive Self: Stories Americans Live By.* Oxford: Oxford University Press, 2006.

———. *The Stories We Live By: Personal Myths and the Making of the Self.* New York: Guilford Press, 1993.

McClendon, James. *Biography as Theology.* Nashville: Abingdon Press, 1974.

McNiff, Shaun. *Art Heals: How Creativity Cures the Soul.* Boston: Shambhala Publications, 2004.

Meisner, Sanford, and Dennis Longwell. *Sanford Meisner on Acting.* New York: Vintage Books, 1987.

Mezirow, Jack. "How Critical Reflection Triggers Transformative Learning." In *Fostering Critical Reflection in Adulthood: A Guide to Transformative and Emancipatory Learning,* ed. Jack Mezirow and Associates, 1–20. San Francisco: Jossey-Bass, 1990.

———. "Learning to Think Like an Adult: Core Concepts of Transformation Theory." In *Learning as Transformation: Critical Perspectives on a Theory in Progress,* ed. Jack Mezirow and Associates, 3–33. San Francisco: Jossey-Bass, 2000.

Miller, Mark. *Experiential Storytelling: (Re)Discovering Narrative to Communicate God's Message.* Grand Rapids: Zondervan Press, 2003.

Moore, Allen, ed. *Religious Education as Social Transformation.* Birmingham: Religious Education Press, 1989.

Morgan, Peter. *Story Weaving: Using Stories to Transform Your Congregation.* St. Louis: CBH Press, 1986.

Morgan, Richard. *Remembering Your Story: Creating Your Own Spiritual Autobiography.* Nashville: Upper Room Books, 2002.

Morton, Nelle. *The Journey Is Home.* Boston: Beacon Press, 1985.

Munsch, Robert. *The Paper Bag Princess.* Buffalo, N.Y.: Annick Press, 1980.

Myers, Ched. *The Biblical Vision of Sabbath Economics.* Washington, D.C.: Tell the World Press, 2001.

Nelson, C. Ellis. *Where Faith Begins.* Atlanta: John Knox Press, 1976.

Neuger, Christie. *Counseling Women: A Narrative, Pastoral Approach.* Minneapolis: Fortress, 2001.

Niebuhr, H. Richard. *The Meaning of Revelation.* New York: Macmillan Co., 1955.

Orenstein, Catherine. *Little Red Riding Hood Uncloaked: Sex, Morality, and the Evolution of a Fairy Tale.* New York: Basic Books, 2002.

Parry, Alan, and Robert Doan. *Story Re-visions: Narrative Therapy in the Post-Modern World.* New York: Guilford Press, 1994.

Patterson, Richard. *Writing Your Spiritual Autobiography.* Allen, Tex.: Thomas More Publishing, 2002.

Peace, Richard. *Spiritual Autobiography: Discovering and Sharing Your Spiritual Story.* Colorado Springs, Colo.: NavPress, 1998.

Pike, R. William. *Act for Health: Using Theater to Teach Tough Teen Topics.* Santa Cruz, Calif.: ETR Associates, 1991.

———. *Stop, Look, Listen Up! and Other Dramas for Confronting Social Issues in Elementary Schools.* San Jose, Calif.: Resource Publications Inc., 1993.

Pitzele, Peter. *Scripture Windows: Towards a Practice of Bibliodrama.* Los Angeles: Alef Design Group, 1998.

Polkinghorne, Donald E. *Narrative Knowing and the Human Sciences.* Albany: State University of New York Press, 1988.

Pollack, Stanley. *Moving beyond Icebreakers.* Boston: Center for Teen Empowerment, 2005.

Prothero, Stephen. *Religious Literacy: What Every American Needs to Know—and Doesn't.* San Francisco: HarperSanFrancisco, 2007.

Risher, Dee Dee. "Roots and Branches: More Than Just Bread." *The Other Side* (September–October 2000): 54.

Rohd, Michael. *Theater for Community, Conflict and Dialogue.* Portsmouth, N.H.: Heinemann, 1998.

Root, Michael. "The Narrative Structure of Soteriology." In *Why Narrative? Readings in Narrative Theology,* ed. Stanley Hauerwas and L. Gregory Jones, 263–78. Grand Rapids: Wm. Eerdmans, 1989.

Rosen, Betty. *And None of It Was Nonsense: The Power of Storytelling in School.* Portsmouth, N.H.: Heinemann Educational Books, 1988.

Rosen, David. *Transforming Depression: Healing the Soul through Creativity.* New York: Penguin Books, 1993.

Ruether, Rosemary Radford. *Sexism and God-Talk: Toward a Feminist Theology.* Boston: Beacon Press, 1983.

Russell, Letty. *Christian Education in Mission.* Philadelphia: Westminster Press. 1967.

———. *Human Liberation in a Feminist Perspective—A Theology.* Philadelphia: Westminster Press, 1974.

Ryan, Thomas. *Soul Fire: Accessing Your Creativity.* Woodstock, Vt.: Sky Light Paths, 2008.

Schipani, Daniel. *Religious Education Encounters Liberation Theology.* Birmingham: Religious Education Press, 1988.

Schramm, Tim F. "Bibliodrama in Action: Reenacting a New Testament Healing Story." In *Body and Bible: Interpreting and Experiencing Biblical Narratives,* ed. Bjorn Krondorfer, 57–84. Philadelphia: Trinity Press International, 1992.

Schutzman, Mady, and Jan Cohen-Cruz. *Playing Boal: Theater, Therapy, Activism.* New York: Routledge, 1994.

Segovia, Fernando F. *Decolonizing Biblical Studies: A View from the Margins.* Maryknoll, N.Y.: Orbis Books, 2000.

———, and Mary A. Tolbert. *Teaching the Bible: The Discourse and Politics of Biblical Pedagogy.* Maryknoll, N.Y.: Orbis Books, 1998.

Segundo, Juan Luis. *The Liberation of Theology.* Trans. John Drury. Maryknoll, N.Y.: Orbis Books, 1976.

Shamana, Beverly. *Seeing in the Dark: A Vision of Creativity and Spirituality.* Nashville: Abingdon Press, 2001.

Shaw, Susan. *Storytelling in Religious Education.* Birmingham: Religious Education Press, 1999.

Sklar, Daniel Judah. *Play-Making: Children Writing and Performing Their Own Plays.* New York: Teachers and Writers Collaborative, 1991.

Smith, Chris, and Melinda Lindquist Dention. *Soul Searching: The Religious and Spiritual Lives of American Teenagers.* New York: Oxford University Press, 2005.

Spolin, Viola. *Improvisation for the Theater.* Chicago: Northwestern University Press, 1999.

Sternberg, Patricia, and Antonina Garcia. *Sociodrama: Who's in Your Shoes.* 2nd ed. Westport, Conn.: Praeger, 2000.

Stone, Kay. "Things Walt Disney Never Told Us." In *Women and Folklore,* ed. Claire R. Farrer, 42–50. Austin: University of Texas Press, 1975.

Stone, Robert. "Narrative Theology and Religious Education." In *Theologies of Religious Education,* ed. Randolph Crump Miller, 255–85. Birmingham: Religious Education Press, 1995.

Stroup, George W. *The Promise of Narrative Theology: Recovering the Gospel in the Church.* Eugene, Ore.: Wipf and Stock, 1981.

Sturkie, Joan, and Marsh Cassady. *Acting It Out: 74 Short Plays for Starting Discussions with Teenagers.* San Jose, Calif.: Resource Publications, Inc., 1990–2000.

Sugirtharajah, R. S., ed. *Voices from the Margin: Interpreting the Bible in the Third World.* Oxford: Oxford University Press, 2002.

Taylor, Joseph. *Reel Youth Ministry: Empowering Young People to Become Agents of Change through Critical Consciousness and Narrative Pedagogies.* Claremont School of Theology, Calif.: unpublished Ph.D. dissertation, 2010.

Thistlethwaite, Susan, and Mary Potter Engel. *Lift Every Voice: Constructing Theologies from the Underside.* San Francisco: HarperSanFrancisco, 1990.

Tinker, George. "Native Americans and the Land." *Word and World* 6 (1986): 66–74.

Trible, Phyllis. *Texts of Terror: Literary-Feminist Readings of Biblical Narratives.* Philadelphia: Fortress Press, 1984.

Turpin, Katherine. "Princess Dreams: Children's Spiritual Formation in Consumer Culture." In *Children, Youth, and Spirituality in a Troubling*

World, ed. Mary Elizabeth Moore and Almeda M. Wright, 45–61. St. Louis: Chalice Press, 2008.

Underhill, Evelyn. *The Spiritual Life*. London: Hodder and Stoughton Ltd., 1937.

Vecchione, Patrice. *Writing and the Spiritual Life: Finding Your Voice by Looking Within*. New York: Contemporary Books, 2001.

Wakefield, Dan. *The Story of Your Life: Writing a Spiritual Autobiography*. Boston: Beacon Press, 1990.

Wangerin, Walt. *The Book of God: The Bible as a Novel*. Grand Rapids: Zondervan, 1996.

Warrior, Robert Allen. "A Native American Perspective: Canaanites, Cowboys, and Indians." In *Voices from the Margin: Interpreting the Bible in the Third World*, ed. R. S. Sugirtharajah, 277–87. Maryknoll, N.Y.: Orbis Books, 1995.

Westerhoff, John H., III. *Will Our Children Have Faith?* New York: Seabury Press, 1976.

Wheel Council. *Storytelling Power Book: Substance Abuse Prevention*. Prescott, Ariz.: Wheel Council, 1997.

White, David, *Practicing Discernment with Youth: A Transformative Youth Ministry Approach*. Cleveland: Pilgrim Press, 2005.

White, Michael and David Epston. *Narrative Means to Therapeutic Ends*. New York: W. W. Norton and Co., 1990.

White, William. *Speaking in Stories: Resources for Christian Storytellers*. Minneapolis: Augsburg Publishers, 1982.

Wimberly, Anne E. Streaty. *Soul Stories: African American Christian Education*. Rev. ed. Nashville: Abingdon Press, 2005.

Wink, Walter. *Engaging the Powers*. Minneapolis: Fortress Press, 1992.

———. *Transforming Bible Study: A Leader's Guide*. Nashville: Abingdon Press, 1980.

Wolfe, Thomas. *Look Homeward Angel*. New York: Scribner, 1957.

Wuthnow, Robert. *Creative Spirituality: The Way of the Artist*. Berkeley: University of California Press, 2001.

Zehr, Howard. *The Little Book of Restorative Justice*. Intercourse, Pa.: Good Books, 2002.

Zipes, Jack. *Creative Storytelling: Building Community, Changing Lives*. New York: Routledge, 1995.

———. *Don't Bet on the Prince: Contemporary Feminist Fairy Tales in North America and England*. New York: Methuen, 1986.

———, ed. *The Trial and Tribulations of Little Red Riding Hood*. New York: Routledge, 1993.